Conscience, Spirituality, and Religion

religions and mental health. There is a great need for such a book as this in a world of so much conflict and confusion."

—CLARENCE E. MCDANAL JR., MD,
Retired Child Psychiatrist

"This book is a fascinating read. I am a retired substance abuse counselor and soon discovered that my clients were most in need of moral rules to follow. Conscience influences every attempt to improve one's life. Dr. Xavier follows the thread of conscience through the history of religion and philosophy. His book highlights the pitfalls of believing in any person or movement that is not firmly grounded in conscience. Without conscience, religions or political organizations soon devolve into cults. This book is a powerful statement on the importance of conscience in the pursuit of spirituality in everyday life."

— MARC'A D. SCOTT,
Retired Substance Abuse Counselor

"This book is as timely as today's news headlines. From international conflict to hometown protests, people have the opportunity to employ either tribal opinions or relationship-building behaviors informed by a conscience of ethical considerations. My thoughts are influenced by forty-seven years' experience of professionally working with groups and individuals who were pursuing personal changes in their daily lives in order to more effectively cope with stress in regard to spiritual formation, substance addiction, and mental disorders. Xavier makes clear how we can progressively change our values, communication, and behaviors from 'parroting' mimicked responses of the superego to ethically based responses of an informed conscience. Xavier's concepts are simple enough to benefit the educationally challenged, yet profound enough to inform the college graduate. The subject matter is not limited in its relevance to our current generation only as some passing fad book. It is perpetual in its relevance. I can see this book being utilized across a broad spectrum of both professional and nonprofessional readers, who seek to improve their problem-solving skills."

—IRA BLANCHARD JR.,
Pastoral Counselor

"As our current environment seems to spawn more and more disunity, disharmony, and outright hostility toward each other, there is no better time for an in-depth probing of the value of conscience. Arising out of spirituality and psychology, conscience allows one to address and overcome imbedded biases and customs which impede our ability to live with each other in peace and harmony. Dr. Xavier has explored in greater detail the value of conscience which, as a psychiatrist and student of world religions, he has explored and written about for more than three decades. This book is not only informative and insightful but written to engage the reader in their own quest for a more honest and direct approach in relating with other people."

—GREGORY T. BITTNER,
Canon Lawyer Priest

"This book is a gentle call to conscientious living with reference to 'Beatitudes' as tools to incorporate into our daily living practices. The relevance of this book is extreme as it offers a clear solution for our age of conflicts across the globe, with a glimpse of perhaps a second Axial Age. Dr. Xavier, as a psychiatrist and with depth of his knowledge of history of world religions, coupled with decades of experiential wisdom, offers his perspectives on current world affairs and calls for individual reflection in pursuit of relinquishing hate, prejudice, and violence in order to promote justice and harmony for a peaceful world."

—ESTHER VEGESINA,
Psychiatric Nurse

"Many of us come across the word conscience but when one asks around it is an eye-opening surprise that hardly anyone does justice to its meaning and perceives the depth of its implications. The way Dr. Xavier wrote in his book, the concept of conscience is as if the creator has installed a sacred temple in every individual. Any religion with conscience is a system of peace and justice while without invoking conscience, and practicing religion with superego, in Dr. Xavier's description, religion is a destructive cult. This is a well overdue book."

—SALEEM I. NAVIWALA, MD,
Consultant Otolaryngology, UPMC Memorial Hospital

"This book provides an all-encompassing overview and offers concrete practical tools that are demonstrated to help misguided individuals and crowds to rediscover the essential ingredients of a healthy, meaningful, and rewarding life. Through observation, empathic listening, and fearless thinking he has identified distorted or absent spiritual concepts as a major source of individual and collective suffering which he faced in encounters with his patients. He describes a practical approach to helping people and society to recover from our contemporary ailments of anger, hate, addictions, egocentricity, and group-think, to name a few, which all seem to be fed by illusions. Using St. Paul's discrimination between 'works of the flesh' (basically 'sin,' addictions, self-centeredness) and 'fruits of the Spirit,' he defines the latter as positive spiritual attributes and forces that help individuals and groups of people alike to 'snap out of illusions,' redirect their life goals, and apply the tools presented. This includes faith, hope, love, compassion, and forgiveness, among others. These tools are distilled from an encyclopedic array of historical, religious, philosophical, psychiatric, and literary sources, which make his book a joy to read."

—GODEHARD OEPEN, MD,
Psychiatrist, Grayson and Associates

"Dr. Xavier's universal understanding of the mind traverses time and space in an epic quest searching for what binds us all—the root of our uniqueness, the heart of our emotions, and the importance of our interconnectedness—a relational model of transformation which challenges us to interpersonal and intrapersonal growth. Through the lens of the fruits of the Spirit, Dr. Xavier unlocks understanding our consciences through this ancient text."

—JULIE CONRADY,
Minister, Unitarian Universalist Church of Birmingham

"One of the great epochs of our world concluded in a revolutionary shift in society and ethics as a result of the evolutionary exploration in beingness. Dr. Xavier's work on this subject, drawing insights from the great philosophical, spiritual, and psychological traditions calls us inward to find a new shore. By returning to the big questions of being, Dr. Xavier points us back to a reality we are still attempting to define with words but is still common to us all regardless of our religious affiliation. This is a powerful and timely work that the world needs to read."

—JESSE EUGENE HERRIOTT,
Spiritual Pastoral Leader, Unity of Birmingham

"Dr. Xavier, a retired psychiatrist and an author of several books on comparative religions, spirituality, and the role of conscience is eminently qualified to write this very timely book. He has a deep understanding of human psychological needs as well as the various world religions and philosophical traditions."

—KAPIL DESAI,
Retired Engineer

Conscience, Spirituality, and Religion

*Evade Extremisms and Enjoy an Enriched Life
with an Axial Age Perspective*

N.S. XAVIER, MD

WIPF & STOCK · Eugene, Oregon

CONSCIENCE, SPIRITUALITY, AND RELIGION
Evade Extremisms and Enjoy an Enriched Life with an Axial Age Perspective

Copyright © 2025 N. S. Xavier. All rights reserved. Except for brief quotations in critical publications or reviews, no part of this book may be reproduced in any manner without prior written permission from the publisher. Write: Permissions, Wipf and Stock Publishers, 199 W. 8th Ave., Suite 3, Eugene, OR 97401.

Wipf & Stock
An Imprint of Wipf and Stock Publishers
199 W. 8th Ave., Suite 3
Eugene, OR 97401

www.wipfandstock.com

PAPERBACK ISBN: 979-8-3852-5244-2
HARDCOVER ISBN: 979-8-3852-5245-9
EBOOK ISBN: 979-8-3852-5246-6

VERSION NUMBER 09/23/25

The Scripture quotations contained herein are from New Revised Standard Version Bible, copyright, 1989, by the Division of Christian Education of the National Council of the Churches of Christ in the U.S.A. Used by permission. All rights reserved.

Although the author has made tremendous efforts to ensure the accuracy of the information contained in this book, the author assumes no responsibility for errors, inaccuracies, omissions, or inconsistencies. Any slights of individuals or groups are unintentional. Readers should use their own judgment and/or consult appropriate experts for dealing with their individual problems. The author has used many examples from his clinical and personal experiences to illustrate his points, but he has significantly altered the identity of private persons to protect their privacy and confidentiality. Some examples are composites of similar cases.

Contents

Acknowledgements | vi

Introduction | 1

PART 1   **CONSCIENCE, RELIGION, AND SPIRITUALITY**

Chapter One   Conscience, the Inner Parrot, and the PIG | 23

Chapter Two   Conscience, Religion, Spirituality, and The Axial Age | 54

Chapter Three   Pro Conscience vs. Anti Conscience: Christian Example | 95

PART II   **CONSCIENCE AND FRUIT OF THE SPIRIT**

Chapter Four   Love | 143

Chapter Five   Joy | 166

Chapter Six   Peace | 173

Chapter Seven   Patience | 200

Chapter Eight   Kindness | 206

Chapter Nine   Goodness | 210

Chapter Ten   Faithfulness | 215

Chapter Eleven   Gentleness | 220

Chapter Twelve   Self-Control | 224

Conclusion | 229

Notes | 235

About the Author | 239

Bibliography | 241

Index | 253

Acknowledgements

My wife, Dr. Anne Valsa Xavier, has been a great help and support in numerous ways. My son Dr. Sudeep Thomas Xavier, a psychiatrist who is also knowledgeable about world religions, especially Christianity, has been very helpful in developing the ideas in this book. My editor, Susan Wood, who had read my first book many years back is an excellent editor and has been a supportive friend helping with various issues around getting published. I deeply appreciate every person who took the time and effort to understand the material and provide a review. For the sake of simplicity, I will list their names alphabetically. Rev. Gregory T. Bittner, Ira Blanchard, Jr., Minister, Rev. Douglas M. Carpenter, Rev. Julie Conrady, Kapil Desai, Dr. Arthur M. Freeman III, MD, Rev. Dr. Jesse Eugene Herriott, Fisher Humphreys, Professor of Divinity, Emeritus, Uma Majmudar, PhD, Clarence E. McDanal Jr. MD, Saleem I. Naviwala, MD, Godehard Oepen, MD, PhD, Fr. Richard Rohr, O.F.M., Marc'a D. Scott, Randall K. Scott, PhD, Rabbi Rami Shapiro, and Esther Vegesina RN, BSN.

    I am grateful to Rev. Ray Wade and Rev. Kevin Higgs for letting me join them to give a presentation on Christian Nonviolence at the Parliament of the World's Religions in Chicago in 2023. I appreciate Josh Reeves, PhD, Director of the Samford Center for Science and Religion for the benefits I gain from attending his discussion group. I'm also grateful to Matthew Wimer and his excellent team at Wipf & Stock as well as Jason Robeck and his management of reprints of my prior two books.

Introduction

"Man is the only animal that loves his neighbor as himself and cuts his throat if his theology is not straight." — Mark Twain[1]

"... having faith and a good conscience. By rejecting conscience, certain persons have suffered shipwreck in the faith." 1 Tim 1:19

"Depart from evil and do good." Ps 34:14

LIFE IS STRESSFUL AND COMPLICATED. We deal with good and bad choices, multiple needs, competing desires and contradictory influences, pressures, and ideals. We are lucky to be blessed with a reliable guide—conscience, if properly used. It is our opportunity and responsibility to understand and utilize it.

What is happening in recent times with conscience, our good old inner voice, if we consider many of the wrong choices people have been making? This book explores ways to understand and utilize conscience more effectively.

An estimated two hundred and thirty-two thousand Americans died from COVID-19 because they rejected the vaccination that was easily available.[2] If people were using conscience to guide their choice, wouldn't they have gotten vaccinated based on good medical reasons? People who refuse vaccination often use their own group's alternate guides, rather than using conscience.

In another tragic case, 107,643 drug-involved overdose deaths occurred in the US in 2023 which was only 3 percent less than in 2022 according to the Center for Disease Control and Prevention. On February

---

1. Twain, *Letters*, 180.
2. Jia et al., "Estimated," 1.

25, 2025, CDC reported provisional data of about eighty-seven thousand drug overdose deaths from October 2023 to September 2024, down from about one hundred fourteen thousand the previous year.[3] The reduction in drug overdoses deaths seems related to increased use of naloxone for reversing opioid overdose and using medications like suboxone to treat opiate addiction.[4] In yet another sad case, according to the CDC, the leading cause of deaths in children and teenagers below the age of eighteen in the US is gun violence.

A Marist poll reported on May 21, 2024, showed 47 percent of Americans think in their lifetime there is likelihood of a civil war.[5] Of these, Republicans are 53 percent, Democrats 40 percent, and Independents 41 percent. Imagine another *Civil War!*

There is so much anger, hate, disputes and quarrels, murder, envying, resentment, drunkenness, and sexual immorality taking place in the world. These are all in the list of evil choices, the "works of the flesh" according to St. Paul (Gal 5:19–21). The two bad choices missing here from St. Paul's list are idolatry and witchcraft.

As against the above, St. Paul gave another list, "the fruit of the Spirit," the good fruits, in Gal 5:22–23: love, joy, peace, longsuffering, or patience, gentleness, or meekness, goodness, faithfulness, and temperance, or self-control. Various religions and ethical philosophies have rather similar teachings. The inner voice of conscience promotes such good choices. Why are these choices on the decline?

The level of wrong choices we're witnessing in the US is surprising and quite concerning given that the American population is 63 percent Christian with 6 percent belonging to other religions according to a December 2021 Pew report.[6] Also, 22 percent identified as spiritual but not religious as per a 2023 Pew report.[7] Isn't living by one's inner voice an essential part of following religion and spirituality? Are people not listening to the inner voice of conscience or is something wrong with the inner voice?

---

3. Centers for Disease Control and Prevention, "Rates," paras. 2–3.
4. NPR, "NPR Exclusive," paras. 1–4.
5. Marist Institute, "Nation," paras. 1–5.
6. Pew, "Three-in-Ten," para. 1.
7. Pew, "Spirituality," paras. 1–5.

TWO KINDS OF INNER VOICES

Two of the most prominent men of the twentieth century had used the phrase "inner voice" with entirely different meanings. In his autobiography relating to his life in South Africa, Mahatma Gandhi, well-known for promoting peace, love, and freedom, wrote that he was guided by his conscience which he called his inner voice. He wrote " . . . I had long since taught myself to follow the inner voice. I delighted in submitting to it."[8] Gandhi used the phrase "inner voice" referring to *conscience*. Adolf Hitler, who caused war and destruction of several million Jews and others used the phrase "inner voice" in a different sense. In 1938, Adolf Hitler was upset that the German people were rejoicing as the Munich Agreement seemed to end the possibility of war. Hitler told a meeting of German journalists to educate the people so that "the inner voice of the people itself slowly begins to cry out for the use of force."[9] I call the inner voice Hitler talked about as the *"inner parrot"* which parrots various ideas it picks up from external sources. *Polly* is known as a parrot that repeats what it hears. President Andrew Jackson reportedly had a parrot which parroted obscenities at visiting dignitaries. So undiplomatic!

I learned something remarkable from a real parrot of a rich Christian couple I knew. The parrot learned to say "Lord" from the pious husband. Occasionally the wife used to get angry with a maid servant and call her "you stupid." The parrot picked it up too. And causing the couple utter shame and guilt, the parrot at times would say "Lord" followed by "you stupid." Societies tend to have various groups with their different ideas and ideals, and they have hierarchies of power and prestige promoting their version of right and wrong. Even in a life-or-death situation like the COVID-19 pandemic, there were voices urging vaccination and voices indifferent to it or even discouraging it.

A Great Example of Transforming People from Following the Inner Parrot to Using Conscience

I have used a very insightful story to explain to people of various religions, agnostics and atheists our two inner guides. Here I am presenting it in more detail. The story is in the Gospel of John 8:2–11.

---

8. Gandhi, *Autobiography*, 134.
9. MacMillan, *War*, 17.

A group of men brought to Jesus a woman freshly caught committing adultery. Apparently, they spared the man, and the blame was on the woman. They reminded Jesus that she should be stoned to death according to the law of Moses. And they asked his opinion as to what should be done to her. Now imagine the emotional state of these men. They probably had sexual thoughts and feelings. The idea of stoning somebody would have aroused aggressive feelings. Moreover, they had a lot of religious feelings because they were testing Jesus to find fault with his teaching. Jesus did not confront the men who were fired up with sexual, aggressive, and religious passions. Confrontation would probably have caused a hostile reaction towards Jesus.

Jesus silently bent down and wrote something on the ground while the men kept asking him what should be done with the woman. Then Jesus stood up and said: "He among you who has not sinned cast the first stone." Then Jesus went back to writing on the ground, again not arguing or confronting them. By saying "he among you" rather than "you all" and by saying "who has not sinned" instead of "who has not committed adultery," Jesus pressured each of them to use his own reason and the spirit of the Golden Rule. Jesus took them out of groupthink. The outcome was excellent. The men left, one by one, starting with the elder, "convicted by their own conscience" according to the King James version of the Bible. In many other versions of the Bible, I have not noticed the word "conscience" used here. It was likely a very insightful addition by the translators of the King James version.

When the men came to Jesus with the judgments that the woman should be stoned to death, they were using their "*inner parrots*," repeating their religious and cultural programming like a parrot parroting something it picked up. Jesus calmed the men by bending down and writing on the ground. When one is too emotional, it's hard to listen to the still small voice of conscience and use reason and the Golden Rule. And by saying "he among you" and freeing them from group thinking, Jesus further pushed them to reflect using their *consciences*. This is a unique example of de-escalation and transformation. Thus, each man came using his inner parrot and left using his inner voice of conscience; these are our two inner guides.

After the men left, the woman must have been feeling greatly relieved from the threat to her life, but she could have been filled with guilt and shame. Jesus asked her whether the men condemned her, and she said no. Jesus told her he did not condemn her either, and instructed her to avoid sin. What she needed was not self-condemnation with excessive guilt and shame which could cause depression, but enough regret and motivation to use her conscience and transform her life for the better. I call it a therapeutic dose of guilt and shame as the therapeutic dose of the right medicine helps to heal but an overdose would cause more harm. So, I imagine she also left using her conscience. Along with reason and the Golden Rule, conscience uses the Golden Mean, or moderation. Aristotle describes virtue as the mean between the extremes, and the extremes on the two sides as vices. Interestingly, Confucius taught the "Doctrine of the Mean," and the Buddha's way is called "The Middle Way," between hedonism and asceticism, both promoting moderation. There is a saying among Hindus that even "Amrit," (heavenly nutrition) has to be taken moderately.

Another factor in using conscience is truth. We need to know the truth about the subject which we are considering applying reason, moderation, and the Golden Rule. In the above story, there was no doubt about the truth of it because the woman did not raise any objection. Many religious thinkers view God as the ultimate reality. Gandhi considered God as Truth. We human beings have the urge to search for truth in scientific, historical, philosophical, and spiritual fields. Truthfulness is a crucial virtue promoted by the great religions. The human tendency to lie to others and even to oneself complicates life. Given our limitations in knowing the exact truth in many situations, what is essential is respect for and commitment to truth. Respect for and commitment to truth involves openness of mind, sincere search for truth, and willingness to accept relevant information, and humble acceptance of limitations.

As spiritual beings and social animals we have two kinds of inner voices or internal guides. Each of us regularly face deciding between right and wrong choices. This internal conflict is often depicted as an angel on the right shoulder encouraging us to do good and a devil on the left shoulder tempting us to do wrong. The choice would be hard because the temptation could be strong. What makes the decision much harder is that besides the angel, there is a parrot on the right shoulder telling us what is right. The parrot considers what is right based on what it picked up from society. The angel promotes what is right based on conscience, our innate human capacity to use reason and the Golden Rule to choose what is good and avoid what is bad. The Golden Rule, "Do unto others as you would have them do unto you," involves empathy, compassion, love, and justice. And we have to consider George Bernard Shaw's famous idea that we must not do to others as we would have them do to us because their tastes might be different. That is in the spirit of the Golden Rule. Reason and the Golden rule require truth and moderation to function well. But the parrot would repeat what it picked up regardless of reason, the Golden Rule, moderation and truth.

Some patients have told me: "In Sunday school I was taught the Golden Rule but the rest of the week I was exposed to the idea that if somebody hit me, I should hit back double or triple hard. Which idea would I follow?" "He is a counter puncher" is a big compliment. Another patient said his mother taught forgiveness and father taught to get even and he chooses whatever he feels like at the time. See the conflict? Can't we empathize with the confused people and help them to integrate conflicting voices? Integrating involves following the voice of conscience and voices of the inner parrot which are in tune with conscience but ignoring parrot's voices out of tune with conscience. On the left shoulder we can imagine the devil and a pig representing physical and emotional needs like pleasure and power which are fine in moderation. When the devil (or the extremism of the individual) pushes a person to meet a human need, such as pleasure, to an extreme, it causes the problem of irrational gratification (PIG).

Regarding conscience, the following statement of St. Paul is often quoted: "They [Gentiles] show that what the law requires is written on their hearts, to which their own conscience also bears witness; and their conflicting thoughts will accuse or perhaps excuse them." (Rom 2:15) St. Paul's expression, "the law written in the heart," reminds me of the history that God told Prophet Jeremiah that He would write His laws on people's hearts. (Jer 31:33) And God told Prophet Ezekiel that He would give people a new heart and a new spirit; and He would change people's stone hearts into hearts of flesh. (Ezek 36:26) Very interestingly, the prophets Jeremiah and Ezekiel lived during what is called the "Axial Age" when many sages promoted the qualities of the tender heart, the core of conscience.

"Axial Age" is a concept used by a German psychiatrist and historian Karl Jaspers in 1949 about BCE 800 to 200 because it was a decisive turning point in the progress of the human race. During the Axial Age, independently in different parts of the world, great visionaries emerged with new profound insights. In Jaspers' words: "The most extraordinary events are concentrated in this period."¹⁰ The sages of the Axial Age included Confucius and Lao Tzu in China: Socrates, Plato, Aristotle, Aeschylus, Sophocles, and Euripides in Greece; Buddha and the authors of the Hindu scriptures, the Upanishads in India; and the Jewish prophets Jonah, Amos, Hosea, Isaiah, Jeremiah, and Ezekiel in Israel. All of them in this list have been connected to religion. Interestingly, in our own times in the US, 19 percent of people in 2012 and 22 percent of people in 2023 reported as spiritual but not religious according to Pew Research.¹¹ Jaspers had included Zoroaster in Persia in this list. Later, historians found out that Zoroaster lived earlier than 800 BCE, probably between 1000 and 1500 BCE. So, he can be considered a transitional sage.

During the Axial Age, philosophers appeared, and great leaders promoted reason, moderation, respect for truth and the Golden Rule. People became aware of their individuality, freedom and responsibility to choose between good and evil options and consequences for their choice. Religions emphasized personal transformation over rituals and sacrifices. The great leaders promoted self-reflection. Beliefs were questioned. Thus, we can see that the various elements of conscience were shaped during this age. The law written in the heart is not a list of do's and don'ts like the Ten Commandments, but the principles of conscience as discussed earlier. With the breakthroughs of the Axial Age, the human potential for conscience could become actualized gradually in people. This is the wonderful spiritual element of human cultural evolution.

About the human cultural evolution and the Axial Age, sociologists Robert Bellah and Hans Joas say in *The Axial Age and Its Consequences,* "Donald [the evolutionary psychologist Merlin Donald] has traced the evolution of human culture through four stages, with the first, episodic culture¹², being shared with other higher mammals. Distinctly human culture begins with mimetic culture in which meanings were expressed through bodily actions and gestures, and language was absent or only incipient, and then goes on to mythical culture where full human language allowed narratives to arise and myth to form the focus of cultural organization. The fourth cultural capacity arose with the emergence of theoretic culture in the Axial Age giving the possibility of universalizable

---

10. Jaspers, *Origin*, 9.

11. Shimron, "Study," paras 1–8.

12. Episodic culture refers to episodic memory or the capacity to remember specific personal experiences.

discourse but not replacing any earlier cultural form."[13] If somebody has to read this quote again to understand it better, I am one. The word "episodic" about the first stage is related to episodic memory, i.e., memory of an event like the memory of the availability of water in a particular location during a drought. It is connected to some level of consciousness. As for the word "mimetic," think of mimicry with a smile. Myths are stories with some deeper meaning or moral element; they are products of human imagination, but theories are products of human reasoning using analysis of evidence. Having reached the theoretical stage using reason, humans have mythical and mimetic capacities too when those are useful. We can recognize conscience as an essential part of the highest level of human cultural evolution.

The word "conscience" was used by some Greek writers from around the fifth century BCE. I will discuss the Axial Age (including the story of King Cyrus the Great) in detail in chapter two. And, in chapter four, I will discuss probably the greatest example of personal transformation by the stimulation of conscience: the case of Emperor Ashoka the Great, the greatest of kings according to H. G. Wells[14] in the third century BCE. It is exciting to note that two of the most admirable rulers in history, Cyrus and Ashoka, were part of the Axial Age.

The word "conscience" is used thirty times in the *New Testament*, twenty-seven times by St. Paul, and three times by St. Peter. St. Paul's statement that some people destroy faith by rejecting conscience (quoted in the beginning of this Introduction) shows the importance he gives to conscience. And the emphasis on conscience by St. Peter is reflected in his following statement: "And *baptism*, which this prefigured, now serves you–not as a removal of dirt from the body, *but as an appeal to God for a good conscience*, through the resurrection of Jesus Christ." (1 Pet 3:21; *italics added*)

Jesus did not use the word "conscience." Jesus's teachings and examples often promoted conscience over the inner parrot. The history of Christianity and other religions show the benefits when they follow conscience, and the destructiveness caused when they contradict conscience. I discuss several examples of this in Christianity in chapter three. To the best of my knowledge, the New Testament is the only scripture where

---

13. Bellah and Joas, *Axial Age*, 3.
14. Wells, *Outline*, 165, 339.

the word conscience is used. Other religions, on their healthy side, foster conscience in different ways.

Historian of religions, Karen Armstrong says: "The first person to formulate the Golden Rule, as far as we know, is the Chinese sage Confucius…"[15] The Golden Rule is a common ethical ground in various religions. In an interesting story,[16] Rabbi Hillel the Elder (110 BCE–10 CE) was promised by a pagan that he would become a Jew if the Rabbi would stand on one leg and recite the whole Torah. Hillel stood on one leg and said: "Don't do to others what you don't want to be done to you; this is the essence of the Torah; the rest is explanations; go and learn."

A story about Prophet Muhammad is that a Bedouin (member of a nomadic tribe) came to the Prophet, addressed him as the "Messenger of God," and requested to teach him something which would enable him to go to heaven. And the Prophet told him to do to others as he would have others do to him and not do to others that he would not want others done to him.[17]

The Psychology of the Inner Voice (Conscience) and the Inner Parrot

The great psychiatrist Sigmund Freud used the word "superego" referring to the part of our personality which judges right and wrong or good and bad.[18] He explained the superego as the internalized external authority. It is the judgment of right and wrong we pick up from family and community and make it our own standard of judgment. If we pick up from society that goodness, kindness and compassion are worth pursuing, and make it our own standard, it is in tune with conscience. But if we pick up from society that racism, sexism and fanaticism are the right choices and we make it our standard we are shaping our superego against conscience because we are not using reason, the Golden Rule, moderation and truth. The superego *is really one's inner parrot, our inner Polly parrot.*

According to the Smithsonian,[19] we, Homo Sapiens, have lived on earth for three hundred thousand years. Sapiens is defined as Wise. As

15. Armstrong, *Twelve Steps*, 9.
16. Armstrong, *Great Transformation*, 379.
17. Wikipedia, "Golden Rule," paras. 40–4.
18. Freud, *New Introductory*, 60.
19. Smithsonian, "What Does," para. 1.

long as there were tribes, tribal rules and ideals, and tribal superegos could have existed. But I believe conscience developed with the Axial Age breakthroughs.

Conscience uses social influences, accepting the influences which are reasonable, moderate and consistent with truth and the Golden Rule, and rejecting the opposite influences. I have come across many people who developed their consciences in spite of wrong influences in their family and community because they rejected the forces which were unreasonable, unfair or extreme. For instance, a man who grew up in a racist family became an active member of a Unity Church, a denomination very open to various races and other religions.

In the field of psychology, ego does not mean pride and superego does not mean super pride. Ego, in a psychological sense, is the part of our personality which keeps us in touch with the reality of our situation and tries to balance the internal and external demands on us. When a person is psychotic [having delusions or hallucinations], his or her ego is not functioning well. Conscience and superego are our inner guides used by our egos. Intense feeling could push the ego to act in the direction of the feeling disregarding inner guidance if the person lacks strong self-control. This often happens in drug addiction when craving for the drug overcomes the opposing superego and conscience.

One big problem with the great psychiatrist Sigmund Freud's theory is that he taught that conscience is the negative—the guilt and shame producing part—of the superego. Conscience, our spiritual guide, as we have seen, uses our innate capacity for reason, fairness, moderation and truth to judge what choice is right or wrong. But the superego judges right and wrong based on what the person picked up from family and social groups and internalized (made it one's own) without processing through reason etc. Please note that I am using the words "conscience" and "superego" differently than how Freud used them.

Prejudices and hatreds are connected to superego and not conscience. Martin Luther King Jr. explained in his famous *Letter from the Birmingham Jail* that his nonviolent direct action was intended to stimulate the conscience of the racist community.[20] The segregationists were obviously guided by their racist superegos in dealing with Blacks. About nonviolent civil disobedience King wrote: "I submit that an individual who breaks a law that conscience tells him is unjust and willingly accepts

---

20. King, *Why*, 85.

the penalty by staying in jail to arouse the conscience of the community over its injustice, is, in reality, expressing the very highest respect for law."[21] And King had a positive response to his effort. King was following the philosophy and technique of nonviolent protest for social and political transformation by Mahatma Gandhi. The enormous success of their approach in changing the course of human history by significantly reducing racism here and colonialism and the caste system in India shows the power of conscience to reform and transform. Gandhi had integrated ideas and ideals from several sources which significantly included Jesus's Sermon on the Mount which he said "went straight to my heart"[22] and Leo Tolstoy's book *The Kingdom of God is Within You*, which also emphasized Jesus' Sermon on the Mount.[23] I believe Gandhi understood how Jesus's teaching of turning the other cheek and the like could stimulate the conscience of the opponent and result in his or her transformation.

E. Stanley Jones, an American Christian missionary and friend of Gandhi, wrote about the Gandhian non-violent activism: "It was really not a passive resistance; it was an active resistance from a higher level. The opponent strikes you on your cheek, and you strike him on the heart by your amazing spiritual audacity in turning the other cheek. You wrest the offensive from him by refusing to take his weapons, by keeping your own, and by striking him in his conscience from a higher level. He hits you physically, and you hit him spiritually."[24]

I have helped a large number of patients with self-hate. When a person hates himself or herself, who is hating who? It is the superego of the person hating the individual for not living according to the standards of the person's superego. I was able to help these patients by teaching them about conscience and superego and how to use the fair and reasonable judgment of conscience to balance the unfair and unreasonable judgment of superego. In many cases the self-hate started from verbal or physical abuse by a caregiver. In some other cases it began from being bullied in school. In a few instances, a very sensitive child felt rejected by a strict (but not abusive) parent or a teacher and developed self-hate. All forms of hatred are connected with superego, not conscience. Empathy is important to understand a person's problem so I could help the person. Helping individuals with self-hate has helped me to better understand

21. King, *Testament*, 294.
22. Gandhi, *Autobiography*, 77.
23. Tolstoy, *Kingdom*, 48.
24. Jones, *Gandhi*, 23.

hatred in general. I have also treated some rare cases of patients who were too proud of themselves and unfairly looked down on others based on excessive praise from others while growing up [see more in narcissistic personality disorder in the notes at the end of the book]. In such cases the solution is using conscience and cutting off the excessive self-flattery making the self-esteem and esteem for others fair and reasonable. Most of my patients were Christians and some belonged to several other religions. When it was useful to address conscience in therapy, hardly anybody had a correct understanding of it. But they appreciated and utilized my explanation.

CONFUSING SUPEREGO FOR CONSCIENCE

In Mark Twain's novel *Adventures of Huckleberry Finn,* the hero's intense inner struggle is very insightful psychologically and spiritually. "Huck" Finn, the adventurous white youth and his friend Jim, a black runaway slave, had many exciting times together as they traveled by the river and did many things in different places. Jim's slave owner was Miss Watson in Huck Finn's hometown and Huck knew her.

On their journey, when they stopped at one place and Jim was out and about, an elderly white man caught him and put him back in slavery. At that point, Huck debated in his mind whether Jim would be better off back with Miss Watson than being a slave under somebody else, but then it occurred to him that his hometown folks may not treat Jim nicely. Moreover, those folks would view Huck so low down for helping a black slave. "The more I studied about this the more *my conscience* (italics added) went to grinding me…" he says.[25]

He also thought Providence was punishing him. He felt that if he had gone to Sunday school he would have learned that people who did what he did with "that nigger" would suffer everlasting fire. It caused him to shiver. He was stressed out. He felt some relief when he wrote a letter to Miss Watson where Jim was. Then he reflected deeply about his relationship with Jim—how good Jim was always to him. Huck didn't come up with anything he could hold against Jim. And he remembered Jim telling him that Huck was his best friend in the world. *He studied deeply his choice* (italics added) while holding the letter. Saying "All right, then, I'll go to hell," he tore up the letter. After that, Huck put the issue out of his

---

25. Twain, *Adventures*, 212.

mind and peacefully proceeded to liberate Jim.[26] Huckleberry Finn made a mistake people often make in thinking that the inner force grinding him earlier was his conscience when it was his superego shaped by social and religious influences.

Conscience and superego overlap. The distinction between them is not at all well known. Superego is not popularly or often properly understood. The big problem is when the superego deviates significantly from conscience. It is possible that the superego is so shaped that it is fully or almost fully in tune with conscience; I have come across it rarely. For our purpose, from hereon, when I use the word superego, I will be referring to the kind of superego which deviates significantly from conscience.

Religious groups may have people guided by conscience and people guided by superego. When a group is doing unfair or destructive activities, it shows the people of superego are in power in that group. The British Colonialists in India and the white segregationists in the US had a deficiency in their religion–a deficiency of conscience at least in their relationship to their victims. The Gandhian nonviolent approaches stimulated the consciences of the oppressors to become fair and reasonable to the others. In over a year, whenever I have used the phrase "religion without conscience," everybody has pointed to the Israeli Palestinian conflict. The decades-old conflict has tragically become intensely violent since October 7, 2023, when Hamas killed twelve hundred innocent Israelis and took about two-hundred and fifty hostages. In retaliation, Israel has killed more than forty-five thousand Palestinians and displaced 90 percent of the population in Gaza in the effort to destroy Hamas, as of this writing in early March 2025. Hopefully, the efforts for peace by the US, Egypt, Qatar, and other countries, including Jordan and Saudi Arabia, will work. And hopefully, in the not-too-distant future, conscience will become a strong guide in the region.

Steps of Using Conscience and Buddha's Teaching to His Eight-year-old Son

When we are faced with deciding on a choice, the first step is awareness of our options and the likely consequences of each option. The next step is applying reason and the Golden Rule to decide on a particular option. In the next step we act on the choice we have made. Then comes

---

26. Twain, *Adventures*, 214.

reevaluating our choice based on the outcome. I use the acronym RADAR, that is, Right Awareness, Decision, Action, and Reevaluation. Consciousness-raising is a very crucial step in nonviolent movements. It is the opposite of slanted propaganda which goes with superego. Interestingly, in Hinduism and Buddhism, ignorance is considered the basic cause of evil.

When his son Rahula was eight years old, the Buddha told him how to make a good choice. Buddha first asked him what a mirror is used for and the boy answered, "for reflection." Buddha told him that before he chooses a mental, verbal or physical activity he should reflect on whether the action would cause benefit or harm to himself or others. If it brings benefit, it is good to pursue, and if it causes harm, it is to be avoided. After the action, he should examine the result. In case it results in harm, then he should consult a wise person and learn from the mistake.[27]

While it is important for a child to consult a wise person, once we develop our own wisdom, we could use it to reevaluate our choice based on the result. It is very interesting that the Buddha taught to rely on one's wisdom mind, not on one's ordinary judgmental mind. The Buddha thereby seems to have been teaching to follow one's conscience and not to rely on the superego. He also taught that compassion is the active aspect of wisdom.

PROBLEM OF IRRATIONAL GRATIFICATION (PIG)

Besides the problems from the superego, people deviate from or contradict conscience because of the problems of irrational gratification (PIG). In these cases, it is intense feelings or cravings that drive the problem. Superego would be involved in a minor role of going along or being carried away by the PIG. In the cases when the person is with a group of addicts or being a member of a gang, the ideology of the group could be a part of the person's superego. The intense feelings connected with certain human needs are the major reason for these individuals to ignore or contradict conscience. Earlier, I said all hatred relates to superego. When hatred is actively strong, intense negative feelings with the motivation to destroy the object of hate exist. Irrational satisfaction is not confined to pleasure: it can be any human need like power or pride.

---

27. Anālayo, "Buddha," paras. 3–8.

In the psychiatric field, I have observed much deficiency in reevaluation by people, especially those with addiction and personality disorder. Personality disorder is a persistent pattern of inner experiences and behaviors significantly different from what is normally expected, without losing touch with reality. *Exception: Borderline personality disorder may rarely have brief psychosis.* For example, paranoid personality disorder involves excessive suspiciousness of others, tendency to assume maliciousness on the part of others, and inability to trust and be close to others. They simply don't use conscience properly. Their awareness is twisted, and they need professional help. Many people have told me that when they get on social media, they shift from using conscience to superego judgment. This is understandable because of the strong social influence of social media.

Utilizing conscience is a very useful approach to deal with addiction and personality disorder. A study of recovery from drug addiction done in the UK by Dr. Yordan Zhekov found using conscience in therapy had very significant benefits. The book on it was published in 2019 entitled *Conscience in Recovery from Drug Addiction* with a Foreword by me.[28] In 2022, he published another book, *Conscience Therapy: Unveiling the Power of Spirituality in Conscientious Transformation*. It explains how to use the power of conscience to recover from addictions, prejudices and marital problems. The Foreword to that book was also written by me. In my view, Conscience Therapy deserves a prominent position among psychotherapies.[29]

Strengthen the Middle Ground and Conscience

We notice the right-wing and left-wing superego attacks in politics, media, and many religious groups, and this is damaging conscience. It is tragic. Even arguments about how to deal with crucial global issues have created so many culture wars, smog of war, and victimization of truth. Climate crisis had been considered a hoax for a long time by many. And it took several months for some political leaders to admit the seriousness of the COVID-19 crisis. There are political and media and religious sources which minimize the impact of pandemic and climate crises and our responsibility to act appropriately. We have to take seriously the death of

---

28. Zhekov, *Conscience in Recovery*, iv–265.
29. Zhekov, *Conscience Therapy*, 9–329.

five and a half million people worldwide from COVID-19. The US alone lost one hundred and sixty-five billion dollars in damage from the climate crisis in 2022. Unreasonable arguments and unbalanced skepticism abound. Affiliation with certain political and religious groups appears to reinforce such choices that are inconsistent with science and conscience. 2024 has been the hottest year on record.

Atlanta based minister Andy Stanley says a number of evangelical Christian leaders have considered the COVID vaccine to be "the mark of the beast," referring to the destructive beast described in the book Revelation in the Bible. Minister Andy Stanley explains his reasons for telling Christians and the church to refuse to participate in the culture wars. "But the dirty little secret of culture war advocates, both religious and nonreligious, is that they cannot afford to claim victory, or they lose followers and funding. So, both sides claim to be *losing*. That's how they *win*. The entire endeavor is fueled by fear. Both sides of any culture war conflict need an enemy to survive…you aren't supposed to love your enemy. Conflict *is* the win. There is no middle ground, and there is no room for compromise."[30] In my experience, it is easy for a person guided by his or her superego to become part of the culture war. This is one more reason to promote conscience.

We hear many ideas opposed to the middle ground. Some argue that if you are in the middle of the road, you will be run over. A similar argument is that the only thing you would find in the middle of the road is roadkill. These sayings about the road traffic are misleading in applying to the middle path in situations where two extreme choices and a middle path exist. Many people are attracted by the intensity of the extremes, distracted by shiny objects.

In an impressive article, "Christian Political Ethics Are Upside Down" (*The Dispatch*, August 21, 2022),[31] David French addresses the contradiction between the reality of American politics and Christian values. "American political culture is a toxic, hyper-partisan, corrupt, and increasingly violent mess." He argues that this should not be because the Republican and Democratic parties depend on the devout Christians for winning elections. French observes that the Christians do not condemn the fruit of the Spirit, but they have made it "secondary values." In comparison, he notes that the civil rights movement maintained the fruit of

---

30. Stanley, *Not in It*, 24–25.
31. French, "Christian Political," paras. 1–4.

the spirit in the face of beatings, dogs and firehoses. In my understanding, the civil rights movement was guided by conscience which promoted the fruit of the Spirit. Several well-informed Christians with whom I discussed the article agreed with French with the exception that they blamed one political party more than the other. In my view, the problem is when Christians are misguided by right-wing or left-wing superegos and not guided by consciences.

Education about conscience is poor. I have asked several dozen people who had studied *To Kill a Mockingbird* whether there was any discussion about conscience. Everyone said no. This is in spite of the powerful insight in the book: "*The one thing that doesn't abide by majority rule is a person's conscience.*"[32] Also, "You never really understand a person until you consider things from his point of view--"[33] I found out that one High school stopped teaching the book, reasoning that it is the white man's perspective. I think it is a good person's perspective. The Catholic Church's official teaching is that one should always obey one's "certain conscience." However, I feel that there is significant room left for many Catholics to differentiate conscience from superego and apply conscience.

A New Testament Scholar and a cross-cultural missionary in their book *Conscience* observe that conscience is one of the subjects "that studying them reaps a harvest far beyond expectations. It is like *buy one, get ten free* . . . . Yet hardly is a topic more neglected in the Christian church . . . "[34]

Rev. Billy Graham's powerful speeches on conscience that I have seen do not address the superego problems and many other issues. Insight into the superego is vital for correct understanding of conscience. Christians, people of other religions, and the "spiritual, not religious" could promote conscience as an integral part of their spirituality.

Religious mystics provide the deeper common ground between religious fanatics on the one extreme and the materialists on the other extreme. Mystics of different religions show deep spirituality and are inclusive of others. They promote love, peace, and goodness. Fanatics tend to hate mystics. The Islamic extremist group ISIS has destroyed several mosques of the Sufis, who represent the mystical side of Islam.

---

32. Lee, *Mockingbird*, 109.
33. Lee, *Mockingbird*, 34.
34. Naselli and Crowley, *Conscience*, 15.

Quantum Questions, edited by Ken Wilber, is a collection of original spiritual writings by eight great modern physicists, six of them Nobel Prize winners including Albert Einstein and Max Planck.[35] I have found this information very useful for many people who struggle with spirituality and science. This information is not as widely known as it deserves to be.

An ideal inner guidance system would have conscience as the master guide and superego under it without it going to extremes. Feelings are a very important part of providing input into our awareness and motivation to express good choices. We can tune out feelings which are harmful or useless. What may be considered negative feelings like envy may be useful in some ways. Envy might make us aware of something superior to us, another person or group has. And it can lead us to make some useful changes. In her book *Holy Envy,* Barbara Brown Taylor points out how jealous feelings about some teachings or rituals in another religion made her modify her Christian perspective. She discusses her experience of teaching a college course on religions including taking students to different places of worship. She envied when she found out that Judaism and Islam do not teach original sin.[36] Although she did not mention it, Christian thinkers like Matthew Fox and John Shelby Spong have rejected the original sin concept. Matthew Fox wrote an entire book against the original sin idea, *Original Blessing.*[37] More recently, Bishop John Shelby Spong wrote against original sin in his book, *Unbelievable.* In the book, he addresses the concept of original sin and calls it "pre-Darwinian mythology and post-Darwinian nonsense," further saying "we have to find a new way to tell the old story."[38] Envy could go in the destructive direction if we let it do so. Therefore, we have to use conscience and choose the right course. On the unhealthy side, different religious groups have promoted misinformation and even hateful propaganda and sometimes violence. These are based on the superego approach, not guided by conscience.

---

35. Wilber, *Quantum,* 1–226.
36. Taylor, *Holy Envy,* 73.
37. Fox, *Original,* 3–367.
38. Spong, *Unbelievable,* 90–99.

SPIRITUAL DEFECT

I think of religion and any kind of spirituality without conscience as "Spiritual defect." People with personality disorders tend to twist their spirituality also along the lines of their disorder. For example, a compulsive or perfectionist person would tend to be nitpicky with his or her spirituality. And a person with a paranoid personality would tend to have suspiciousness and insecurity about his or her spirituality.

The famous theologian who formulated the "serenity prayer,"[39] (God grant me the serenity to accept the things I cannot change; courage to change the things I can; and wisdom to know the difference.) Reinhold Niebuhr, analyzed "a constant and seemingly irreconcilable conflict between the needs of society and the imperatives of a sensitive conscience."[40] His analysis showed that "the highest moral insights and achievements of the individual conscience are both relevant and necessary to the life of society."[41] *Gandhi and King proved this point.*

---

39. Niebuhr, "Serenity Prayer," 87.
40. Niebuhr, *Moral*, 257.
41. Niebuhr, *Moral*, 257.

Part 1

Conscience, Religion, and Spirituality

PLEASE NOTE:

"PIG" stands for "Problem of Irrational Gratification"

Conscience is the human capacity to judge what is a right or wrong choice using reason, the Golden Rule, moderation, and respect for truth.

Superego, or the inner parrot, is the judgment of right or wrong based on what a person picks up from external sources (and uses without processing with reason, Golden Rule, moderation, and respect for truth).

I think of social values which do not significantly deviate from conscience as part of conscience.

In many matters, such as international peace or dealing with the climate crisis, most people may be quite limited in what they can do. But in democratic countries people can support with contribution and votes for the leaders who promote good policies.

Chapter One

Conscience, the Inner Parrot, and the PIG

"The heart is like a garden. It can grow compassion or fear, resentment or love. What seeds will you plant there?" — Buddha[1]

"[For] there are two things inside me competing with the human self which I must try to become. They are the Animal self, and the Diabolical self. The Diabolical self is the worst of the two. That is why a cold, self-righteous prig, who goes regularly to church may be far nearer to hell than a prostitute. But, of course, it is better to be neither." — C.S. Lewis[2]

IN THE INTRODUCTION, I observed that conscience guides us to choose what is good by using the principles of what is good or useful, reasonable, in tune with the Golden Rule, moderation and respect for truth. Related to these principles, in this chapter, I will explore a large number of different tendencies between conscience and the inner parrot (the superego) like self-reflection vs. self-defeating defenses, depth vs. superficiality, conscience psychology vs. behavior psychology, perspective vs. angle of argument, and so on. I will also discuss Extremism which relates to

---

1. Kornfield, *Buddha's*, 11.
2. Lewis, *Mere*, 95.

superego and addiction which relates to the Problem of Irrational Gratification (PIG).

The Animal Self that Lewis refers to above is the PIG (problem of irrational gratification) which I discussed in the Introduction and the Diabolical self is the Superego. In fact, for the Diabolical self, Lewis gave the example of a "cold, self-righteous prig who goes regularly to church."[3] In this chapter, I will use three quotes from Shakespeare's King Richard III. (*A point of caution: looking at the quotes from Shakespeare, nobody needs to be concerned that this chapter, or the book, will be a tough academic exercise. Read on and experience the down-to-earth practical and significant approach that I take. I will provide explanations to make it easy, especially for the third quote, which is the complicated one. Enjoy the keen insights and beautiful expression of Shakespeare.*)

First, we will look at the bard's description of why a professional murderer avoids using his conscience because the way conscience works on people. He misinterprets that conscience would make him a coward but, in reality, conscience would have made him courageous instead of foolhardy, committing severe crimes.

> "I'll not meddle with it. It makes a man a coward; a man cannot steal, but it accuseth him; a man cannot swear, but it checks him; a man cannot lie with his neighbor's wife, but it detects him: 'tis a blushing shame-faced spirit that mutinies in a man's bosom; it fills one full of obstacles: it made me once restore a purse of gold that by chance I found; it beggars any man that keeps it: it is turned out of all towns and cities for a dangerous thing; and every man that means to live well endeavors to trust to himself and live without it." (Act I, Scene IV)[4]

We can note the cold-blooded calculating superego of a hired hitman consciously blocking his conscience to do his dastardly deeds with inner comfort. There is a method in his manipulations internally as well as externally. Next, let us view Shakespeare's brilliant portrayal of an intense inner conflict of a very disturbed character, King Richard III, in the play named after him. King Richard III has intense internal conflicts about the evil deeds like the murders he had committed. Then, in the third quote, the King deals with his inner conflict by playing games with his conscience using his superego.

3. Lewis, *Mere*, 95.
4. Shakespeare, *Tragedy*, Act 1, Scene 4.

> "O coward conscience, how dost thou afflict me–
> The lights burn blue–It is now dead midnight
> Cold fearful drops stand on my trembling flesh.
> What, do I fear myself? There's none else by:
> Richard loves Richard; that is, I am I.
> Is there a murderer here? No;---yes I am:
> Then fly. What, from myself? Great reason why,--
> ..." (Act V Scene III)[5]

The intensity of the conflict is due to the severity of the subject. Now, see his decision-making process using his superego.

> "Conscience is but a word that cowards use,
> Devised at first to keep the strong in awe:
> Our strong arms be our conscience, swords our law.
> March on, join bravely, let us to't pell-mell;
> If not to heaven, then hand in hand to hell— ..."[6]

We can see in the first two lines how he is devaluing conscience, falsely arguing like it is fake—something created to control the strong people. Then he provides his alternate ideology: might is right. And he promotes the idea of marching on or staying the course without reevaluation and useful change of course. He claims the virtue of being brave, which is false again, because going against conscience is foolishness, not courage. This kind of evil deed, arguing that it is a virtue, is one of the worst distortions. For example, many religious fanatics hatefully attack people who are different from them in the name of love of God. And he finally appeals for group support which reinforces the superego. That is literally the bottom line. I have seen people trying to smooth away guilt and shame from conscience with superego arguments like "everybody does it." We frequently observe certain politicians engaging in unethical behavior, backed by their base of supporters. Amazingly, in five lines, Shakespeare has shown the five common ways people con their consciences.

STEPS OF USING CONSCIENCE OR SUPEREGO

As mentioned in the Introduction, there are four steps in using conscience: Right Awareness, Decision, Action, and Reevaluation (RADAR).

5. Shakespeare, *Tragedy*, Act 5, Scene 3.
6. Shakespeare, *Tragedy*, Act 5, Scene 3.

Superego may take the same steps with different values. In the awareness step, conscience would try to have a broad perspective, awareness, or information about the matter in consideration. But superego tends to limit information to a narrow perspective. For instance, more and more people seem to be in an information bubble, limiting their exposure to information only from either right-wing or left-wing sources. Limiting relevant information reduces respect for truth and use of conscience. In the step of decision, conscience would apply reason, the Golden Rule, and moderation but superego would follow the party line or the group's ideal. In the step of action, conscience would keep an eye on whether the impact of the action seems to be desirable or not. Conscience would reconsider and change course if it noticed undesirable outcomes occurring, but superego would tend to keep the course. In the step of reevaluation conscience makes a sincere and open observation and impartial judgment of what was done being ready to feel guilt/shame or feel good. Superego tends to make a skewed evaluation. For example, a fanatical Christian had much guilt about any fleeting sexual thoughts but no guilt about hateful ideas about Muslims which he promoted among others.

Please note: In the following sections, the distinction of the two sides that I've contrasted is that they represent divergent tendencies, not absolute or exclusive extremes.

SELF-REFLECTION VS. SELF-DEFEATING SELF-DEFENSE

"Do not be conformed to this world, but be transformed by the renewal of your mind, that by testing you may discern what is the will of God, what is good and acceptable and perfect." Rom 12:2

Self-reflection is very important for all and very difficult for many. In a memorable statement, German Philosopher Friedrich Nietzsche stated: "I have done that, says my memory. I cannot have done that–says my pride–and remains unshakable. Finally–my memory yields."[7]

Psychologically, Nietzsche prevented feeling guilt and shame about his wrongdoing by this denial. Obviously, it was the victory of one part of him or one need, his pride, at the expense of his total self and his integrity. Similarly, one could be protecting one part, like one's power, or pleasure, or identity, or relationship, and so on at the expense of the whole person.

---

7. Nietzsche, *Beyond*, 59.

CONSCIENCE, THE INNER PARROT, AND THE PIG

We tend to identify closely with our group, and so, like our individual pride, our group's pride, power, identity, relationships, etc., becomes very important for us. And denial of our group's wrongdoing also gains personal importance for us. Neutral observers can notice this tendency more or less on the part of religious and political groups to deny or minimize the wrongdoing by the group. If the wrongdoing was way back in history, the group members may be less defensive about it. Catholics seem to be not too sensitive about reference to the Crusades. In fact, Pope Francis, like some other Popes before him, has described the Crusades as shameful actions.[8] Polarization of right-wing and left-wing has become intense in politics and media, and many Christian groups. Such polarization prevents a broad perspective with better understanding and chance for good resolution of problems.

Moreover, individuals could get stuck with the group's ideology and agenda, becoming unable to be authentic. One big tragedy these days is the denial or minimization going on in many Christian groups regarding the dangers of the climate crisis and the need for taking action to deal with it. Group identity appears to be a major reason many Americans were not wearing masks and taking vaccines to protect themselves and others from COVID-19 infection, against the recommendations of medical experts.

Denial is often impractical when the wrongdoing is blatant. Rationalization is a common defense in such situations. We can notice many people's tendency to rationalize; however irrational their choices are. They use twisted reasoning in the name of personal freedom or anti-government or anti-science arguments. Rationalization protects the person from guilt or shame about the wrongdoing, but it also removes the motivation to face the truth, to change for the better, to grow, and transform.

Another age-old defense is shifting blame from oneself to other people or other sources. It is often said that Adam blamed Eve and she blamed the serpent. Interestingly, the serpent did not blame the attractive fruit or the tree. Televangelist Jimmy Swaggart's blaming the devil for his sex scandal became news.[9] Some Christian groups tend to blame the devil a lot. If that is one's understanding of evil, still, one has to take responsibility for one's role in going along with the devil. If we don't take

---

8. Pope Francis, "Dialogue," 1–3.
9. Balmer, "Still Wrestling," paras. 1–10.

responsibility for our wrongdoing and face the guilt or shame, we miss the motivation to learn and change.

Blaming others or the circumstances; finger pointing when soul searching is needed is rather common in psychiatric cases, especially in people with addiction or personality disorder. Personality disorder is an enduring pattern of inner experience and behavior that deviates markedly from the expectations of the individual's culture, according to psychiatry. Within the US population, 9.1 percent are reported to have a personality disorder.

An important feature of personality disorder is that the person is unaware of the problem; the person doesn't feel that he or she has that problem whereas a person with depression or anxiety feels distressed from the symptoms. People with personality disorders would feel the abnormality is on the part of others and not on themselves.

A brief understanding of personality disorders is very important for two reasons: (1) if other people imply or you get an inkling that you may have a personality disorder, then it is crucial to find more information and consider professional help, and, (2) if somebody in your relationship shows features of a personality disorder you have to seriously consider its impact and be cautious. Be extremely cautious of criminal or antisocial personalities. They do criminal acts and have an extreme deficiency of empathy, compassion, and conscience. If you happen to be in a relationship with such a person, working with the legal system could be crucial. Even in politics, if a leader shows evidence of a personality disorder, you must be cautious about believing and supporting the person. Refer to the Notes section at the end of the book for more details and brief descriptions of the most commonly seen personality disorders.

People with any personality disorder do not use their consciences properly. They have difficulty with every step (RADAR) of using conscience. And their superegos are loose, except for perfectionists, who have rigid superegos. Learning about conscience and superego and how to use their consciences help them tremendously. Psychotherapy helps especially if the problem with conscience is addressed. People with personality disorders benefit from religious groups promoting balanced self-reflection and 12-step groups taking "fearless moral inventory" and working on "defects of character." However, religious groups which promote superegos with rigidity or conspiracy theories or hate make personality problems worse. Good friends and family members or companions could gently bring up the problem to the attention of such people and persuade them to get help. Therapists benefit greatly by getting information from close family or friends of the patient (client) because the patient may not reveal the true picture. In psychotherapy, the therapist may have to use "supportive confrontation" discussing the issue in a friendly, pragmatic, and optimistic way to open the minds of people with personality disorders. It is similar to the way Martin Luther King Jr. described nonviolent direct action to cause creative tension. Since personality disorders do not cause internal tension to change, external pressure is needed to stimulate the creative tension. It is like the saying that some people see the light only when they feel the heat. When family and friends do an "intervention" with an addict who is in denial, they are using this approach. Indeed, crises provide the opportunity for change, but it is crucial for it to be nonviolent, creative, not destructive.

All the above defects are closely connected with the superego. In therapy, I have found it especially useful to explain the benefits of healthy guilt and shame when we have done wrong or fallen short of reasonable expectations. Healthy guilt and shame lead us to regret the wrong, repair damage, if possible, prevent repetition, add the lesson from the experience to our wisdom and end positively, rejoicing in the transformation. I point out Jesus's statement to remove the log from our own eyes before removing the speck from another's eyes. As people overcome the problem, they become adept in helping others with similar problems. Unhealthy guilt and shame can be either too much or too little.

DEPTH VS. SUPERFICIALITY

"Unless your righteousness exceeds the righteousness of the Scribes and Pharisees ye shall in no case enter the kingdom of heaven." Matt 5:20

The Scribes and Pharisees were preoccupied with rituals and traditions. Those could be done without the inner transformation of loving God and neighbor that Jesus emphasized. I became aware of this kind of problem from childhood because of a man in our community. He was mockingly called "saint" by a lot of people. He prayed the loudest in our church. He even used to go to other churches in the surrounding area and pray loudly particularly on special days of the church. Many Catholics used to wear a Catholic scapular (a necklace with a picture of St. Mary or Jesus). He wore a scapular several times bigger than that of other Catholics. It reminds me of how Jesus criticized the Scribes and

Pharisees for wearing big phylacteries (small leather boxes with scripture passages inside) which they wore on their foreheads showing off their religiosity. Interestingly, this "saint" was the only person known to be a child abuser in the community. He used the proverb "spare the rod and spoil the child" to justify his action. Sometimes he used a branch of a rose bush as his rod, just removing the thorns enough for him to hold it without hurting his hand. Others had intervened to protect his children.

A patient in her thirties who finally overcame her rigid superego by learning to be guided by her conscience declared: "I am like a butterfly now having come out of a cocoon in which I lived for decades." She had grown up in a family which overemphasized fear of God and focused much on hellfire and damnation. She had developed a harsh superego and self-hate for not being perfect. She was superficial, both psychologically and spiritually. She used to keep her affiliation with her Christian community. Learning about conscience and superego and living by her conscience was the crucial step in her transformation. With that change she became, overall, much deeper in her perspective within her faith and in her life. For many years she was on medicines and therapy for anxiety and depression. These treatments had helped to some extent with those symptoms. But reading my book, *Fulfillment Using Real Conscience*, dealing with her religious issues using conscience, with the help of therapy, made a dramatic difference in her life. Previously, she used to get stressed and anxious whenever she was around some family members who expressed extremist Christian views.

Another person, Mathew (not his real name), grew up with the ideal "pray, pay, and obey" from his church; a broader understanding of faith, especially any doubting, was discouraged. He was told if he doubted any teachings of his church, he would be out of God's blessing. While in therapy for anxiety, he became aware that doubting and questioning are part of spiritual growth. As he practiced meditation, learned about conscience and superego, and handled his needs with conscience, he overcame his anxiety and became spiritually strong. Since we live at a time when we have access to a great deal of information about our potential choices and their consequences, we could make a lot of choices guided by our consciences. When we are children, we need simple lists of right and wrong but as we grow, we can use the principles of conscience in making choices. He realized that similar to Socrates's statement that an unexamined life is not worth living,[10] an unexamined faith is not as worthwhile as a faith with a deeper perspective.

Some people are almost deathly afraid of depth, afraid of the unknown, and scared of going astray. In one case, a lady struggled for many years about believing in the spiritual as she thought science was against religion. She had grown up in a traditional Christian family. She admired science and was exposed to some atheistic arguments. She struggled between Christian Fanaticism and atheism. She knew the ideas of atheists like Richard Dawkins. I recommended her to read *Quantum Questions* edited by Ken Wilber which I mentioned in the Introduction of this book. When she finished reading it, she gained a new and exciting spiritual outlook, integrating deeper spiritual and scientific views.

She was joyful and wanted to share her new understanding and excitement with her husband. But he refused to listen to her because he was too scared to touch on his beliefs from his Sunday school days in his youth. He kept his belief like an extremely fragile treasure which might explode if he touched it. There is a profound common ground of spirituality among mystics of different religions and the great scientists with spiritual orientation.

Richard Dawkins, in his well-known book, *The God Delusion*, doesn't address the mystical experience, religious mystics, and conscience.[11] Even in his discussion about Einstein, Dawkins did not say anything about Einstein's idea of the three stages of religion: religion of fear, religion of morality, and the highest stage—cosmic religious feeling. Einstein gave the examples of Democritus, Francis of Assisi, and Spinoza in the cosmic religious feeling level. Einstein also stated that the strongest and noblest motive for scientific research is the cosmic religious feeling. He observed that science "contributes to a religious spiritualization of our understanding of life."[12] Dawkins argues against not only extremist religion but also against mild and moderate religions because they might become extreme. In my experience, healthy spirituality guided by conscience and a good connection to religion is the best solution for religious extremism.

The other famous atheist Steven Pinker, in *Enlightenment Now*, doesn't address mysticism or conscience. Pinker admits the contributions of religions in the fields like education and healthcare. He advocates

---

10. Plato, *Apology*, 38a.
11. Dawkins, *God Delusion*, 34–41.
12. As quoted in Wilbur, *Quantum*, 111.

praising religious groups for their specific good contributions and condemning the religious groups for their particular wrongdoings. Pinker claims that humanism is the moral alternative to theism.[13] As a life member of the Association for Humanistic Psychology, I can say we have hardly been active for many years and then somewhat active in a few recent years. Humanistic psychology is inclusive of spirituality. Abraham Maslow, the most prominent humanistic psychologist, had a friendly and respectful relationship with the mystical side of religion. His book *Religions, Values, and Peak-Experiences* has fostered mystical religious experiences. Humanistic philosophy seems rather active, but it seems materialistic.[14]

Those who are sincerely seeking could find comfort in Jesus's own words: "So, I say to you, ask, and it will be given to you; seek, and you will find; knock, and it will be opened to you." (Luke 11:9) In my experience, some children get so scared from hellfire and damnation preaching or angry responses to genuine questions about faith that they quit seeking. Some of them become agnostic or atheistic, and others stay superficial believers. Respect for truth—whether historical, scientific, psychological or any other—is in harmony with conscience.

CONSCIENCE PSYCHOLOGY VS. BEHAVIORAL PSYCHOLOGY

According to behavioral psychology, rewarding a behavior increases the behavior and punishment decreases the behavior. We use this approach with domestic animals. Reward and punishment approaches are very common in our daily lives. We use rewards by increased salary or promotion for good work and demotion for poor performance. Incarceration is one of the stiffest punishments. I wonder why incarceration is so high in the US, with around 65 percent of the population being Christian and yet, 25 percent of the incarcerated people in the world are here in the US. It seems to me that a behavioral approach is heavy in our culture including among the Christians and the media.

Rollo May, the humanist psychologist, expresses his strong opposition to the famous Behavioral psychologist B.F. Skinner's scorn for the idea of human freedom as untrue and a block to progress; May compared

---

13. Pinker, *Enlightenment*, 430.
14. Maslow, *Religions*, 59–66.

Skinner to Dostoyevsky's Grand Inquisitor.[15] Both were opposed to freedom; Skinner denied the very existence of freedom while the Inquisitor admits its existence but claims it is dangerous for the public. Of course, it is very useful for us to be aware of how our freedom is limited by our superegos and various external forces.

People using conscience go beyond the reward/punishment paradigm and choose what is right and pursue it. Nonviolent activists in civil rights movements have taken punishments and kept their commitment. Their satisfaction or good feelings are based on their commitment to the cause and their ideals. Many people have a hard time understanding this. It is our special human capacity to pursue our meaning and ideal irrespective of reward or punishment. It is not being masochistic either. Accepting suffering is only when necessary to pursue a conscientious cause.

In order to use conscience properly, one has to be open-minded because a broad awareness is inevitable to apply reason, the Golden Rule, and moderation. Prejudices and various negative feelings tend to narrow or close the mind. Such are fear, anger, hatred, and disgust. On the other hand, positive feelings like empathy, compassion, courage and love open the mind. Religious and political leaders who stimulate too much negative feelings are often manipulating people away from using their consciences.

It is useful to remember how Jesus calmed the guys who brought the adulteress to him by bending down and writing on the ground. Once we have made a decision using our conscience, strong feelings of courage, love, compassion, and the like would be important to strengthen willpower especially if the choice is difficult to make and implement. An open-minded person would give a chance to understand another view before accepting or rejecting it. At the same time, an open mind is not a hole in the head; one has to be choosy about what ideas one chooses to examine because of our limitations of time and energy.

Being able to use feelings appropriately is very important to live by one's conscience. We have to be aware of our feelings and what signals and motivation the feelings are causing. Then we can take the useful next step. Some feelings could be ignored. Some other feelings may be important to act on. We can learn to tune up or tune down feelings by the way we think about them and focus more or less on them. Practice of meditation helps one to have good skills in this process.

15. May, *Freedom*, 199.

RATIONAL VS. IRRATIONAL THINKING AND ACTION

This approach involves changing irrational beliefs causing symptoms like anxiety or depression. For example, a belief that one must be perfectly successful to be valued. In therapy, the therapist would help the client to recognize and correct the irrational belief. Superego is connected with all kinds of negative thoughts and conscience can neutralize them. In the spiritual field, our pattern of thinking is given much importance. Buddhist Scripture Dhammapada opens with a statement: "What we are is a result of what we have thought."

Interestingly, the Buddha identified three problems of the mind, the three poisons: greed, hatred and delusion (ignorance). Opposing these poisons are the three wholesome or positive attitudes: generosity, loving-kindness, and wisdom. Buddhist practitioners identify the thoughts that give rise to the three poisons, not dwell on those thoughts, and nurture thoughts that give rise to positive attitudes. Living by conscience involves using conscience in various choices.

PERSPECTIVE VS. ANGLE OF ARGUMENT

In his rather humorous book, *Bigfoot . . . It's Complicated,* former Congressman and former Intelligence Officer Denver Riggleman describes his experiences with Bigfoot believers' unreasonable convictions about Bigfoot. He explored the beliefs of many Bigfoot believers and went on a Bigfoot expedition where they did not find any Bigfoot but it did not change true believers' belief. Some of the believers had an interesting curiosity about Bigfoot's genitals. He says that he had similar feelings of curious dread while running for office in Virginia and listened to activists on the far left and the far right.[16] As the philosopher Nietzsche had suggested, we must have the courage to attack conviction, not just the courage of conviction. Of course, the courage of right conviction is important.

Some people use various angles of arguments for justifying their prejudice. A Methodist lady said her father was against Catholics moving to their neighborhood because Catholics would have too many children and make the neighborhood noisy.

The struggle between two pastors, John Cotton and Roger Williams, in the seventeenth century in New England illustrates the difference

---

16. Riggleman, *Bigfoot,* 174.

between a superego approach and a conscience approach. Cotton supported religious persecution against people who did not follow Christian orthodoxy. He argued that it was God's will to separate the sick element from the healthy part of society. In his view, it was needed to keep social order. Authoritarians like to use their power over others and the argument for law and order is a big stick they use to support their approach. Cotton emphasized the inherent sinfulness of people. He argued that the presence of dissidents and heretics would corrupt society, so they must be punished. If they don't reform, they must be banished. There was much fear of Satan's presence in the community and witch-hunts. Cotton did not care for the freedom of conscience, but his opponent Roger Williams was a champion of conscience.

Roger Williams sternly opposed persecution which he called "Soule rape." He promoted religious liberty and emphasized conscience. He had experienced goodness, dignity, and integrity outside Christian orthodoxy. And he appreciated the love, peace, gentleness, and goodness of the natives, and had a very friendly relationship with them. He promoted love and respected human dignity, and Williams established the Rhode Island colony. Cotton provides clear examples of the angle of argument supporting superego and Williams shows the broad perspective of conscience.[17]

Right-wing and left-wing angles of argument bombard us, especially during the election season. Take the example of the climate crisis. Right-wing arguments include the idea that what we experience with climate change is just a natural cycle. Another argument is that in some places there is more snow sometimes and so global warming is false. Some people argue that climate crisis talk is a hoax. There are people who say it is Chinese propaganda. The left-wing extreme seems to cause fear and resistance to their ideas by proposing radical changes like decarbonization by 2025. Calls for extremely radical changes cause some people to be afraid it would cause an economic catastrophe and lifestyle crisis. Both extremes predict doom if the other side wins the election. As the old saying goes, truth is the first casualty of war. In culture wars too, truth is an ongoing victim. In the feverish heat of battle, people tune down or even turn off their consciences. What is needed is more awareness of the problem and better use of conscience. It was a great step when in 2022 President Biden passed the Inflation Reduction Act with three hundred and seventy-nine billion dollars for clean energy. The US being a leader

---

17. Nussbaum, *Liberty*, 46–9.

in fighting the climate crisis is consistent with conscience, but we can hear strong objections to this step by people with unreasonable superego judgements.

The vast majority of climate scientists believe climate change is increasingly damaging our planet because of human activity. According to a Pew research report in November 2022, only 34 percent of evangelical Christians agree with it compared to 68 percent of black Protestants, 55 percent of mainline Protestants, 70 percent of people without religious affiliation, and 57 percent of the general population and Catholics.[18] Many Christians think there is not enough evidence for the scientists' view, many others believe God is in control and whatever change is part of His plan. The group Young Evangelicals for Climate Action, who promote environmental protection, gives hope for positive change. Dr. Katherine Hayhoe is a climate scientist and Evangelical Christian who has been promoting climate science. I heard her inspiring speech at Samford University, a Baptist institution in Birmingham, in February 2024.[19]

Pope Francis was a very active leader in fighting the climate crisis. In 2015, he dedicated an Encyclical (Laudato Si') to climate issues. He has urged Catholic institutions and people and governments to act on fighting the climate crisis.[20] There have been objections to the Pope's efforts by people who don't believe in humanly caused global warming or who think the Pope should stay out of issues with political implications. Pope Francis had an 83 percent favorable rating in the October 2021 Pew report among US Catholics.[21] But some Catholics are critical of him. One Catholic said: "Pope Francis talks a lot about mercy but not about justice." Justice meant hell for sinners in this person's view. Some Catholics considered Pope Francis as Antichrist. I got an email from some group showing the Pope either about to go in or come out of an airplane and reminding people of the Pope's preaching to live a simple life. The propaganda apparently was that the Pope was hypocritical about his climate stance. Did those people expect the Pope to walk to Africa or take a public bus? In reality, Pope Francis was well-known to live a simple life compared to Popes in general.

In September 2021, a total of two hundred and thirty-three health journals in the world published the same editorial calling for urgent

18. Pew, "How Religion," paras. 1–6.
19. Hayhoe, "Climate," 80 min.
20. Pope Francis, *Laudato Si'*, 1–184.
21. Pew, "Two-thirds," paras. 1-13.

action to limit global temperature increase below 1.5 degree C, maintain biodiversity, and protect health.[22] They warned about catastrophic harm to health that would be impossible to reverse if the urgent steps are not taken. The editorial noted that in the previous twenty years, heat-related death among over sixty-five-year-olds had increased over 50 percent. Higher temperatures have caused an increase in the following conditions: dehydration, loss of renal function, skin cancers, tropical infections, allergies, mental health problems, pregnancy complications, and cardiovascular and pulmonary illnesses. Additionally, global warming since 1981 has caused the decline of global yield potential for major crops by 1.8–5.6 percent. Food and water security is eroded by the widespread destruction of nature. The side effects of the environmental crisis fall more on the poor who have less resources. I consider these editorials as an example of the awakened conscience of the editors. Opposite to this, we can notice the unreasonable skepticism and even minimization of the climate crisis among some other media, showing the underlying superego problem. "The Conscience" was the title of *Time Magazine*'s article on Greta Thunberg, the young Swedish environmental activist, who was chosen as the "Person of the Year" for 2019.[23] So appropriate!

A lady I dealt with some years ago was an outspoken Christian. One time she had the opportunity to take a man to the cleaners in a lawsuit using a legal technicality and unfairly gain a considerable sum of money. Knowing how her legal action would go against St. Paul's emphatic objection to Christians suing fellow Christians, I asked her about the conflict. She quoted from the King James version of the Bible: "[But] brother goes to law with brother, and that before the unbelievers. Now therefore there is a fault among you, because you go to law one with another." Then, she said she was fine with her legal action because he was not her brother.

As a doctor, I am well aware of the US healthcare system. And I know about the universal healthcare systems in Canada, England, Germany and Australia from media sources and personal sources on the provider side and consumer side from close relatives. With such perspective, I can see how mistaken the angle of argument here is that it would be a step towards communism if the US adopts such a system. It is one thing to discuss the practical merits and defects of the other health care systems compared to our current system, but it is so extreme to invoke

---

22. Atwoli et al., "Call," paras. 1–18.
23. Worland, "Conscience," paras. 1–9.

fear of communism about it. Such extreme fear is reminiscent of a Baptist Professor in the novel *Elmer Gantry* telling people not to drink ginger ale because they might slip into drinking ale.

Several media personalities express their angle of arguments which makes it difficult for a lot of people to have a broad perspective. We find the opinions of reputable historians and views on world issues by journalists who have real international experience useful. Those analysts and propagandists who promote wrong impressions and ideas deviate the audience from conscience to superego.

BOTH/ AND, OR NEITHER/ NOR MENTALITY VS. EITHER/ OR

Jesus is often quoted saying: "He who is not with me is against me." (Matt 12:30) But Jesus also said: "Whoever is not against us is for us." (Mark 9:40) Interestingly, we rarely find this quote used. In the first case, Jesus was dealing with spirits. When the choice is between good spirits and evil spirits, there is only one good choice. In the second case, Jesus's disciples stopped a man casting out demons in Jesus's name. Jesus told them not to stop the man and explained that those who were not against them were with them. The man was largely on the side of Jesus although he was not a disciple.

Of course, a woman cannot be a little bit pregnant. The lady is either pregnant or not pregnant. But she could well be socially liberal and financially conservative as well as neither a Republican or a Democrat; she is independent. The devil—no, the angel—is in the details. Get a perspective!

In his farewell address, President George Washington had warned that partisanship would "make the public administration the mirror of the ill-concerted and incongruous projects of faction, rather than the organ of consistent and wholesome plans digested by common counsels and modified by mutual interests."[24] In recent decades, partisanship has become damaging.

An interesting example of destructive rivalry is what an Alabama football fan did in his opposition to the rival Auburn football team. In 2010, Harvey Updike poisoned two huge oak trees at the Toomer's Corner on the Auburn campus which were important for the Auburn team in

---

24. Washington, "Farewell," paras. 1–42.

their celebrations. And he bragged about it to a radio host without giving his name. But authorities traced him, and he got a jail term and a fine. The trees did not survive long.[25]

Superego could easily take a black or white mentality. It is a prominent problem for perfectionists. Gray areas are often pushed to the black side by these folks to be on the safer side. Rivalry between two parties can cause much damage to the middle ground. There is a saying that when elephants fight, the grass gets trampled. More importantly, when parents fight, children suffer. When political parties polarize excessively, democracy suffers as has been happening in our country. We need to build more common ground by promoting conscience, and authentic Christianity can play a crucial role in it.

My first book was *The Two Faces of Religion: A Psychiatrist's View* which discussed the healthy and the unhealthy sides of religions. Several media persons who interviewed me told me that the book would have been much more popular if I had written only about one or the other side of religions. I appreciate their honesty and helpful attitude, but had I done that, I would have been selling my soul.

AUTHENTIC INDIVIDUALITY VS. AUTHORITARIANISM AND DEPENDENCY

Conscience promotes authentic individuality, but superego tends to promote authoritarianism and dependency. Authentic individuality involves making choices using conscience, utilizing reason and the Golden Rule. All our choices are connected with our needs. Authentic individuals use their awareness to explore their needs and choices. They consider the pros and cons of each choice weighing consequences and applying reason and the Golden Rule. Both reason and feeling are involved in this process. Then they choose to pursue the best option.

Authoritarian leaders are guided by superegos with rigidity, self-righteousness, selfishness, dogmatism, superficiality and manipulation. They have a strong need for controlling others and guilt or shame about failing in their agenda, not much in causing problems for somebody else. The dependent followers are also guided by superegos. Their superegos misguide them to be submissive and dependent. They tend to have significant self-doubt and much guilt or shame if criticized by authority figures.

25. CBS News, "Alabama Fan," paras 1–19.

An example is an interesting story I believe was told by the Christian author Martin Marty. He had noticed for several years in Thanksgiving celebrations one lady used to be critical of people drinking alcohol. Then one year he noticed the same lady drinking wine. When he asked the lady about the change she said: "I have a new pastor."

Among many books written by people in politics or economics with "Conscience" in the title, *"Conservatives Without Conscience"* by John W. Dean discusses conscience. Dean discusses Authoritarian Personality extensively, the right-wing variety, and their submissive followers. Dean has used social psychologist Stanley Milgram's and Bob Altemeyer's insights regarding authoritarianism.[26]

Milgram is famous for his experiments about obedience to authority. His experiments showed that 65 percent of apparently ordinary people were willing to subject protesting victims ("learners") to increasingly painful electric shocks. The people administering the shock were following the instructions of a scientist wearing a lab coat in a lab. The authority figure ordered an increasing level of electricity to determine whether it would make the learners learn faster. The learners expressed increasing pain although they were pretending for the experiment and they were not being shocked. According to Milgram, a person's conscience becomes subservient to the group when the person joins a group. In my experience, it is the superego that changes by joining a group.[27] Conscience changes if truth, reason, moderation, and the Golden Rule requires the change.

Dean also used psychologist Bob Altemeyer's findings about rightwing authoritarianism. I have no comments about the leaders Dean wrote about. As for Dean's description of right-wing authoritarianism, I consider it as insightful but it is only part of right-wing superego. Moreover, there is also a similar left-wing superego. Conscience functions at a deeper and balanced level.

Ben Shapiro, who is popular with the right-wing, argues that the battles in the newsrooms in America currently are not between conservatives and liberals but between authoritarian leftists and liberals. He further explains the battle between people who may largely agree on policy preferences, but who disagree on whether robust discussion should be allowed. The authoritarian left argues no. The liberals argue yes.[28] I have

26. Dean, *Conservatives*, 40–49.
27. Dean, *Conservatives*, 41.
28. Shapiro, *Authoritarian*, 173.

no comments on this except a question: any moderates around in this situation?

FEELINGS, IDENTITY AND DEALING WITH CHANGE

Superego tends to be connected with strong negative feelings like fear, anger, guilt, and shame. We can notice it in perfectionistic people who have rigid superegos. Superego tends to be weak in feelings of empathy, love, and compassion which are connected more with conscience.

Identity involves our sense of our individuality and our sense of belonging to or being part of groups. Superego tends to promote a rather superficial sense of self and a narrow sense of belonging. For example, a sexist male's biggest identity would be as a man. His macho identity would affect his various relationships. In the meaning field, he is likely to hang on tightly to his group's ideology, rituals, and power structure. Changes that challenge his identity and security could cause much fear and anger in him. If such feelings are intense, he is likely to act out.

Adjustment to significant changes, especially negative changes, is difficult for most. It is worse for people guided by superego than the ones using conscience. Using ways to appeal to the consciences of both sides and authorities and influential people helping to reduce the real problems are crucial. A great deal of human conflicts, especially group conflicts with other groups, are based on identity differences along with other factors like economic and power issues. Differences in religious groups, nationality, race, and the like cause conflict when people use superiors attached to the difference. Look at the history of Catholic and Protestant conflict, Sunni and Shia Muslim fights, Hindu Muslim conflict and so on. If people are more guided by consciences, they would focus on their common humanity and spiritual identity.

In the US, the demographic change of increasing minority groups has been causing significant anxiety. I recall two cases in particular. In one of those cases, the mother was a middle-aged white woman. She was very unhappy and insecure when her divorced son started dating a young lady from a third-world country. With much effort from her son and his girlfriend, the mother gradually became close to her son's girlfriend. In another case, the elderly white Christian woman was at first negative about her son's Muslim girlfriend who used to cover her hair. Again, the young lady overcame the older lady's hair-raising issues by love and goodness. I have also seen some young people with rigid superegos showing no empathy about their parents' problems with immediate and total acceptance of homosexuality or inter-racial marriage and damaging their relationship with parents.

I noticed an interesting case in the news in January 2021. On January 6, Officer Mike Fanone was defending the Capitol, and the rioters were attacking him, even talking of killing him with his own gun. Pleading for his life, when he said he had children, some rioters protected him.[29] I believe the officer's mention of his children touched the consciences of the people who protected him. It is remarkable, especially in a crowd that was apparently stirred up by the superego approach.

BALANCED VS. EXCESSIVE OR DEFICIENT FEELINGS

As I have discussed in *Fulfillment Using Real Conscience*, feelings have four functions: they give signals, act as motivating forces, give pleasant or unpleasant sensations, and moods, and modulate relationships. For example, fear signals danger, motivates fight or flight response, unpleasant sensation and mood, and causes a negative reaction to the source of fear to others. If the fear is realistic and the response is appropriate, the system is functioning well. Superego's judgment can be skewed based on past experience. Based on a spouse cheating on them, many people become irrationally suspicious of their current spouse. Conscience would promote a realistic level of trust with caution. As we discussed before, a therapeutic dose of feelings is useful.

Superego tends to cause excessive negative feelings. And people guided by harsh superego would try to stir up negative feelings in others. Recall the objection to gay marriages arguing that it would lead to some gay people marrying their pets. Excessive feelings make it difficult to stay balanced. When feelings are too low, it would need to be boosted up. We can notice in history how great leaders boosted feelings of love, courage, compassion, and so on.

BALANCED VS. EXCESSIVE RITUALS

Many people overdo rituals, going overboard with rituals or involvement with religious organizations leading to problems like neglecting family's

29. The Guardian, "I Yelled," 79 secs.

needs. People with perfectionistic personalities tend to overdo rituals. They may do so because of doubt that they did not do the ritual correctly or because the ritual relieves their anxiety temporarily. For example, Catholic patients with perfectionism might repeatedly confess about an old sin. They become balanced when they learn to be guided by their consciences instead of their superegos.

There is an insightful story of how Buddha helped a follower with excessive ritualism. This young man was doing so much walking meditation that he was bleeding from his feet. Buddha found out from others that the guy enjoyed playing violin. Buddha got hold of a violin and went after the man following the blood marks. Buddha had loosed the rungs of the violin. After handing the violin to the man Buddha told him to play it. The man played the violin, but it did not sound good. The man tightened the strings and played the violin, and it sounded good. Then Buddha took the violin, tightened the strings even more and asked the guy to play it. When he played this time, it did not sound good. He told Buddha that it did not sound good because the strings were too tight. Buddha explained to him that his meditation practice was too tight, and he needed to loosen up and be balanced. We can notice that conscience helps to keep balance.

RATIONAL VS. IRRATIONAL GRATIFICATION OF NEEDS AND CONSCIENCE

We human beings need the three P's, pleasure, power, and pride (or esteem) besides biological needs like food and social needs of belonging. Any of these needs can be taken to extremes.

Overeating causing obesity is a serious and widespread problem. Anorexia is much less prevalent, but it can cause serious medical and psychological complications. These are complex issues often requiring psychiatric and medical intervention. Along with 12-step programs or similar therapies, utilizing conscience is highly beneficial. People who live by conscience would be open to recognize and seek proper help rather than using denial and resisting help.

Steps four, five, and six of the twelve steps of AA are very closely linked to conscience. Step four involves taking a fearless moral inventory of oneself. Addicts tend to resist taking this step as it would cause guilt and shame. We find it very helpful to explain to the addict about conscience and superego and the benefits of healthy guilt and help him or her to recognize and ignore unhealthy or excessive guilt. Step five involves admitting the wrong and step six is working on the defect of character or the pattern of unhealthy choices. Many people who had trouble believing in a Higher Power accepted conscience as their Higher Power.

In our society, meeting the need for comfort and pleasure by abusing drugs has become a severe problem affecting millions of individuals and their families. The Christian Celebrate Recovery programs, and the Buddhist Refuge Recovery programs utilize conscience in their own ways, but my understanding is that they do not discuss conscience. As far as addiction to power and control, and craving for esteem, these are part of certain personality disorders. All personality disorders can benefit from learning about and using conscience.

Gerald G. May, MD, addictionologist and spiritual teacher, in his book *Addiction and Grace* says: "the five essential characteristics that mark true addiction" are (1) tolerance, (2) withdrawal symptoms, (3) self-deception, (4) loss of willpower, and, (5) distortion of attention.[30] Referring to Paul Tillich's idea of God as the ultimate concern, May points out that the addictive object becomes more important than God.

In my clinical experience, alcohol as well as drug addicts who followed up with AA or another 12-step program did far better than those who did not have such follow up. Yordan Zhekov in the UK has researched the role of conscience in recovery from alcohol and drug addiction. He is promoting Conscience Therapy's new treatment modality for addiction utilizing the transforming power of conscience. Zhekov had eighteen cases showing the way conscience works in recovery. I'll share one of the cases–John's story.

John's story opens with his childhood problems with eyesight and appearance concerns. Also, he failed to measure up to his family's high expectations. With low self-esteem and emotional stress, he started drinking to manage these issues. Working as a bar attendant made matters worse and his alcoholism led to stealing, conflicts with siblings, and sexual immorality. His conscience was suppressed during this period of his life. His marriage failed. He had detox and relapses several times. Then he entered a Christian rehabilitation program where he got involved with Christian faith and a spiritual transformation using his conscience.

---

30. May, *Addiction*, 26.

Besides staying sober, he developed character strength, and virtues which manifested in his good work as well as good relationships.[31]

There are medications which can significantly help in the treatment of addictions to alcohol and drugs. So, it is important to seek professional help. There are plenty of support groups. It is important to be aware of risk factors. Those who have a parent or family member with alcohol or drug addiction have a much higher risk than others. While dealing with significant distress, people are more vulnerable to addiction. AA has a saying that addicts should change playmates and playgrounds to stay away from tempting situations of being around addicts. People guided by conscience would use precautions and appropriate treatments. I have experienced many times the joy of addicts recovering and discovering their consciences to follow.

The famous radio host Glenn Beck, in his book *Addicted to Outrage*, discusses his addiction to outrage and recovery from it. Beck had an alcohol addiction in the past and had recovered from it with the help of AA's 12-step program. Later on, he got addicted to outrage. It appears that he got pleasure from it. Beck admits that outrage takes on the identity of the addict. He goes on: "They surrender the responsibility of developing a caring, rational human person…Rather than actual empathy for the misfortune or suffering of others, addicts respond with oversized and obnoxious levels of self-righteous indignation, always scattering blame against alleged perpetrators of the crime, against some victims, or against humanity itself. Rather than quiet, reasoned introspection, instead, addicts make a grossly obvious, grand spectacle of their sympathy and protestations that speaks of their inner disquiet and self-loathing. Wrongdoers don't simply make a mistake, they have acted in a subhuman manner and must be castigated by the tribe, and ultimately destroyed."[32] And Beck goes on to say that such victory is to fill the hole in the addict because of the lack of a real human soul. In this description, I notice the emotional intensity and harsh judgment of an unfair superego. Where he says lack of a soul, I would say lack of conscience. Beck used AA principles to overcome his addiction to outrage. He emphasizes respect for all regardless of their political or other differences. He also emphasizes the final step of AA, helping other addicts to recover.

---

31. Zhekov, *Conscience in Recovery*, 30.
32. Beck, *Addicted*, 28.

CONSCIENCE VS. EXTREMISM

In *Extremism, one* of MIT Press' *Essential Knowledge* series, J.M. Berger says: "Extremism refers to the belief that an ingroup's success or survival can never be separated from the need for hostile action against an out-group. The hostile action must be part of the in-group's definition of success. Hostile acts can range from verbal attacks and diminishments to discriminatory behavior, violence, and even genocide."[33]

One of the oldest extremist groups in history is the zealots, a Jewish sect well-known for its opposition to pagan Rome and its polytheism. They despised the Jews who cooperated with the Roman authorities. They objected Jews from complying with a Roman order for a census of Galilee in six AD, arguing that complying with the order would imply agreeing with the Roman rule. A subgroup of Zealots called the Sicarii (dagger men) assassinated Jews who cooperated with Rome. In seventy-four CE, the Sicarii committed mass suicide rather than surrender to Roman authorities in a siege on their mountain redoubt.

Interestingly, the word "assassin" comes from an Arabic word "Hashishin" meaning hashish smoker, an Islamic sect of extremists who terrorized crusaders and Muslims who they considered as not living up to the standard. They used to smoke hashish before going to assassinate their object. They were extremists in their belief system and terrorists by their tactic. They were clearly guided by their superegos.

Unfortunately, extremisms of various types are prevalent now. Let us look into a story of the spiritual transformation of a former extremist, the story of Tony McAleer, based on his book *The Cure for Hate*. Tony grew up in Vancouver, Canada. His parents—father a psychiatrist and mother an airline stewardess—were from England. Until he was seven, his mother did not return to work and until he was ten, she took jobs only on local flights and did not work at night. He was doing well at school and at home. Tony idolized his father.

The first night his mother was working, Tony noticed a naked female with his father, and he told mother about it. She decided to stay in the marriage but used separate rooms. Tony's grades fell and the efforts of the teacher, including spanking at his Catholic school, failed to improve his performance. So, he was dismissed. Then he was sent to England for school. Tony was rebellious in school and his parents brought him back home. By age sixteen, in his search for identity, he joined the skinheads.

---

33. Berger, *Extremism*, 44.

The skinheads' tendency for violence served his purpose. He wore the mask of a mean, angry, and nasty person to cover up his sensitive, shy, and soft self.

He continued drinking, fighting, and enjoying his skinhead status. As a leader, he got connections and respect from leaders of other extremist groups like leaders of the KKK, and Nazi Nationalist Party. Through the skinhead network, a woman, Michelle, started living with him. Three months later, she was pregnant. He and Michelle had an emotionally abusive relationship like many around them. The experience of holding his newborn baby girl, especially when she opened her eyes for the first time and saw his face, started an internal change for love but he continued his racist identity and activities.

He was a quite involved father. When his daughter was two, his son was born. Two more years passed when Michelle and Tony separated, and he took care of the children. Michelle left with an Australian man. His very loving relationship with his children and his mother's pressure on him led him to leave the racists. He experienced friendship with a Sikh lady which would have been a taboo for the racists. Through a friend whose wife was a Hindu, he got interested in Eastern philosophies and attended an intense meditation. His mother shared her spirituality with him. Tony got counseling and visited a Holocaust memorial center. He gained insight into the toxic shame at the core of his problem and compassion for himself and others as the solution. In my experience, toxic shame is based on superego judgment and compassion is a part of using conscience. Tony became co-founder of a nonprofit organization, Life After Hate, to help people leave hate groups.[34]

Breaking Hate by Christian Picciolini provides the author's involvement in white supremacist group for eight years. His parents were Italian immigrants. Living in Chicago, his parents were busy with work. During childhood, he was mocked for his surname which rhymes with weenie. He was bullied and had no close friends. In his youth, he was befriended by a white supremacist man who showed him respect and interest. Picciolini became a white supremacist. He honored the racist Fourteen Words' mission: "*We must secure the existence of our people and a future for white children.*"[35] He says he became an extremist because of life's "potholes" — "the unresolved traumas buried deep within us. He says he missed

---

34. McAleer, *Cure*, 1–320.
35. Picciolini, *Breaking*, xxxi.

three important needs: identity, community, and purpose"[36] (ICP). In other racists he has known, the same ICP deficit caused their extremism. In fighting, he experienced the thrill of combat and when he was leading a group, it was stronger. His interest and skill in writing music and performing gave him more power and respect.

He fell in love with a loving and open-minded young woman. He continued his leading role in skinhead movement and music. After they got married and their first child was born, he had to open a shop selling records besides his job in construction. In his business, he dealt with a variety of nice people, and it opened his eyes to his prejudices. He and wife had many arguments because he was spending so little time at home. He cut down his involvement with the skinhead group. One of the close members of his group was shot and killed by some black youths.

In November 1994, when he was twenty-four and his first son was two, his second son was born. One night when he got home late again, Lisa left him. He moved back with his parents, went through regrets about his past wrongdoings like his racist activities. Then he started working part-time, then attending college and got a job with IBM. He kept a friendly relationship with his ex-wife and he loved his sons. He fell in love with a lady working for IBM and they married after dating for three years. Then tragedy hit—his brother who was with skinheads was killed by some blacks. He felt guilty about his wrong influence on his brother. In 2009, he, along with Tony McAleer and four others, co-founded the nonprofit organization, Life After Hate, on Martin Luther King Jr.'s birthday to help people safely leave extremist groups. We can notice how his superego had been shaped by the skinhead influences, but loving experiences later promoted his conscience and helped him to depart from evil and do good.

In his book *Hateland*, Daryl Johnson, an expert on domestic extremist groups, describes many cases of radicalization and deradicalization. Derek Black is one case. Derek grew up in a KKK family. His father was a grand wizard of the Klan. The well-known David Duke of KKK fame was his godfather. After homeschooling, he joined a liberal arts college. There, he became friends with a Peruvian immigrant and dated a Jewish woman. After a while, someone outed him as a white supremacist. He received negative reactions from most students, but a Jewish friend invited him for Shabbat dinner. He met a woman, Gornik, at the dinner

---

36. Picciolini, *Breaking*, xxxii.

and later on, they became romantic partners. Derek and Gornik had many discussions about racial issues. Gormik asked him angrily one time how his idea of a white homeland would work. He asked his father the same question. The answer was that the nonwhites would be forced to leave, perhaps violently. His mind gradually changed, and he finally cut his ties with white nationalism. In another case in Johnson's book, a neo-Nazi, Frank Meeink, began to change when he was in jail for kidnapping and torturing a rival leader and in jail, he experienced more common grounds with the African Americans than with the Aryan gang. And his change became much stronger after he got out of jail and a Jewish man offered him a decent job in spite of a swastika tattooed on Meeink's neck. His final turning point is very interesting. On a long ride, his boss kept telling him to stop calling himself dumb. It was the first time Meeink heard somebody tell him that and he decided he was done. We can see that his self-hate was the reason he used to call himself dumb. It was his superego judgment. His loving boss stimulated his conscience—to transform to love himself and others.

Daryl Johnson observes about our socio-political situation: "... America's addictive social media, irresponsible cable news pundits, divisive political parties, unforgiving paramilitary culture, and an unbalanced economy with shortcomings that are easily exploited by extremists."[37] I feel there is an urgent need for conscience to deal with this situation.

VIOLENT EXTREMISM, JIHADIST IDEOLOGY

About the increasing terrorism problem in the US, the Center for Strategic and International Studies compiled a dataset of eight hundred and ninety-three incidents that happened between January 1994 and May 8, 2020 in the US. Both attacks and foiled plots were included, and the ideology was coded into five types: left-wing, right-wing, religious and ethnonationalist, and others. All the religious plots and attacks were done by terrorists with Salafi-jihadist ideology. Right-wing incidents were the majority of terrorist plots and attacks, especially in the 1990s and 2010s. The total number of right-wing incidents have increased substantially since 2016. In 2019, right-wing extremists committed about two-thirds of the incidents. And in 2020, the right-wing caused 90 percent of the incidents between January 1 and May 8. Religious extremists

---

37. Johnson, *Hateland*, 243.

were responsible for the most fatalities because of the 9/11 attacks but the right-wing perpetrators caused over half of all annual deaths during fourteen out of twenty-one years. Of the eight hundred and ninety-three incidents, 57 percent were by the right-wing, 25 percent by left-wing, 15 percent by religious terrorists, 3 percent by ethno-nationalists, and 0.7 percent by others.[38]

In the 1990s, most right-wing attacks targeted abortion clinics but since 2014 they have targeted individuals (because of religion, ethnicity or race) and religious institutions and people connected with the government. Deaths caused by the incidents: religious terrorism caused three thousand and eighty-six deaths including two thousand nine hundred and seventy-seven deaths from the 9/11 attack; right-wing attacks caused three hundred and thirty-five deaths; left-wing attacks, twenty-two deaths and ethnonationalist attacks, five deaths.[39]

Right-wing terrorism has three types: white supremacists, anti-government groups, and incels. In recent times, they have also used the Internet to organize. Incels are involuntary celibates, a loosely organized group of men who tend to commit violence against women. Left-wing terrorists include Anarchists, Earth Liberation Front, Animal Liberation Front, and Antifa. Antifa is a far-left militant group. They tend to wear black clothes and cover their faces and tend to disrupt far right gatherings. So many people are not guided by conscience! Varieties of misleading superegos!

SOLITUDE AND INTERDEPENDENCE VS. LONELINESS AND CLANNISHNESS OR INDIVIDUALISM

Surgeon General Dr. Vivek Murthy, in his book *Together,* and Senator Ben Sasse, in his book *Them,* observe that America's biggest problem currently is loneliness. While they don't address the issues of superego and conscience, we can see that the two inner guides impact people tremendously.

Murthy discusses three dimensions of loneliness: (1) intimate or emotional as having a confidant, (2) social or relational loneliness that is lack of social connections and friendships, and (3) collective loneliness, which is lack of a network of or larger community. Murthy emphasizes

---

38. Center for Strategic and International Studies, "Escalating," 1–10.
39. Center for Strategic and International Studies, "Escalating," 1, 4–5.

the difference between loneliness and solitude. Loneliness is a state of tension from unmet need for human connection and feeling unhappiness, but solitude is a state of peace and happiness. Examples of solitude are the monks and nuns who joyfully practice solitude.

Murthy notes that Dr. Julianne Holt-Lunstad's study showed that people who have strong social relationships are 50 percent less likely to die prematurely compared to people with weak such relationships. He says: "Even more striking, she found that the impact of lacking social connection on reducing is equal to smoking fifteen cigarettes a day, and it is greater than the risk associated with obesity, excess alcohol consumption, and lack of exercise."[40] With the findings of experts on the evolutionary roots of human need for connectedness, Murthy points out the benefits people have in cooperating in groups for safety and nurturing. We can appreciate the saying that there is safety in numbers. Although compared to many animals, the physical strength of humans is less, people have often more than compensated by joining together. Imagine how people trained wild elephants. Estimates are that hunter-gatherers spent a third of their time working, another third sleeping, and yet another third socializing and playing with kids.

We are wired for connection in the sense that social support decreases the body's stress response, feeling more calm and secure. This reaction is supported by hormones and neurotransmitters, including oxytocin, endorphins, and dopamine. Oxytocin, which is well-known for its role in labor, lactation, and mother-child bonding, also strengthens social bonding. Endorphins, our naturally occurring opioids, help to reduce pain and provide some euphoric feeling. Dopamine helps us to focus, strive, and find things interesting.

Loneliness can cause anxiety, substance abuse, depression, and suicide. Chronic loneliness can also paradoxically cause many people to become excessively defensive and reject offers to socialize. People guided by conscience tend to have significantly more solitude and less defensiveness, thereby reducing their chances of loneliness. But people with rather rigid or harsh superegos tend to have less solitude and more defensiveness towards others. Both Murthy and Sasse emphasize the benefits and importance of being members of good organizations, good tribes.

I recall a patient who had experienced rejection from his arrogant and critical successful older brother and had also failed to find a

---

40. Murthy, *Together*, 13.

compatible girlfriend. He had grown up in a fundamentalist Christian Church and grown out of it because of intellectual conflict and experiences of hypocrisy. He was seriously depressed and found it difficult to socialize, partly because of his own introverted personality. I was able to persuade him to join a meditation group with broad spiritual interests. It made a world of difference for him.

Sasse's analysis of what he calls "anti-tribe" is quite relevant. He explores "known anti-tribes—of news consumption more than political activism—have cropped up to try to fill the void left by the collapse of the natural, local, embodied, healthy tribes people have traditionally known."[41] Sasse points out that the anti-tribes are poisoning our national spirit critically. People connect against a common enemy with contempt for their enemy. He observes the unhealthy state of the country where increasingly disconnected people watch news that riles them up. " . . . liberals and conservatives no longer believe in the same things, we don't understand how our opponents believe what they believe, and we soothe our lonely souls with the balm of contempt."[42] And he says "contempt" is big business. We can notice it in several media outlets, more or less. I see some media personalities gaining high ratings by promoting contempt. In my view, this situation promotes unhealthy superego and damages conscience. It is a double tragedy as it promotes the evil side at a time when there is much potential to enhance goodness. Sass writes admiringly of Martin Luther King Jr., for his nonviolent struggle against promoters of segregation, trying to change their hearts but not hating them—using the Gandhian approach of meeting physical force with soul force.

CONSCIENCE AND THE SEVEN SOCIAL SINS AS PER GANDHI

The following are the seven social sins Gandhi discussed: (1) wealth without work, (2) pleasure without conscience, (3) knowledge without character, (4) commerce without morality, (5) science without humanity, (6) religion without sacrifice, and (7) politics without principles. By sacrifice, he meant service to others, not animal sacrifice or other rituals. About commerce without morality, Stephen Covey wrote: "In his book *Moral Sentiments*, which preceded *Wealth of Nations*, Adam Smith explained

---

41. Sasse, *Them*, 13–14.
42. Sasse, *Them*, 103.

how foundational to the success of our system is the moral foundation: how we treat each other, the spirit of benevolence, of service, of contribution. If we ignore the moral foundation and allow economic systems to operate without moral foundation and without continued education, we will soon create an amoral, if not immoral, society and business."[43] While Gandhi is right from the angle of conscience, some people's superegos consider these sins as smart lifestyles.

WEAK, SEARED, DEFILED, WOUNDED, AND EVIL CONSCIENCE

These are terms Paul used in the Bible. Weak conscience is weak because it does not use good reasoning, or it is not based on broad awareness. Defiled conscience is polluted or damaged by the person's superego or PIG. Seared conscience is damaged by habitual defilement. Wounded conscience is usually wounded by acting against conscience. Evil conscience gives the wrong direction. So, it is not conscience in the usual sense; it is evil superego or evil PIG or a combination, like the broken moral compass of a person with a criminal superego and drug addiction when the moral compass points south instead of north. It is really not a functioning conscience.

CARL JUNG'S CONCEPT OF THE TWOFOLD CONSCIENCE

Jung discussed two kinds of conscience: "moral conscience" and "ethical conscience." The moral conscience is based on the social mores and so it is basically the superego I have been describing. "The ethical conscience most often arises when critical reflection is brought to bear on a conflict of duties, where society's mores provide no clear answer, and the solution can arise only through the creative ethos of the whole personality, that is, a creative conscious and the unconscious, or, theologically, reason and grace."[44] An example would be if you know an abused wife is hiding in a place and if the husband asks you where she is, you break the social rule of telling the truth and tell the husband that you don't know.

---

43. Covey, "Way," 75.
44. Robinson, *Conscience*, 215.

Chapter Two

Conscience, Religion, Spirituality, and The Axial Age

"We are not human beings having a spiritual experience; we are spiritual beings having a human experience." — Pierre Teilhard Chardin[1]

"When a man follows the way of the world, or the way of the flesh, or the way of tradition (i.e., when he believes in religious rites and the letter of the scriptures, as though they were intrinsically sacred), knowledge of Reality cannot arise in him." — Philosopher and Hindu reformer Shankara[2]

A PEW RESEARCH CENTER report published in December 2023 showed 83 percent of US adults believe people have a soul or spirit and 81 percent say there is something spiritual besides the natural world. Regarding life after death, 71 percent Americans believe in heaven, 61 percent believe in hell and 60 percent believe in both. About half of US adults are both religious and spiritual and 22 percent spiritual but not religious [SBNRs]. SBNRs are more likely to see spiritual forces in nature, such as in rivers and mountains.[3]

---

1. Furey, *Joy*, 138.
2. Shankara, *Crest*, 91.
3. Pew, "Spirituality," 2–95.

Another Pew Research report in May 2018, "*Attitudes toward spirituality and religion*," noted in the US 48 percent described themselves as both religious and spiritual. According to this study, Europeans who consider themselves religious but not spiritual (median 15 percent) tend to believe in the God of the Bible, believe they have a soul, and religion helps them to choose what is right. In my opinion spiritual people tend to have ethics along the line of conscience. I think of people whose spirituality is beyond their particular religion as spiritual and religious.[4]

A Pew report in January 2024 gave details about the 28 percent US adults who are classified as "religiously unaffiliated." The religiously unaffiliated are widely called the "nones." Among the nones, 17 percent are Atheists, 20 percent Agnostics and 63 percent Nothing in particular. Disbelief or skepticism is the cause most nones report for being unaffiliated with religion. The nones are also less involved in civic life. Their attitude towards religion is interesting: 43 percent think religion does more harm than good, 41 percent think religion does equal harm and good, and 14 percent think religion does more good than harm.[5]

In my psychiatric practice, in the initial evaluation, I routinely asked patients whether they have any religious connection. Religiously unaffiliated patients would typically say they reject religion for the harm it causes. And I would say something like "It sounds like you have a conscientious objection to religion. We can use your conscience as a strength."

Let me give a very interesting example of a great person who was religious and spiritual, and another person who seemed to have been just religious. In December 1968, the Catholic monk and famous writer Thomas Merton visited the Buddhist pilgrimage place in Polonnaruwa, Sri Lanka. The place has four statues of the Buddha, two sitting, one standing and one reclining, all cut from granite rock. The reclining statue is forty-six feet long and depicts his passing away, and standing by him with folded arms is his favorite disciple, Ananda.

Merton approached these figures barefoot like a pilgrim and had a wonderful mystical experience which he wrote about beautifully: "Looking at these figures, I was suddenly, almost forcibly, jerked clean out of the habitual, half-tied vision of things, and an inner clearness, clarity, as if exploding from the rocks themselves, became evident and obvious.... The thing about all this is that there is no puzzle, no problem, and really

---

4. Pew, "Attitudes," 38, 39, 1–168.
5. Pew, "Religious 'Nones,'" 1–96.

no "mystery." All problems are resolved and everything is clear, simply because what matters is clear. The rock, all matter, all life, is charged with dharmakaya[6]...everything is emptiness and everything is compassion. I don't know when in my life I ever had such a sense of beauty and spiritual validity running together in one aesthetic illumination . . . I don't know what else remains, but I have now seen and have pierced through the surface and have got beyond the shadow and the disguise."[7]

Merton's description of the experience, especially with it occurring in the week before his death, is a reflection of his deep spirituality. Interestingly, the vicar general of the local Catholic diocese who accompanied Merton stayed back "shying away" from "paganism" at some distance from the statues. I don't know anything more about the vicar general, but my impression is that this priest was a Catholic religious person who had a narrow Catholic identity and belief and was prone to have negative views about other religions. People who have a narrow rigid identity and ideology tend to miss mystical experience, as Psychologist Abraham Maslow noted. And the vicar general probably missed the opportunity to discuss with Merton about interfaith matters.

Merton's spirituality was not part of any deficiency in his being a Catholic, but it was in addition to his Catholicism. He was fully and deeply a Catholic, as a committed Trappist monk. But he transcended to a deeper and broader spirituality. His broader spirituality included knowledge and understanding, as well as respect for and appreciation, of other great religions of the world. Moreover, Merton's interest in history, mysticism, and psychology greatly enhanced his spirituality. An integral part of spirituality is that it reinforces and spreads spirituality in others. Thousands of people have benefited from Merton's spirituality.

MYSTICAL EXPERIENCES

William James described four features of mystical experiences: (1) ineffability or defying description, (2) noetic quality or keen insight into deeper truth, (3) transiency, that is, short-lived experience. James mentioned that these experiences last, at most, one-half to one hour. The mystical experiences I have come across have lasted only a few minutes,

---

6. Merton, *Asian*, 233–36.
7. Merton, *Asian*, 233–36.

and (4) passivity, that is, the person having a mystical experience has no control over it.[8]

Humanistic psychologist Abraham Maslow who studied "peak experiences" observes: "Apparently, it is one danger of the legalistic and organizational versions of religion that they may tend to suppress naturalistic peak, transcendent, mystical or other core-religious experiences and to make them less likely to occur, i.e., the degree of religious organization may correlate negatively with the frequency of "religious" experiences.[9] He viewed the prophets or founders of religions as "peakers" or people who had peak experiences and the organization people or the legalist ecclesiasts as "non-peakers." Maslow's observation fits well in the case of Merton and the vicar general. Maslow noticed that people who are extremely rational or "materialistic" and those who are extremely "practical" i.e., exclusively means-oriented tend to be non-peakers. I feel these non-peakers could benefit greatly if they could experience and understand the mystical aspect of life because many extremely materialistic or extremely practical people tend to be quite influential in society.

THE SPIRITUAL EXPERIENCES OF TWO GREAT RELIGIOUS FIGURES

(1) The Story of St. Paul's Conversion

St. Paul, the apostle to Gentiles, is the most consequential leader of Christianity. His conversion from a leader of Jewish persecutions of Christians to a devout Christian and successful promoter of Christianity is a highly remarkable story. He grew up in Tarsus and was a Roman citizen who had studied under Rabbi Gamaliel, a grandson of the famous Rabbi Hillel. Before conversion, he, also known as Saul, was a Pharisee, a zealot extremely attached to his Jewish faith. He had dragged the followers of Jesus from their homes and put them in prison. As part of the persecution of the Christians, he witnessed St. Stephen being stoned to death. It is said that he was the watchman for the ones who were stoning St. Stephen, the first Christian martyr. As he was dying, St. Stephen prayed to God to forgive his persecutors. St. Augustine speculated later on that this attitude of forgiveness of his enemies by St. Stephen laid the seeds of

---

8. James, *Varieties*, 292–93.
9. Maslow, *Religions*, 33.

radical change in Saul. After this, Saul was riding on his horse to Damascus to persecute more Christians.

As he was close to Damascus, a bright light from the skies flashed around him and Paul fell off the horse and landed on the ground. And he heard a voice: "Saul, why are you persecuting me?" Saul asked who was talking to him. The voice answered: "I am Jesus whom you persecute." And the voice told him to go to the city and there he would be told what to do. When Saul opened his eyes, he couldn't see. His companions helped him to get to Damascus.

In Damascus, a man named Ananias had a vision of Jesus giving him instruction to place his hands on Saul and gave him details of where Saul would be. Ananias followed Jesus's instructions, and, as he laid his hands on Saul, something like fish scales fell from Saul's eyes and he could see after being blind for three days. Saul stood up and got baptized. He evaded the Jews who were trying to harm him. Subsequently, he spent three years in Arabia. What exactly he did in Arabia is unclear. The speculation is that he spent time in prayer, meditation, and preparing for his mission as the Apostle of the Gentiles. Then, he went to Jerusalem, met with apostles Peter and James, after which he went on, tirelessly shaping and promoting Christianity emphasizing faith, conscience, love, and goodness until his own martyrdom.

Paul's transformation is psychologically and spiritually fascinating, but I can only make educated guesses because of limited information about his life, especially before his conversion. Eric Hoffer, a recipient of the Presidential Medal of Freedom, wrote about the tendency of people in mass movements to change their allegiance from one group with one ideology to another group with the opposite ideology. They change ideology while keeping their extremist personality. Discussing such tendency in mass movements, Eric Hoffer observed: "A Saul turning to Paul is neither a rarity nor a miracle."[10] But, in the case of Paul, he changed from being a fanatic Pharisee to an enthusiastic Christian. The root meaning of fanatic is being possessed by a deity but being enthusiastic means being inspired by a deity. Being possessed means losing one's control and balance. While he kept his dynamic personality, he became balanced and loving, not a hateful Christian persecuting others.

---

10. Hoffer, *True*, 17.

(2) The Divine Vision of Shankara

Adi Shankara, the greatest thinker in Hinduism, who lived most likely in the eighth century CE, rejuvenated and reformed Hinduism. He is often called Shankaracharya, meaning Shankara, the great teacher. It is hard to believe that in his life of thirty-two years, he learned much of the existing teachings of Hinduism, wrote about them and established spiritual centers, one each in the east, west, north, and south of India. Nobel Prize winning Quantum physicist Erwin Schrödinger has been among the numerous modern intellectuals who have supported his teachings of *maya* and *Advaita*, teachings rooted in the Hindu Scriptures. *Maya* means illusion; the world is really not like it appears to us. *Advita* is nonduality; the ultimate reality is one, transcending dichotomies.[11]

When Shankara was living in Varanasi, which is a holy city of Hinduism, on a noon day in Summer the acharya was walking with some students towards the holy river Ganges to perform his mid-day ritual. On their way, they came across a hunter, an outcast, with four dogs. They asked the hunter to move away based on the practice of untouchability and unapproachability (the practice of low caste and outcast people could not touch or be close to the upper caste to prevent polluting the upper caste). The hunter questioned how the acharya could ask him to move away since he was teaching that the body comes from the same source and the same function in everybody, and the Atman is same in all, irrespective of being a brahmin or an outcast. Struck by the Advaita wisdom of this outcast, Shankara spoke respectfully to the chandala as his guru. Then, the hunter disappeared, and, in his place, Lord Shiva appeared and the four dogs as the four Vedas, the scriptures. And Shankara glorified Shiva with a hymn of praise. The Caste System has been very much a part of Hindu society for thousands of years. It is said that it started as a division of labor. So, I believe it was part of Shankaracharya's superego until this experience stimulated his conscience on this issue. These kinds of spiritual experiences help at least some people who are very skeptical of a spiritual realm to overcome some of their doubts. In the case of St. Paul and Shankaracharya, the Divine voice questioned their superego approach.

---

11. Wikipedia, "Erwin Schrödinger," paras. 3, 31, 35–40.

RELIGION AND SPIRITUALITY - DIFFERENCES AND SIMILARITIES

Both religion and spirituality deal with issues of our beliefs about life, especially about a life beyond this world, belonging to a religious community or not, sense of right and wrong, rituals and religious or spiritual exercises. Religions have a significant impact on both aspects of our identity as individuals and members of different groups.

The religions we can fairly easily recognize are: Hinduism, Zoroastrianism, Judaism, Shintoism, Taoism, Buddhism, Jainism, Confucianism, Christianity, Islam, Sikhism, and Baha'i faith. Interestingly, Sikhism, which originated in India in the fifteenth century, rejects the caste system, vows of celibacy, and professional priests. They promote gender equality and don't discredit other religions. They don't cut their hair but they have no dietary restrictions except meat from a ritual slaughter. Anybody attending a service at a Sikh gurdwara or temple would be invited to share a meal prepared and served by the worshippers. And the Baha'i Faith, which originated in Iran in the nineteenth century, teaches the essential worth of all religions and promotes gender equality, democratic structure, and acceptance of science, reflecting human progress by the time of its origin. Religions are community-based organizations with group and individual identity, particular sacred rituals, ethical ideals of right and wrong, sacred books, and sacred places, and most of them believe in life hereafter. Religions have their founders. Belief in God or a spiritual realm is common. Religions foster loyalty to them. Religions have religious organizations with their structure, hierarchy, rules and functions. Many religions, like the Abrahamic religions (Judaism, Christianity and Islam), tend to be exclusive. Most of the religions have branches, and some branches have major conflicts between them.

There are some people belonging to minority religions such as Satanists, Shamanic, Wiccans, Scientologists, Druids, and Free thinkers according to the UK's Office of National Statistics. I have not studied them with sufficient depth to make any remarks on them.

Spirituality is more open-ended and flexible. While religions tend to emphasize their organizations, spirituality promotes more inner growth. Inner growth includes deeper understanding, expanding wisdom, enhancing love, and practicing spiritual exercises. Spiritual people tend to feel free to pick and choose beliefs and rituals or practices which the person feels most suitable to oneself. Spirituality tends to be consistent with conscience in my experience. Religions promote partly conscience and partly superego depending on the particular religious group's beliefs and values.

While spiritual people tend to be open to adopting spiritual exercises connected with another religious tradition like yoga and meditation, religious people tend to be resistant to such activities. In recent times, lots of people practice yoga poses like physical exercises and many people practice meditation with no religious connotation. In Alabama Public Schools, teaching yoga exercises were prevented in 1993 at the urging of the conservative Eagle Forum. However, in 2021, Republican Governor Kay Ivey signed a Democrat-sponsored bill allowing yoga to be taught. But because of conservative Christians' and Atheists' fears of kids embracing Hinduism, lawmakers caveated the bill by banning any aspect of Eastern Philosophy, religious training such as saying "namaste" or meditating. Also, special permission is required for practicing the one-footed tree pose. This change indicates some opening of mind which is a positive step in spirituality.[12]

In China, before the communist takeover, millions of people belonged to three religions: Confucianism, Taoism, and Buddhism, for centuries. And the combination worked well enough. Pew Research in India had several interesting findings. Sufism, the mystical branch of Islam, has followers among the members of all the major religions of India. The percentages of people with Sufi identity along with their other religious identity are as follows: Jains 12 percent, Muslims 11 percent, Sikhs 9 percent, Christians 7 percent, Hindus 5 percent, and Buddhists 2 percent. The percentages in Northern India were Muslims 37 percent, Hindus 12 percent, and Sikhs 10 percent. Incidentally, a Pew Research study published in June 2021 involved a face-to-face interview of twenty-nine thousand nine hundred and ninety-nine people. The study also found that dietary restrictions were too important to Hindus and Muslims. 72 percent of Hindus believe a person who eats beef cannot be a Hindu but only 49 percent of Hindus think an atheist cannot be a Hindu. Similarly, 77 percent of Muslims believe somebody who eats pork cannot be a Muslim but only 60 percent believe that atheists can't be Muslims.[13] I imagine people who follow strict religious dietary restrictions would disagree with Jesus's

---

12. Cason, "Gov. Kay," paras. 1–16.
13. Pew, "Religion," 1–233.

statement: "It is not what goes into the mouth that defiles a person, but it is what comes out of the mouth that defiles." (Matt 15:11)

One of the biggest benefits of spirituality versus religion is how spirituality contradicts religious fanaticism. Fundamentalism and fanaticism are closely linked. Fanaticism is a more intense form of fundamentalism. Even one of the most famous Christian fundamentalists, the late Rev. Jerry Falwell, the founder of the political activist group "The Moral Majority" and the founder of the world's biggest Christian University, Liberty University, admitted this in the book, *The Fundamentalist Phenomenon*. Jerry Falwell, Ed Dobson, and Ed Hindson give the features of what they call "hyper-fundamentalism" or excessive fundamentalism: intolerance, absolutism, militancy, separatism, inflexibility, weak social emphasis, confrontation, and proclamation as opposed to dialogue. They admit that many characteristics of fundamentalism become weaknesses when taken to extremes.[14] Such are the lack of self-criticism, overemphasis on external spirituality, resistance to change, excessive importance given to minor issues, authoritarianism and excessive dependence on leaders, too much concern over labels and associations in the belief that they alone are saved. These are the same features of religious fanaticism except the belief about being saved is an especially Christian feature.

Religious fanatics hate not only outsiders but also members of their own religion, especially those who are a challenge to them, such as the mystics or genuinely spiritual people in their own religion. As noted earlier, the Islamic fanatic group ISIS had bombed several mosques belonging to the Sufis, a Muslim mystic group. Violence based on religion continues to be a tragic defect of humanity because of religious fanaticism. It is well known that Gandhi was assassinated by a Hindu fanatic,[15] Anwar Sadat by a Muslim fanatic,[16] and Yitzhak Rabin by a Jewish extremist.[17] Religious fanaticism is consistently connected with superego. The fanatic superego may be programmed by influences from religious groups, and may be a religious leader, family, media, and so on. Such fanatics miss the wonderful benefits of conscience and authentic spirituality.

Fanatics' tendency to resist change and to isolate themselves from people with different ideologies and identities become tragic traps that prevent them from exposure to better choices and useful sources to

14. Dobson et al., *Fundamentalist*, 6–11.
15. Wikipedia, "Mahatma Gandhi," paras. 1–9.
16. Wikipedia, "Anwar Sadat," paras. 1, 7–11.
17. Wikipedia, "Yitzhak Rabin," paras. 1–19.

change. And people living in communities with very unbalanced superego guidance makes it easy to become fanatical.

Historically, one of the most interesting examples of religious conflict between two brothers occurred in the family of emperor Shah Jahan who built the Taj Mahal, one of the wonders of the World. Shah Jahan's oldest son Dara Shikoh was a scholar especially interested in mysticism. His spiritual mentor was the Sufi saint, Miam Mir. Dara had translated fifty verses from the Upanishads to Persian and had written a biography of Sufi pirs (spiritual guides) by 1657. He searched for the common ground between Islam and Hinduism. His effort was to promote interfaith harmony as his great grandfather Akbar the Great had done. Akbar had intellectual discussions at his palace involving learned men of different religions. His closest minister was a Hindu. He had three wives: one Hindu, another Muslim and the other a Christian. Akbar actively promoted religious harmony.

Dara's younger brother Aurangzeb was interested in the fundamentalistic side of Islam and became a fanatic. He was into the Sharia. Shah Jahan became seriously ill in 1658. Dara assumed the ruling role, but Aurangzeb fought against the older brother. In 1659, Dara was caught and brought to Delhi where Aurangzeb's clergy sentenced him to death for deviating from Islam. His dead body was placed on an elephant and paraded in Delhi. Aurangzeb, who had gotten his younger brother Murad's cooperation by promising him the crown, after getting rid of Dara one day, got Murad drunk and two slaves killed him. He had another brother, a son, and a nephew executed. So much for the fanatic's loyalty. He was a teetotaler and prohibited alcohol and appointed a morality police chief to watch out for blasphemy, enforce prayer, and fasting and even to ensure the right length of Muslim beards. So many hair-raising issues! Some years into his rule, he prohibited music, too. He imposed poll tax on Hindus and martyred a Sikh guru. He discriminated against various religious groups except Sunni Muslims. Shah Jahan was imprisoned by Aurangzeb for the last eight years of his life. From his prison cell, the old former emperor watched the Taj Mahal, which he had built in memory of his favorite wife, at a distance. Tourists visit where Shah Jahan was imprisoned and view the Taj Mahal from there. So did I. Aurangzeb's fanaticism damaged the spirit of Akbar's interfaith harmony and contributed to religious conflicts subsequently.[18]

18. Wikipedia, "Mughal," paras. 1–24.

Sigmund Freud, who had considered religion as a universal neurosis of mankind had speculated a decline of religion as science advanced and people became more knowledgeable. Secularism and Marxism have caused a decline in religion in different parts of the world. Religions have had members with fundamentalistic mindsets over the centuries. Christian Fundamentalism grew in the US from the 1910s. Since the 1970s, in the US, Christian Fundamentalism has been highly successful socially and politically. It shows the power of religion and the human needs behind it. Fundamentalists tended to avoid political involvements until the 1970s because they considered political activism as a sinful domain.

Fundamentalists tend to oppose secularism, and a scientific worldview which differs from traditional views of their particular religion. They are not open to other religions and resist the deeper, mystical sides of their own religion. Psychologically, also, they tend to remain superficial, mostly believing in the behavioral level of thinking that rewards or punishments are the ways to change behavior. Fundamentalists tend to believe God uses natural disasters to punish groups of people they consider sinners. It is not rare that fundamentalistic leaders use the fear of disasters to control people. Close-knit social connections, emotionally exciting religious services, and the absolute beliefs they promote are among their attractions for some people. With the advent of modern education and exposure to multiple cultures, the negative features mentioned above have decreased significantly in modernized communities.

Traditionalists resist modernity. What is called the Axial Age was a crucial period in the progress of humanity's religious and spiritual basis, and the emergence of conscience that we will explore next.

AXIAL AGE

Let us build on the information about the Axial Age in the Introduction. In 1949, Karl Jaspers (1883–1969) published a book in German, *The Origin and Goal of History*, in which he discussed what he called the Axis Period or Axial Age, the period between about 800 and 200 BCE. Karen Armstrong gives the dates as between 900 and 200 BCE.

Before the Axial Age, people's identity was as a member or a part of a family and a tribe; individuality was not part of the person's identity. With individual identity came the sense of freedom and responsibility to make the right choice. Before the Axial Age, the function of religion was for people to assist the natural forces which were considered divine forces to maintain the world functioning well. People offered prayers, hymns, and sacrificed animals and made other offerings to gods for this purpose. During the Axial Age, the function of religion shifted to personal transformation, although many people continued some of the earlier practices too. I believe the Axial Age was thus the great stage in human evolution that people could make authentic choices using conscience–using reason, the Golden Rule, the Golden Mean, and respect for truth.

Axial Age spirituality's emphasis on reason naturally included questioning beliefs and practices. But empathy, compassion, and love connected with the Golden Rule, and moderation made reasoning itself more reasonable to produce good results rather than angles of arguments leading to extremism. Respect for truth involves searching for truth. The Golden Rule became the ideal far above the "Might is Right" view and the "Iron Rule" of an eye for an eye, or even worse. whatever the powerful chooses to do. These changes were in attitude and behavior.

Myths were turned into parables and the Mythical Age was ending. There was recognition that God wanted practice of mercy and righteousness rather than rituals and sacrifices. In Jasper's words: "In this age were born the fundamental categories within which we still think today; and the beginnings of the world religions, by which human beings still live, were created. The step into universality was taken in every sense."[19]

THE TWO CHINESE RELIGIONS OF THE AXIAL AGE

Confucius

Confucius, who lived between 551 and 479 BCE, is the greatest Chinese thinker. In China, he was known as Kongzi or Master Kong. He was the youngest of twelve children; he had one brother and ten sisters. His father died when he was three. His poor mother struggled to support the family and to educate him. To her delight, he was an excellent student. He was financially rather poor but open-minded and eager to learn and teach others all his life. He was particular about living a moral life and teaching it and passionate about the arts, especially singing and music. A one-man university, he could teach divination, government, history, mathematics, music, poetry, propriety, and sports.

19. Jaspers, *Origin*, 10.

He was not an ascetic; he enjoyed socializing, dining out, participating in good fun, and drinking moderately. His remarks were often pragmatic with a touch of humor. When a skeptic sarcastically seared "if someone said, 'there is a man in the well' the altruist would go after him," Confucius remarked that even the altruist would make sure that there really is a man in the well before taking action. It reminds me of the saying: "Look before you leap." When somebody suggested to think thrice before acting, Confucius remarked: "Twice is enough."

Confucius lived during a time of terrible anarchy and violence in China. So, naturally he focused on ways to bring social harmony and order. Confucius was keenly aware of the history of peace and harmony in the country in some centuries past when people lived by certain traditions. Those harmonizing traditions had lost their power especially as people became more individualistic. The two schools of thought prevalent in those years of chaos and violence were the Realists and the Mohists. The Realists believed in the use of force and punishment to make people behave well but Confucius recognized that this approach does not result in good character. Mohists promoted universal love as the solution for the chaos and violence. This ideal of universal love is sentimental and not pragmatic by human nature. As for loving the enemy, for example, Confucius taught to be fair, or just, to the enemy. We can see how Jesus's teaching went beyond being just and fair to loving the enemy.

Confucius' solution to the problem of anarchy was promoting a new, improved, and deliberate tradition. Huston Smith, author of *The World's Religions,* points out five elements in the new tradition: Jen, Chun tzu, Li, Te, and Wen. (1) Jen is translated as goodness, benevolence, love, and human heartedness. It involves self-respect and humanity towards others. The master promoted the Golden Rule. (2) Chun tzu means humanity-at-its-best or the Mature person. Such a person is confident, gracious, competent, peaceful and not boastful. Such members form strong, stable and harmonious societies. (3) Li which includes propriety, the Doctrine of the Mean and appropriate rites. The Doctrine of the Mean is the same as Aristotle's Golden Mean which is virtue, and the extremes are vices. Extremists may claim "smart alecky" ideas like "what is in the middle of the road is roadkill" but other people can appreciate the wisdom of moderation and middle ground in these days of extremisms. (4) Te which means power, especially the power of virtue. This is particularly true for people in leadership in different fields. A good example of a virtuous person obviously has a good influence on others around the person. 5) Wen which refers to "the arts of peace": music, art, poetry and the like. What Confucius valued most about art was its power to transform human nature to become more virtuous. The deliberate tradition was protected by social prestige. Scholars were at the top of social respect and soldiers were at the bottom.[20]

These elements of the deliberate tradition are consistent with conscience but people with distorted superegos might easily misapply the principles. For example, an older brother who grew up under an authoritarian father might automatically be unfairly demanding of his younger brother justifying his action by the Confucian ideal of regard for elders. Each person has five relationships and with it five duties: to his or her ruler, to parents and children, to their spouse, to siblings and friends. Familial duties are specially emphasized. Individuals are strongly encouraged to build their character based on the Confucian ideals. While the word "conscience" is not used in the above values, we can note the spiritual benefits of these values like living by one's conscience.

Confucius' teachings were translated to European languages by Christian missionaries in the sixteenth century. Compared to most other religions, Confucianism does not teach about God or gods. Also, it does not deal with death and any life after death. While Buddhism doesn't believe in God, it has elaborate teachings on life after death and reincarnation. Confucius promoted rituals like ancestral worship which produced several benefits: cooperation among people, development of deeper perspective by individuals, enhancement of fun and gaining blessings of Heaven. Sacrifices were ordered for Confucius in all urban schools in AD 59. In the seventh and eighth centuries, temples were erected as his shrines. China synchronized three religions in an interesting way: Confucianism in public life, Taoism in personal life, and Buddhism in matters of death and life hereafter.

Confucianism has been a great influence in China, Japan, Korea, and Taiwan over the centuries. Confucius' works became an official imperial philosophy and material for civil service exams in 140 BCE until the end of the nineteenth century almost continuously. In 1905, the Qing dynasty abolished the imperial civil service exams based on Confucian texts. After the Communists gained power in 1949, Confucianism lost its public influence until more recently. During the cultural revolution, gangs of Red Guards blew up Confucius' tomb in his hometown Qufu.

---

20. Smith, *World's*, 172–80.

In the mid-1980s, the birthday of Confucius could be celebrated again. President Xi Jinping visited Qufu in 2013 soon after gaining power. And he called for new and positive roles for Confucianism including teaching Confucianism in schools.

Confucius did not use the word "conscience," but he recognized the function of shame. He taught rulers to guide people by showing people good examples of being virtuous themselves. He explained that if people are forced to behave well by punishment, they won't develop a sense of shame. He claimed that one hundred years of moral rule would eliminate killing in the kingdom.

Confucius did not write any books. It was Mencius who was born a century after Confucius' death, who gathered the teachings of Confucius and organized them as books. *The Book of Analects* is the best known of these books.[21] Confucius believed that he had the mandate of heaven to promote his teachings among people. Confucius has been known as the First Sage of China and his follower Mencius as the Second Sage of China. About the efforts in China to fuse Confucianism and Marxism, *The Economist* magazine in November 4, 2023 reported: "In the early 2000s, Chinese scholars debated whether Confucianism might even replace Marxism as China's guiding ideology. Mr. Xi is putting an end to that debate. Marxism is the "soul" and Confucianism the "root" of Chinese culture, he says. Neither ideology can be abandoned. Instead, they must be merged."[22]

Taoism

Based on tradition, Taoism originated with a sage known as Lao Tzu. The name is translated as "the Old Fellow'" or "the Old Master." He is believed to have lived in the Chou province of China in the sixth century BCE. The story is that he was frustrated by the failure of his attempts to help people to enhance their natural goodness, and in his old age, he was running away towards what is now Tibet. At the border, a guard talked him into writing down his ideas before he would proceed. In three days, he wrote a book of five thousand Chinese characters, *Tao Te Ching* or The Way and its Power. Lao Tzu promoted simple living close to nature, self-reflection, meditation, unselfishness, cleanliness, and calmness. There are

---

21. Confucius, *Analects*, 1–352.
22. The Economist, "Xi Jinping," paras. 1–5.

three meanings to Tao: (1) Tao is the ground of all beings. It is immanent and transcendent. Tao is the greatest of all great things, (2) It is spirit rather than matter. It is the driving force in nature. It is graceful, flowing, and generous. (3) It is the way of human life when it is harmonious with the Tao of the universe. The "Te" in the title of *Tao Te Ching* stands for power.[23]

There are three kinds of Taoistic power: (1) Efficient Power, which is acting in ways that reduces friction or conflict whether it is in dealing with human relationships or inner conflicts in our minds. Going with the flow is an example of this. Don't think the only thing that goes with the flow is dead fish. (2) Augmented Power, by increasing *chi* or vital energy. This is done by body movements like *tai chi chuan* and martial arts or removing blocks to the flow of *chi* in the body by acupuncture. My wife who had done acupuncture along with other treatments at a university clinic here had encountered some patients who were afraid that the devil might get inside them through the needle!! Taoist meditation is another approach. (3) Vicarious Power, in religious Taoism which includes exorcism, shamanism, and herbal therapy. Taoism emphasizes the relativity of all values and complementarity of opposites like day and night. The traditional Chinese yin/yang symbol depicts this.

In Chinese spirituality, Earth and Heaven are complementary, a continuum. In case of a drought, the king used to confess his and his government's failure and offer a sacrifice at the Earth altar in the southern part. In Taoism and in Confucianism, there is belief in an unseen higher power. In Taoism, it is the Tao and in Confucianism, it is Tiam. Both religions provide their own angle of how to live in harmony with the higher power and contribute greatly to our overall perspective in life. Taoism promotes naturalness, goodness and simplicity. An interesting Tao idea is "wu wei" that is action by inaction. For example, letting a river flow around a rock rather than removing the rock by force. The symbol of Taoism shows the two basic forces: yin (female) and yang (male). Yin is dark, negative, and passive. Yang is white, positive, and active. But we can notice a white area in the dark and a dark area in the white. Neither the female force nor the male force is totally one way. And they are complementary and not contradictory. An awakened person is simple, upright and useful like a bamboo. Taoism promotes self-discipline and goodness.

---

23. Lao Tzu, *Tao Te Ching*, 13–17.

In my work, I have used the idea behind two poems by the Taoist poet Chuang Tzu. In one poem, an archer was very good at archery if he were relaxed. But if he were in a small competition, he became somewhat nervous and he somewhat missed the mark. And if he were in a big competition for a big prize, he became very anxious and significantly missed the mark. I used the poem as showing do not get too hung up on your goal and fear of missing the goal. In the other poem, a wheel-maker notices that if he is too tight, the wheel becomes wobbly. And if he were too loose, the wheel would fall apart. I used it to mean the importance of balance and moderation.[24] Taoism promotes conscience by emphasizing a harmonious and balanced life by using virtues like compassion, self-discipline, and aligning with the Tao.

GREEK AXIAL AGE

Socrates *(470–399 BCE)*

Socrates promotes a deeper perspective in various aspects of life. He was guiding his students to discover in themselves an intuitive wisdom from previous life experiences. The Socratic approach was to question the person's assumptions, opinions and beliefs to knowledge and self-knowledge. Socrates believed that he was commanded by God to do this. He lived by and taught the idea that "an unexamined life is not worth living." He gave much importance to virtues. In discussing the virtue of courage with two military generals, he showed them that without other virtues courage could be foolhardiness or stupidity. For him, philosophy was about learning to live well, not a way to speculate about different matters in life. Acting truly with courage would involve the virtues of goodness, justice, temperance, and wisdom. For him, the reason for so much evil in the world is because of the human ignorance of life and morality. According to Karen Armstrong, goodness was his main preoccupation[25]. While Christianity considers pride as the force behind human evil, we could notice ignorance behind pride.

Socrates had a daimon, a guiding spirit that warned him when he had a thought of doing something wrong. But this inner voice did not tell him what to do, according to Plato, Socrates's student. But Xenophon

---

24. Merton, *Way*, 83.
25. Armstrong, *Great Transformation*, 259.

CONSCIENCE, RELIGION, SPIRITUALITY, AND THE AXIAL AGE 71

(430–354 or 355 BCE), another student of Socrates, wrote that the daimon told Socrates what to do as well as what not to do.[26] Many people think of this inner voice as his conscience. Very interestingly, Socrates taught against the custom and ideal of his society to retaliate or render evil for evil. He instructed that this is good for the soul. He believed that every person has an immortal soul which is set free at death. Also, he believed in reincarnation.

In Athens, there was suspicion and fear about Socrates, which is not an unusual risk for leaders teaching something radically new. He had lived according to the laws of the land. He was accused of corrupting the youth, introducing new gods and not recognizing the gods of the state. Socrates was imprisoned, and at his trial he denied the charges. The judges gave him the option of death or exile. At his advanced age he did not want to be exiled; so, he accepted death by drinking hemlock. His inner voice did not object to it. On the day of his death, he washed himself to avoid women from having to wash his body after death. He expressed his appreciation to his friends and even his jailor who was kind to him and made some jokes and died peacefully after drinking hemlock. Plato, his great student, witnessed the trial and death. And Plato said of Socrates: " . . . of all the men of his time whom I have known, he was the wisest and justest and best."[27]

Plato (428/427–348)

Plato was born into an aristocratic family in Athens. He was a brilliant student of Socrates. Plato was thirty when Socrates was forced to drink poison and die. That incident made a lasting impression on Plato. He withdrew from society, then traveled the eastern Mediterranean, Egypt and Syracuse, and met many interesting people. He returned to Athens in 387. Plato established a school of mathematics and philosophy called the Academy in a sacred grove dedicated to the hero Academia. In one form or another, the Academy lasted for nine hundred years and became a model for the Western universities.

The teachings in Plato's academy were by discussion and dialogue in the Socratic style. He was not a dogmatist; he allowed expression of different views. Often, he presented his views indirectly, playfully, and in

---

26. Sorabji, *Moral*, 21.
27. Plato, *Phaedo*, §117c-118a.

parables. He aimed to stimulate independent thinking by his students. Plato was not a mathematician, but he was reputed as a good teacher of mathematics. He gave great importance to mathematics, so much so that over the door of his academy was inscribed the motto: "Let no one unacquainted with geometry enter here." Studying abstract mathematical concepts helps one to attain knowledge of the essential forms. He believed in the equality of men and women except in physical strength. The ideal ruler is a philosopher king based on merit, not heredity. When a part of society suffers, the society suffers as a whole.

Socrates and Plato believed that each human being has a soul (*psyche*) which is eternal and goes through many reincarnations. In *Timaeus,* Socrates located the three parts of the soul in the following parts of the human body: Reason is located in the head, Spirit is located in the upper third of the torso, and the appetite located in the middle third of the torso down to the naval. Deep within us we have the wisdom from past experiences. By the Socratic approach of reasoning and clarifying one's understanding of different matters, we recollect what we learned from previous lives. Greek education became more spiritual in the Academy.

Plato promoted spirituality in individuals and societies by teaching them to pursue virtues. In the *Republic,* he described four virtues: wisdom, justice, courage, and moderation. Wisdom involves knowledge of the whole including self and society. Justice is fairness to one and all. Courage is the ability to stand in defense of good values. Moderation is the mutual consent between the rulers and the ruled that promotes happiness and peace for all.[28]

Philosopher Alfred North Whitehead famously said: "The safest general characterization of the European philosophical tradition is that it consists of a series of footnotes to Plato."[29] Towards the end of his life, Plato had become authoritarian and even suggested the death penalty for people who opposed his view. He disapproved of poetry and tragedy in his ideal Republic because such arts stimulated irrational feelings and reactions. These steps were deviations from the spirit of the Axial Age and conscience. Interestingly, Plato's best student Aristotle wrote in *Poetics* the benefits of tragedy by stimulating pity and fear affecting catharsis, showing his psychological insight.[30] It has been said that Plato's Academy consisted of Aristotle's brain and the brawn of the rest.

28. Plato, *Republic,* Book IV, 428–35.
29. Whitehead, *Process,* 39.
30. Aristotle, *Poetics,* 6, 36–37.

Aristotle (384–322 BC)

Aristotle's father was a court physician to the Macedonian king. At age seventeen, Aristotle joined Plato's Academy where he continued for twenty years. In 347, he left Athens when Plato died. Aristotle was invited by King Philip of Macedonia to tutor his son Alexander. In 342, King Philip became master of Greece, but he was assassinated in 330 and Alexander succeeded him. The next year, Aristotle returned to Athens and founded his own school called the Lyceum as it was located close to the temple of Apollo Lyceus. Over the course of time, Alexander became Alexander the Great.

Aristotle invented the discipline of logic. He showed how to construct arguments to support one's position and how to find weaknesses in the arguments of others. He did a great deal of scientific research, especially in marine biology and zoology. He classified animals into genus and species, and he investigated over five hundred species.

Plato and Aristotle considered theology, the study of God, as the first philosophy as it dealt with the highest cause of being. Both of them believed in the cosmic religion, viewing the universe as divine. Aristotle had observed that everything that moved had something else activating it. So, he viewed God as the Unmoved Mover. Aristotle taught that everyone must do philosophy. He viewed even arguing against philosophy as a kind of philosophy. The best type of philosophy is the contemplation of the universe of nature; God gave us our intelligence for this purpose. In his view, the search for truth for its own sake is a great goal for man. Aristotle did not believe in reincarnation. He believed a person's intelligence (*nous*) *as divine and immortal.* He did not believe in traditional religion, but he thought religion may be useful in society and some people could progress from religion to contemplation, which is quite desirable.

Aristotle gave much importance to virtues which are acquired by practice and lost by disuse. Unlike feelings or passions such as anger or fear which are often momentary, virtues are lasting. The idea of following the middle ground has been in Greek culture long before Aristotle. In the myth of Daedalus and his son Icarus, Daedalus had built feathered wings for them to fly. Icarus ignored his father's instruction to fly the middle course between the sea and the sun and got the wax of his wings melted and he fell into the sea by flying close to the sun. The saying "Nothing in excess" was carved on the temple at Delphi. Socrates and Plato also promoted this idea. Aristotle gave the golden mean between excess and defect even more importance. The virtuous golden mean applies to passions and actions. There are some actions which are bad in any amount; Aristotle gave the example of murder, theft, and adultery in this category.

Aristotle called *eudaimonia* (Greek word translated as happiness or well-being or flourishing) the highest human good. He views happiness as the activity of the rational soul in harmony with virtue.[31] Compared to animals, we humans are gifted with reason, and good human functioning is the functioning of humans using reason in tune with virtue. In my view, this is living by conscience. Superego does not use proper reasoning, often using distorted ideals.

Aristotle was historically the first scientist. His Lyceum was the first research institute and the library there was the first research library. He laid the foundations of Western science, sociology and logic. His book *Poetics* is the first significant work of literary criticism. His teachings significantly influenced Christianity.

Greek Drama

Athens had a tradition of drama for three days in March every year from the late sixth century. It was to welcome spring and honor Dionysus, the God of tragic art. The plays were held in a stadium for twenty thousand people, and it went on for three consecutive days from morning to evening. Three tragedians chosen by the organizers competed in presenting.

The plots were usually taken from Greek mythology and focused on conflict in a great family of the past with contemporary issues added. Different aspects of the dramas were discussed by the citizens. People could get exposed to the display of human passions, fears, conflicts, and resolution of conflicts in a controlled setting. They could reflect on such issues, discuss with others, and learn to handle such matters better. One of the most impressive aspects of the Greek tragedies was when the plays depicted the suffering of the enemies of the Greeks and the audience was encouraged to cry in empathy of the enemies. That is so psychologically insightful and spiritually elevating. By opening the mind, stimulating feelings useful for self-understanding and empathetic views of others, literary works enhance the function of conscience and overcome superego problems.

---

31. Aristotle, *Nicomachean*, 1094a15.

Karen Armstrong puts the effect of Greek tragedy in beautiful and insightful words: "The Greeks put human misery onstage so that the Athenian audience could learn sympathy for the Persians who had devastated their city a few years earlier. In the tragedies, the chorus regularly instructed the audience to weep for people whose crimes would normally fill them with abhorrence. Tragedy could not be denied. It had to be brought right into the sacred heart of the city and made a force for good—as at the end of the *Oresteia*, the vengeful Erinyes were transformed into the Eumenides, the "well-disposed ones," and given a shrine on the Acropolis."[32]

Merlin Donald wrote about the transformation in Greece from around 700 BCE: "In Greece human thought suddenly came into its own simultaneously in a number of fields: philosophy, mathematics, geometry, biology, and geography, to name a few."[33] He further notes: "The evolution of writing was complete: the Greeks had the first truly effective phonetic system of writing, so successful that it has not really been improved upon since."[34] The Greek Axial Age promoted conscience by the emphasis on self-knowledge, goodness, reason, empathy and virtues.

THE INDIAN ROLE IN THE AXIAL AGE

The Upanishads

In India during around 1500 to 500 BCE four collections of Hindu sacred texts called "Vedas" were formed. These are the revealed knowledge directly received by the Rishis, the ancient Indian sages. The Upanishads are also known as Vedanta because it is the end or concluding part of the Vedas. The earlier parts of the Vedas consist of prayers, hymns, rituals and ceremonies. The Upanishads were largely composed probably during the Axial Age. The word 'Upanishad' means 'sitting nearby devotedly', referring to students sitting near a guru listening to the teaching. These texts internalize the sacrifices and worships described in the earlier texts, the Vedas which described the performance of Vedic rituals. Towards the Axial Age period, people needed to go beyond rituals and deal with the issues of death. Indicative of this need is the story of a young boy,

---

32. Armstrong, *Great*, 396–97.
33. Donald, *Origins*, 340.
34. Donald, *Origins*, 341.

Nachiketa, who went to the underworld to find out from Yama, the god of death about the secret of death. The details of that story will be discussed under *Katha Upanishad*. The Upanishads do deal with the issues of death but also explore our mind and spirit and provide deeper understanding of our inner world. There are over two hundred Upanishads. Of these, only ten are principal ones according to philosopher Shankara.

There are four main teachings in the Upanishads: (1) Brahman, the Ultimate Reality, pervades all the universe. Our inner soul is a tiny part of the Brahman, and it is called Atman. (2) The Atman is eternal and becomes reborn with each reincarnation. (3) The shape of our reincarnation depends on our karma which is the consequence of our actions in the current life. (4) The cycle of life, death, and rebirth continues until the person gains enlightenment or self-realization. Eknath Easwaran, a translator of the Upanishads, observes: "The rest of the Vedas, like other great scriptures, look outward in reverence and awe of the phenomenal world. The Upanishads look inward, finding the powers of nature only an expression of the more awe-inspiring powers of human consciousness."[35]

The Upanishads give the principles to lead a righteous life and the effects of proper knowledge on the person. Chandogya Upanishad names Ahimsa (nonviolence), truthfulness, sincerity, charity, and self-discipline as essential virtues. A story in the Brihadaranyaka Upanishad is that gods, men, and demons met with the Supreme Master seeking to know how to live a righteous life. The Supreme Master uttered the syllable "DA" three times which meant: self-control (damyata), charity (in Sanskrit datta), and kindness (dayadhvam). Each time the master verified, the listeners understood the instruction. The heavenly voice of thunder repeats this. Yajnavalkya teaches that with the attainment of proper knowledge, the person's attitude and behavior changes; the person becomes calm, patient, restrained, composed, and introspective. These features are consistent with living by conscience. Now, focus on Shankara's statement quoted in the beginning of this chapter. Those who follow the way of the world or the way of the flesh or tradition miss the proper insight into reality and live by the wisdom from such insight.

The Katha Upanishad is the most widely known among the Upanishads. In this Upanishad, the young boy, Nachiketa, noticed his father was giving away his possessions in preparation for increasing his spiritual life. So, the boy asked his father to whom father would give Nachiketa.

---

35. Easwaran, *Upanishads*, 21.

CONSCIENCE, RELIGION, SPIRITUALITY, AND THE AXIAL AGE

The boy asked the question twice. When he asked for it a third time, the father got angry and said: "I will give you to Death." So, Nachiketa decided to learn more about death and went to the underground abode of Yama, the god of death. Yama was away for three days doing his regular work. Upon his return, Yama offered Nachiketa three boons as compensation for causing the boy to wait for three days.

The first boon Nachiketa asked Yama was for his father to be not angry but to be loving when he goes back home. The second boon was for Yama to teach Nachiketa about the sacred fire sacrifice. After teaching the boy about the fire sacrifice, Yama moved on to the third boon: the secret of what lies beyond death. Yama explained that each of us has a choice between the path of joy and the path of pleasure. The one who follows the path of joy gets good results and the other gets bad results in the end. Similarly, we face the choice between the path of wisdom and the path of ignorance. Those who are deluded by wealth, the childish ones and careless people, don't see the importance of life hereafter. Some people foolishly think there is nothing beyond this life.

Yama talked about the Atman hidden in the heart of all beings. It is neither born nor dies. The Atman is eternal; it does not die when the body dies. Atman is compared to the Lord of a chariot; the body is the chariot. Reason is the charioteer; and the mind is the reins. The senses are the horses; and their paths are the objects of the senses. A person whose chariot is driven by reason and holds the reins of mind correctly reaches the supreme Spirit. A person becomes free from the jaws of death when he or she lives by the good consciousness of the Atman. The mind is beyond the senses; reason is beyond the mind; the individual Spirit is beyond reason; the Universal Spirit is beyond the individual Spirit. Meditation can help to enable people to go deeper and deeper into consciousness and might reach the wisdom in the Self. After the body of a person dies, the person's individual spirit, or atman, survives and it might reincarnate in another person.

The belief in reincarnation was present in Axial Age Greek thinkers Socrates and Plato, but it did not become a popular belief among the masses as it did in India. While some Native Americans and West Africans had also believed in reincarnation, the belief in karma was a special contribution of India.[36] At the University of Virginia where I got my Psychiatric training, there is a Department of Perceptual Studies doing

---

36. Muesse, *Age*, 64.

research on Near Death Experiences and reincarnation studies. There, I knew Professor Ian Stevenson who did years of research on reincarnation cases. What was most impressive to me in his findings was many cases of children claiming reincarnation who had birthmarks corresponding to the wound by which the person he or she was in the previous life died. Reincarnation is a very important theme in Hinduism, Buddhism, Jainism, and Sikhism, the Indian religions.

Quantum physics theory and the Vedantic philosophy share significant parallels especially in their concepts of interconnectedness. Erwin Schrödinger is particularly remarkable in this connection. Schrödinger demonstrated that electrons could have the properties of either particles or waves, but they are neither the one or the other; their state can be calculated only with a degree of probability. Schrödinger shared the 1933 Nobel Prize in Physics for this discovery.[37] Around 1918, he was exposed to the writings of the German philosopher Arthur Schopenhauer who had said of the Upanishads: "In the whole world, there is no study so beneficial and so elevating as that of the Upanishads. It has been the solace of my life. It will be the solace of my death." Schopenhauer, a lifelong bachelor, had a series of poodles each named "Atman."[38]

We can notice the phrase, "all in all" used on the side of quantum physics (talking about the Universe) and the side of Vedanta (talking about Brahman), meaning everything is interconnected. About the mystic vision, Schrödinger wrote: "[No, but], inconceivable as it seems to ordinary reason, you—and all other conscious beings as such–are all in all.[39]" I think here a statement in the *Isha Upanishad* is quite relevant: "Who sees all beings in their own self and their own self in all beings, loses all hatred and fear."

Biographer Walter Moore in *Schrödinger: Life and Thought* wrote: "In 1925, the worldview of physics was a model of the universe as a great machine composed of separable interacting material particles. During the next few years, Schrödinger and Heisenberg and their followers created a universe based on superimposed inseparable waves of probability amplitudes. This new view would be entirely consistent with the Vedantic concept of the All in One"[40].

37. Wikipedia, "Erwin Schrödinger," paras. 1–3.
38. Wikipedia, "Arthur Schopenhauer," paras. 20, 28–29.
39. Wilbur, *Quantum,* 97.
40. Moore, *Schrödinger,* 173.

Catholic monk and religion scholar Bede Griffiths, an Englishman who settled in India and was keenly knowledgeable of Hinduism, wrote about the wisdom of the Upanishads: "It is only when we learn to see the immanent (the material world) in the transcendent (the divine) and the transcendent in the immanent, that we find the truth. Both materialism and idealism can lead us astray. It is the consciousness which transcends the opposites and all dualities that reaches the truth. The discovery was made that the "gods" are nothing but names and forms of the one Reality beyond name and form. This is a lesson for all religions."[41]

About the importance of Griffiths' work, William Johnson, an Irish Jesuit and a professor of religious studies, observes: "In the twentieth century, however, who spoke most eloquently and wrote most prolifically about universal wisdom was Bede Griffiths. . . . Griffiths saw that the wisdom of the great religions was necessary for the survival of a world in crisis."[42]

Impressive is the efficient way the profound wisdom of the Upanishads is imparted effectively. For example, the father of Svetaketu, a young man, asked him to bring the fruit of a banyan tree. Then, the father asked him to cut the fruit. Asked about what he saw, the young man answered: "very small seeds, Sir." Next, the father told his son to cut a seed and asked him what he saw. Svetaketu answered: "Nothing, Sir." Then, the father explained: "Son, from the invisible essence of the seed comes the big banyan tree." "Son, an invisible and subtle essence is the Spirit of the Universe. That is Reality. That is Atman. You Art That." Then, the father told the son to mix some salt in water, and they would talk about it the next day. On the next day, the father asked the son where the salt was, and he answered that he could not find it. Then, Svetaketu tasted the water in different spots as his father asked him to and it tasted salty every time. And the father concluded: "Son, you can't see the Spirit, but he is really here. A subtle and invisible essence is the Spirit of the whole universe. That is Truth. Thou Art That."

"Thou Art That" is a great saying. It means your Self is identical to Brahman–eternal and conscious.

The Upanishads promoted conscience by ethical teachings, emphasizing good karma and teaching our true identity as Atman, a part of Brahman.

41. Griffiths, *Universal*, 29.
42. Johnson, *Arise*, 46.

I will end this part with a beautiful and meaningful prayer called pavamana [being purified] mantra from the Brihadaranyaka Upanishad:

> Om
> Lead me from the unreal to the real,
> Lead me from darkness to light,
> Lead me from death to immortality.
> Om Peace, Peace, Peace[43]

Buddhism

Prince Siddhartha Gautama or Gotama was born in 563 BCE. His father was the king of the sakyas, a tribe of the Gautama's living at the foothills of the Himalayas in northern India. According to a legend his father was told by an astrologer that this prince would become a great king if he is not exposed to suffering and become a great teacher otherwise. Since the king wanted his son to become a king, he was brought up shielded from suffering. He was handsome and physically and psychologically strong. At sixteen, he married a beautiful princess, Yashodhara, a cousin.

At age twenty-nine, Gotama went outside of the palace grounds and got exposed to what are called "The Four Sights": a sick person, a very old person, a dead body being carried off to the charnel ground, and an apparently happy wandering monk. These sights shattered his superficial outlook on life and sent him into a search for enlightenment. He renounced his royal life and his wife and newborn son. For six years he lived as an ascetic. He practiced yoga and self-mortification. Self-mortification only increased suffering. On an occasion when he was extremely weak from ascetic practices, a farmer's wife named Sujata offered him milk rice which helped him.

Gotama left asceticism because it did not bring enlightenment. Self-mortification only added to suffering. He had five followers when he was practicing asceticism, but they left him when he changed. Then, for seven weeks, he tried mindfulness meditation sitting under a peepal tree (which came to be called the bodhi tree, bodhi meaning wisdom). In spite of temptations of sensual pleasure and taunting him with doubts and threats by the demon Mara, he continued the meditation until he got enlightened or became awake (Buddha means the "awakened one"). He

---

43. *Brihadaranyaka Upanishad*, "Pavamana," Vol. 15, 2.

had rejected the sensual life of a prince, and he renounced the opposite extreme of asceticism and pursued "The Middle Way."

After Gotama became the Buddha, he searched for and found his five previous followers who were living in a Deer Park near Benares. The five followers became his disciples.

It is at the Deer Park that the Buddha delivered his first sermon called "Turning the wheel of Dhamma" (Dhamma in Pali or Dharma in Sanskrit has been translated as truth that leads to liberation). The sermon covered the core of his teachings: the four noble truths and the eightfold paths.

He taught "The Four Noble Truths."

1. The first of these is translated as "life is suffering" but the spirit of it is that life involves a lot of suffering.
2. There is cause for the suffering.
3. Attachment or emotional clinging is the cause. Aversion is a form of attachment.
4. The Eightfold Path is the solution for this problem.

The eightfold path consists of the following: right intent, right speech, right conduct, right occupation, right effort, right mindfulness, and right concentration. Right conduct involves not killing, not stealing, not lying, being chaste, and not drinking intoxicants.[44] Buddha gave so much importance to the mind that the Buddhist scripture Dhammapada opens with a statement: "All that we are is a result of what we have thought."[45] As for an example of a wrong occupation, the Buddha gave the case of a traveling salesman probably because he may be able to evade social consequences to cheating in his work. Buddha worked for forty-five years and died at the age of eighty.

Buddha's teaching of the four reliances is particularly interesting for us.

1. Rely on the teachings, not the teacher's personality.
2. Rely on the meaning of the teaching, not just the words.
3. Rely on the deeper meaning, not the superficial meaning of the teaching.

---

44. Muesse, *Age*, 109–32.
45. Easwaran, *Dhammapada*, 78.

4. Rely on your wise mind, not your ordinary judgmental mind.

Doesn't the fourth reliance sound quite like saying rely on your conscience, not your superego? Buddhism promotes conscience by the emphasis on good karma, compassion, goodness, wisdom, humility and a healthy identity.

He taught about samsara, karma, rebirth and nirvana. Samsara is the repeated cycle of birth, mundane life, death and rebirth with its accompanying suffering. He emphasized that karma is based on intentional actions. Nirvana is a state of no more rebirth and suffering. There are two types of nirvana: nirvana with a remainder in which case the person lives after the nirvana, and nirvana without a remainder (the person dies). Enlightenment is the process of being awakened to profound truths and the final fruit of it is nirvana. Bodhisattva is an enlightened being who is postponing his or her nirvana for living to help others, to become enlightened. Buddhism does not believe in anything permanent like a soul or God. Upon death, it is the end of the body of the person, but the spirit (consciousness) is reborn in one of six realms: heaven, human being, Asura, hungry ghost, animal, or hell. Again, this state is not permanent. There is no eternal damnation.

Buddha rejected the caste system of Hinduism. While Buddhism teaches the impermanence of everything, Hinduism teaches that everything is impermanent except the Atman and the Brahman. Both religions promote the practice of meditation. In some Hindu teachings, Buddha is considered the ninth incarnation of God. Supporting this, S. Radhakrishnan (late Hindu philosopher, former President of India and former professor at Oxford) explained why Buddha was considered an incarnation of God or an Avatara: "All those who adhere to the essential framework of the Hindu religion and attempt to bring it into conformity with the voice of *awakened conscience* (italics added) are treated as *avatars* (divine incarnations)."[46]

I think the phrase "awakened conscience" is applicable to the whole Axial Age progress. Historically, it is remarkable that Buddha's initial hesitations were overcome by the influence of his cousin and close disciple Ananda and Buddha's aunt who raised him (when his mother died seven days after he was born), he allowed women to become Buddhist nuns. In the upcoming chapter on Peace, I have written about the enormous contribution of Ashoka in spreading Buddhism. Buddha's cousin Ananda's

---

46. Radhakrishnan, *Indian*, 171.

sharp memory helped to transmit his speeches, and the oral transmission continued for around four centuries.

THE JEWISH PROPHETS OF THE AXIAL AGE

Prophet Jonah

Jonah was a servant of God during the rule of King Jeroboam (792–753 BCE). God gave Jonah instruction to go to Nineveh, the capital of the Assyrian empire. He was to cry out against the wickedness of the people and ask them to repent. He did not want to follow this instruction and ran away in the opposite direction and got on a ship. The ship faced a mighty storm. In his discussion with the distressed sailors, Jonah admitted that the storm was because of him and told them to throw him into the sea. They threw him into the sea, and he was swallowed up by a big fish which was provided by the Lord. Jonah spent three days and nights in the belly of the fish. Then, as instructed by God, the fish spewed him onto the dry land. Now that he was safe and sound, he heard God's words a second time telling him to go to Nineveh and deliver God's message. This time, Jonah followed God's instruction. The people, including the King, took God's message seriously. They fasted, prayed, and turned away from their sinful ways. And so, God decided not to cause them a calamity.

Jonah did not follow God's instructions the first time because the Assyrians were enemies of Israel. For the same reason, he waited outside the city hoping God would change his mind and destroy the city. Jonah was very angry that God did not destroy Nineveh. Interestingly, God asked him: "Is it right for you to be angry?" For me as a psychiatrist, it reminds me of how I posed a question to a patient to ponder over. Then God proceeded to teach him compassion. One night, God created a bush to give Jonah shade, and he was very happy. But the next day God created a worm that destroyed the bush which made Jonah "angry enough to die." God asked Jonah whether it was right for him to be angry about the bush. Further, God explained that Jonah was concerned about the bush although he did not work to grow it. Then God posed a big question whether God shouldn't be concerned about thousands of people and many animals? The story of Jonah shows many aspects of conscience.

Prophet Amos *(Active in 760–755 BCE, Died in 745 BCE)*

Amos was a sheep herder and sycamore fig farmer who preached in the northern Kingdom of Israel in the eighth century BCE. It was a more peaceful time. Religious practices were focused on rituals and sacrifices. The rich were very rich, and the poor were very poor. The rich exploited the poor. And the political system was corrupt. Amos had a vision of Yahweh standing in the temple of Bethel and ordering the divine council to destroy the temple and the people of Israel for their injustice and corruption.

Amos conveyed this message to the king and people of Israel in his prophetic style. He explained that what Yahweh wanted was not sacrifices and festivals but practice of justice and integrity. For Amos, Yahweh is the only God, and he is the God of all people and all nations. Karen Armstrong notes that Amos attacked the pride of Israelites in their special relationship with God which was an example of self-surrendering instead of false pride by denying wrongdoing.[47] *The Book of Amos* in the *Hebrew Bible* is attributed to him. God told Amos: "But let justice roll down like waters, and righteousness like an ever-flowing stream." (Amos 5:24)

Prophet Hosea *(Active in 750–722 BCE)*

Hosea was active in the kingdom of Israel from around 750–722 BCE, highly cultured, and belonged to the upper class. The Lord had Hosea marry Gomer, a sacred prostitute in the fertility cult of Baal. Gomer kept going back to prostitution and Hosea continued to love her and pursue her. This story is symbolic of God's love for Israel as Yahweh continued to love Israel in spite of Israel worshiping other gods like Baal and practicing theft, adultery, and violence. Hosea taught that what God wants is love and compassion, not rituals. Hosea considered God as a loving God.

Interestingly, Jesus quoted Hosea saying what God wants is mercy not sacrifice. Yahweh is a God of Love. When He punishes Israel, it is from love, not hate. Hosea urged people to be deeper in their understanding of God and be self-reflective of their attitude and behavior. It is people's personal responsibility. A tragedy of religion is when the followers are stuck with rituals and superficiality. Hosea's writings are the first of the *Old Testament* books of the Minor Prophets.

---

47. Armstrong, *Great Transformation*, 88–89.

Prophet Isaiah *(Active in 749–700 BCE)*

Isaiah was active in around 749 to 700 BCE in Jerusalem in the Southern Kingdom of Judah. He was an aristocrat well aware of political affairs and the victimization of the poor and the powerless by the ruling class and the wealthy, and he spoke up for the victim. He had a powerful vision of God in amazing glory needing a messenger to warn his people of Israel about their impending doom and its meaning. Isaiah accepted the tough role and carried it out.

His prophecies came true with the Assyrian conquest of Israel in 722 BCE, which was a punishment from Yahweh for the sins of the people. The punishment was remedial, for a change of leadership and an increase in the spiritual strength of the people. Isaiah's prophecies also expressed for the first time Israel's messianic hope. Messiah means the "anointed one." This is the person chosen by Yahweh for a particular purpose. The biblical book of Isaiah has been very important in Judaism and Christianity. A part of the *Book of Isaiah* was written by him.

Prophet Jeremiah *(650–570 BCE)*

Jeremiah grew up in a village near Jerusalem. He was a member of a priestly family. He began his prophetic work in 627/626 BCE. When he got the call from the Lord, he was unsure. But with Yahweh's reassurance, he accepted the very tough mission. He condemned false worship and social injustices and emphasized the need for repentance and reform. He proclaimed that an enemy from the north was coming. In his famous "Temple sermon," he criticized people for excessive dependence on the temple and urged them to make genuine ethical reform. He predicted that God would destroy the Temple if they did not transform. He was arrested, tried and acquitted but may have been prevented from preaching there again. He commended King Josiah for promoting justice and righteousness and criticized King Jehoiakim for his injustice, selfishness and materialism.

Jeremiah emphasized personal transformation with self-reflection, sincerity and change of heart. Like the prophets before him, he views external rituals meaningless unless they help the person's spiritual transformation. His very important prophecy for the future was about a New Covenant [Jer 31:31–34] with Israel when Yahweh would write his law upon the hearts of people. It would supersede the Mosaic Law written on tablets of stone. The prophet is the author of the *Book of Jeremiah* in the *Old Testament*.

Prophet Ezekiel *(possibly 622–possibly 570 BCE)*

Ezekiel was born in a priestly family in Israel. At the age of thirteen, he had a call from God to become a prophet. He had many visions, and he prophesied the destruction of Israel and the Temple. Jerusalem surrendered to the Babylonians in 597 BCE. Before this, he was working as a priest connected with the Temple. He was deported to Babylon along with a large number of Israelites. He became a comforter of his fellow exiles. In Babylon, Jews learned that they could worship God away from the temple. They organized places to gather for formal Jewish worship, "synagogues" which also provided schools for Jewish education. Prophet Ezekiel was opposed to the idea that "the sins of the fathers are visited upon the children." He taught that each person would be responsible for his or her right or wrong deeds.

In 539 BCE, King Cyrus invaded Babylon, and he liberated the Jewish exiles. Ezekiel and fellow Jews returned home, and Ezekiel continued his work as a priest. He had prophesied the restoration of Israel. God told him that He would remove the people's heart of stone and give them a heart of flesh. The Book of Ezekiel is believed to have been primarily written by him. He has had great influence in Judaism and Christianity.

Prophet Zechariah *(prophet from 520–518 BCE)*

Zechariah was a prophet at a time when a lot of Jews were returning from their Babylonian captivity and rebuilding Jerusalem and the temple. His prophecies were based on his visions. He had a long series of visions. God told him to love one another, to judge truthfully, and keep peace. A lot of his visions were about rebuilding Jerusalem and the Temple and the destruction of Israel's enemies.

All the above Jewish prophets emphasized justice, compassion, righteousness, the law written in the heart, the heart of flesh and individual responsibility, features which are consistent with conscience. They were monotheists and courageous activists.

ZOROASTRIANISM

Persians believed in Mazda as the greatest and wisest of the ahuras or divine beings. Zoroaster became a priest at age fifteen and a prophet at age thirty following a vision in which he saw Ahura Mazda and six other radiant beings. This vision caused him to determine to teach people to seek what is right. He had several more visions which reinforced his new path in life.

Zoroaster passionately promoted the worship of Ahura Mazda and he divided the spirits and gods, the daevas and ahuras into two: daevas as wicked gods and the ahuras as the ethical gods. Our term "devil" derived from the daeva. (Incidentally, the asuras are the demons and devas are the divine spirits in Indian mythology.) Zoroaster also conceived a chief god among the daevas called Ahriman who is totally evil as opposed to the totally good Mazda. People have the responsibility to choose between following the good or the evil path and their destiny would depend on this choice.

Four days after death, people would be judged at a palace at the sacred mountain High Hara. The good people would be led across a bridge accompanied by a beautiful maiden to heaven. The evil people would be led by an ugly old woman to cross an extremely narrow bridge, and the people would fall to hell. In hell, which is ruled by the Evil One, people get punished for their sins, but hell is not eternal. The struggle between good and evil would go on until a spectacular war when the good would destroy evil along with hell and its inhabitants. The good people in heaven would resurrect on earth and live in paradise along with the good people who would be living on earth at the time of the ultimate war. A savior-judge figure [a Saoshyant born from a virgin who got pregnant by bathing in a lake in which Zoroaster's semen would have been preserved] would appear in the end. And he would lead Ahura Mazda's forces to victory.

Cyrus the Great (590–529 BCE) became king of the Achaemenid dynasty when his father died. He expanded the kingdom by several conquests, including Babylon, and the kingdom became the largest the world had known. The "Cyrus Cylinder" is a football-size barrel made of baked clay on which in Babylonian cuneiform is written about Cyrus' conquest of Babylon and his intention to give freedom of worship to various communities. So, the Cyrus Cylinder is also considered the first bill of rights, and a copy of the cylinder is kept at the UN headquarters in

New York. Cyrus was a tolerant, benevolent, and magnanimous ruler. Greek historian Xenophon considered him an ideal ruler. The special inspectors, "the King's ears," informed the central administration about local matters. There was an effective courier service and legal cases could be appealed to the King. He liberated the Jews from their Babylonian Captivity and helped them to return to Jerusalem and build the Second Temple. Cyrus was strongly influenced by the teachings of Zoroaster. In the Old Testament, the Prophet Isaiah says that the Lord anointed Cyrus. The Hebrew word *messiah* means anointed. Cyrus is the only non-Jewish person anointed by the Lord, according to the *Old Testament*. Thomas Jefferson owned two copies of Xenophon's book on Cyrus and was inspired by Cyrus' example. In 1971, Iran celebrated the two thousand five hundredth anniversary of the founding of King Cyrus' kingdom. Wouldn't it be great if Iran and Israel would follow his enlightened spirit?

Goodness is the ideal in Zoroastrianism: good thoughts, good words, and good deeds. Karen Armstrong points out that Zoroaster belonged to the old spiritual world in his teaching of the cosmic contest between good and evil, but he looked forward to the Axial Age by his passionate ethics. His teaching of individual choice and responsibility was impressive. The moral obligation of individuals to distinguish between good and evil and pursue the former that Zoroaster passionately advocated became part of the Axial Age. We can notice the presence of many of Zoroaster's concepts in other religions, especially in the Abrahamic religions, Judaism, Christianity, and Islam. With the spread of Islam in Persia, Zoroastrians spread to India where they were known as Parsees.[48]

THE GREAT TRANSFORMATION IN THE AXIAL AGE

Various elements of conscience–self-reflection, reason, search for truth, moderation, and the Golden Rule—developed during the Axial Age. Some of these factors were stronger in some areas and some other factors in other areas. For example, reason was given much importance by Socrates and the Golden Rule by Confucius. The stage was set for further refinement and wider utilization of conscience.

The word conscience first used in Greek and then in Roman writings got a great boost in The New Testament. Literary luminaries like Shakespeare, Tolstoy, Victor Hugo, and Harper Lee nurtured it. A book

---

48. Muesse, *Age*, 107–41.

Thirukkural written in the South Indian language Tamil in the first century AD has used the word for conscience. It was from a German translation of that book that Tolstoy learned the concept of nonviolence, according to an English translation of the book. Gandhi and King applied conscience in the socio-political sphere.[49] Various nonviolent movements have promoted conscience. By differentiating conscience from superego, we can make the best of both.

In his book *Immortal Diamond*, Richard Rohr states: "Unfortunately the monumental insights of the Axial periods that formed all of us in foundational and good ways began to dry up and wane, descending into the extreme headiness of some Scholastic philosophy (1100–1500), the antagonistic mind of almost all church reformations, and the rational literalism of the enlightenment."[50]

Ewert H. Cousins has written about the twenty-first century as what he calls "the second Axial Age."[51]

I differ from this view and when I use the term Axial Age, I am talking about Jasper's view. See more about this under the notes section at the end of the book.

THE PERENNIAL PHILOSOPHY

In his book with the above title, Aldous Huxley observes: "*Philosophia Perennis*–the phrase was coined by Leibniz: but the thing–the metaphysic that recognizes a divine Reality substantial to the world of things and lives and minds; the psychology that finds in the soul something similar to, or even identical with, divine Reality; the ethic that places man's final end in the knowledge of the immanent and transcendent Ground of all being–the thing is immemorial and universal." [52]

Rabbi Rami Shapiro, who has used the ideas of the Perennial Philosophy in his book *Perennial Wisdom for the Spiritually Independent*, discusses the five questions central to the spiritual quest: (1) *Who am I?* (2) *Where did I come from?* (3) *Where am I going?* (4) *How shall I live?* and (5) *Why?* [53] These are issues the religions and the spiritual with or

---

49. Rajaram, *Thirukkural*, 176–87.
50. Rohr, *Immortal*, 115.
51. Cousins, *Christ*, 10.
52. Huxley, *Perennial*, vii.
53. Shapiro, *Perennial*, preface.

without religion deal with. During the Axial Age, there were leaders who addressed these concerns.

Bede Griffiths, in *Universal Wisdom,* expresses Sufism, the mystical branch of Islam, as a great example of the Perennial Philosophy. He viewed the Jewish mystical group Kabbalah similarly. Earlier in this chapter, I noted the Pew Research Center survey regarding the percentage of people of different religions in India who identify as Sufis also. Sufism emphasizes introspection and spiritual closeness to God. Sufis seek spiritual knowledge, reject materialism, exercise purification of the soul, and mystical contemplation on God.[54]

CONSCIENCE AND THE QURAN

Allah wants people to be just to others and avoid gossip, backbiting, suspicions, grudges, envy and jealousy. Conscience helps people to believe in God. Living by conscience leads to gaining heaven after death and living against conscience leads to hell hereafter. Yahya says the devil (shaytan) is real. Not Harun Yahya, a Turkish Muslim author, in his book *The Importance of Conscience in the Quran* says: "Conscience is a spiritual quality that bids man good attitude and thought and helps him think straight and tell right from wrong."[55] He further states: "Conscience will surely show man what is right, even if nobody else will. However, what matters for man is to take recourse to his own conscience. Listen to what it says, and act on it. For this reason, we can say that conscience is the main component of religion."[56]

If a person does not accept the guidance of conscience, it is because of selfishness. The devil (shaytan) is real, not mythical. Each person has two angels with him or her, one on the right writing every good action the person does and the angel on the left writing all the wrong deeds the person commits. After the person's death, God judges the person based on the two accounts and provides rewards or punishments. The punishment in hell is really hellish.

---

54. Griffiths, *Universal*, 31.
55. Yahya, *Importance*, 9.
56. Yahya, *Importance*, 10.

SPIRITUALITY AND NEAR-DEATH EXPERIENCE (NDE)

Raymond Moody's groundbreaking study published as *Life After Life* in 1975 discusses common features of Near–Death Experience (NDE). These are the experiences of people who were declared clinically dead but became obviously alive briefly. Many of those who had a Near–Death Experience describe hearing that they were pronounced dead, hearing distressing noise, moving fast through a dark long tunnel, meeting departed relatives and friends, having out of body experience, and a being of bright light appearing. This "being of light" reviews the person's life in a panoramic vision and compassionately stimulates the individual to reflect whether he or she has gained love and knowledge. And the knowledge is like wisdom based on further information the NDEers gave. In Moody's studies, the review of one's life by the being of light has a gentle and loving feel unlike the tense and scary feel of the judgment upon death Christians often talk about when God judges whether the person should be sent to heaven or hell. After the review of life, some NDErs experience a border or a limit like a fence or a door or a body of water before they reluctantly return to their body. The NDErs return to their bodies reluctantly because the experience is so wonderful.[57]

On September 14, 2023, *Science Daily* published an article about a new research study's result which indicated some patients recall death experiences up to an hour after a cardiac arrest. The study was led by Sam Parnia, MD at NYU Grossman School of Medicine in cooperation with twenty-five hospitals mostly in the US and Britain. The study named "AWAreness during REsuscitation (AWARE)-II study" followed five hundred and sixty-seven hospitalized patients. A subset of eighty-five patients received brain monitoring with EEG during resuscitation. Also, additional testimony from one hundred and twenty-six patients from the community with self-reported memories of cardiac arrest were used. The EEG recordings showed higher mental function connected with the experience of death. Perception of separation from the body, observing events without distress or pain, and meaningful evaluation of the person's relationships and actions throughout life were part of the death experience. The EEG studies helped to rule out hallucinations, delusions, illusions, and dreams or CPR–induced consciousness.[58]

---

57. Moody, *Life*, ix–181.
58. Parnia, "New Evidence," paras. 1–9.

On October 19, 2024, *Epoch Times* had an article by Yuhong Dong MD, PhD about a congenitally blind person, Vicki, who had a near-death experience after sustaining a head and neck injury from a car accident. During her NDE, she saw her body and her wedding ring for the first time.[59] Vicki was part of the research on NDE by Dr. Jeffrey Long, a radiation oncologist in Kentucky who has researched over four thousand cases of NDEs and published it on his website, the Near-Death Experience Foundation (https://www.nderf.org). Vicki's NDE had the usual features. One exception was that she had a 360-degree vision during the experience. After the NDE she gained knowledge about math, science, and God easily and understood languages she did not previously know.

The personal transformation of people going through near–death experience includes more love and compassion, deeper search for meaning in life, overcoming fear of death, sense of unity with others, discarding any suicidal ideas, happiness and peace, and psychic abilities in many cases. These are really spiritual changes. In the 2015 edition of *Life After Life*, Eben Alexander, a neurologist who has written about his own near-death experience, wrote that our brain works as a filter that limits our consciousness. In his words: "Consciousness is elemental–it is primary in our universe. Near–death experiences teach us that the spirit survives physical death."[60]

Bede Griffiths believed Love and Wisdom as the most important aspects of religions. Guided by conscience, healthy spirituality, and religion promote love and wisdom. When we live by conscience, we manifest love and wisdom. Wisdom involves knowledge, reason and imagination, and insight into these in the practical situations in life. In the words of Paul Tillich: "It is insight into the meaning of one's life. Into its conflicts and dangers, into its creative and destructive powers, and into the ground out of which it comes and to which it must return."[61]

EXCLUSIVISM VS. UNIVERSALISM

Being born again and believing in Jesus as one's Lord and personal Savior are essential for one's salvation according to many Christian groups. Jesus had said that none could enter the kingdom of God without being born of

---

59. Dong, "From Blindness," paras. 1–49.
60. Moody and Alexander, *Life*, xv.
61. Tillich, *Eternal*, 167.

water and Spirit. It is often taken to mean getting baptized and accepting Jesus as one's personal lord and savior as the conditions for salvation. Or else you go to hell. Protestant theologian Marcus J. Borg points out that the phrase "being born again" is a metaphor for personal transformation into a life in Christ. Borg says: "the result of being 'in Christ' is a new way of being, a new identity, a new creation."[62] Borg quotes St. Paul: "There is no longer Jew or Gentile, there is no longer slave or free, there is no longer male and female, for all of you are all in Christ Jesus."[63]

Borg explains the statement in John 14:6: "I am the way, and the truth, and the life. No one comes to the father except through me." Showing the commonality of "the way" in the other world religions, Borg states: "The image of following "the way" is common to Judaism, and "the way" involves a new heart, a new self—centered in God. One of the meanings of the word "Islam" is "surrender": to surrender one's life to God by radically centering on God. And Muhammad is reported to have said, "Die before you die"....At the heart of the Buddhist path is "letting go"–the same internal path as dying to an old way of being and being born into a new one. According to the *Tao Te Ching*, a foundational text for both Taoism and Zen Buddhism, Lao Tzu said: "If you want to become full, let yourself be empty; if you want to be reborn, let yourself die."[64]

Borg admits how this commonality of spiritual pathways could be disconcerting to Christians sometimes given the history of believing Jesus as the only way. Moreover, he says the commonality of the path gives credibility to Christianity because if Jesus is considered the only way, it would be suspect. In my experience, Christians who are guided by conscience are glad about such inclusiveness. But others who are guided by superegos, sadly, tend to reject it and hold on to their old ways of exclusiveness.

Thomas Merton expressed quite similar views. In *Contemplation in a World of Action*, he says: "The notion of "rebirth" is not peculiar to Christianity. In Sufism, Zen Buddhism, and many other religions or spiritual traditions, emphasis is placed on to fulfill certain obscure yet urgent potentialities in the ground of one's being to "become someone" that one already (potentially) is the person one is truly meant to be."[65] Merton further described the features of such a person: "transformed,

62. Borg, *Heart*, 110.
63. Gal 3:28.
64. Borg, *Heart*, 119.
65. Merton, *Contemplation*, 220–21.

"reborn" to a new and more complete identity, and to a more profoundly fruitful existence in peace, in wisdom, in creativity, in love. When rigidity and limitation become ends in themselves, they no longer favor growth, they stifle it."[66] It is noteworthy that Borg, from the Protestant side, and Merton, from the Catholic side of Christianity, expressed similar views. Quite interestingly, both of them had mystical experiences.

The idea of universality is reminiscent of Mother Teresa's famous statement that her view of conversion is helping a Hindu to be a better Hindu and a Muslim to be a better Muslim.[67] In a similar spirit, the imam of the Atlanta Masjid of Al-Islam told students of Barbara Brown Taylor: "Our desire is not that you become Muslim, but that you become the best Christian, the best Jew, the best person you can be…"[68] Such openness to other religions may be held by a minority of religious people but it is an increasing minority in my experience.

Jaspers says: "The claim to exclusive possession of truth, that tool of fanaticism, of human arrogance and self-deception through the will to power… can be vanquished by the very fact that God has manifested himself historically in several fashions and has opened up many ways to Himself. It is as though the deity were issuing a warning, through the language of universal history against the claim to exclusiveness in the possession of truth."[69]

In recent times, scientists from various fields have explored spirituality. Geneticist Dean Hamer says: "Spirituality is based in consciousness, religion in cognition. Spirituality is universal, whereas cultures have their own forms of religion. I would argue that the important contrast is that spirituality is generic, while religion is based on culture, traditions, beliefs and ideas."[70] We live at a time when there are plenty of chances to awaken conscience, understand its difference with the superego and the PIG, and make good choices promoting healthy spirituality, preventing superego, or the PIG, from causing wrong choices.

---

66. Merton, *Contemplation*, 221–22.
67. Mother Teresa of Calcutta, "Mother Teresa on Religion," paras. 1–19.
68. Taylor, *Holy Envy*, 79.
69. Jaspers, *Origin*, 28.
70. Hamer, *Adi Shankaracharya*, 188.

Chapter Three

Pro Conscience vs. Anti Conscience: Christian Example

"To the corruption of Christianity I am, indeed opposed: but not to the genuine precepts of Jesus himself." — Thomas Jefferson[1]

"[Religion] has two faces: one the face of truth, the other the face of deception."— Arthur Schopenhauer[2]

CONSCIENCE IS GIVEN GREAT importance in the *New Testament*. But Christians often seem to be guided by superego inconsistent with conscience. The history of Christianity shows plenty of examples when Christian groups have followed their consciences and other examples when Christians went against consciences and followed their superegos or their PIGs (Problem of Irrational Gratification). In this chapter, I explore this issue.

THE WORD "CONSCIENCE" IN THE NEW TESTAMENT

The word "conscience" is used twenty times in St. Paul's letters, five times in Hebrews, three times in 1 Peter and twice in Acts. The one-time conscience is used in the story of the adulteress seems to be only in the King

---

1. Jefferson, "Benjamin Rush."
2. Schopenhauer, *Essays*, 180–82.

James' version, as noted before. The importance of conscience is shown by the strong expressions by both Apostles Paul, observing that rejection of conscience causes destruction of faith, and Peter, who considers baptism as "an appeal to God for a good conscience." (1 Pet 3:21)

St. Paul connected the judging right or wrong function of conscience with the law written in the heart in Rom 2:14–5 as we addressed in the last chapter. Paul saw conscience which judges right and wrong as part of being human, not something confined to Christians. In the story of the adulteress, we can notice that Jesus used the law written in the heart over the law of Moses. Jesus explained that he came to fulfill the law, not to abolish laws. Fulfilling the law involves understanding the spirit and purpose of the law in the broad perspective and what would be fair and reasonable for those involved.

In the above description, we can see conscience judges right and wrong based on the law written in the heart which uses reason, truth, moderation, and the sense of fairness, the Golden Rule. The phrase "the law written in the heart" obviously emphasizes the role of empathy, compassion, and love. With it comes reasonable flexibility in applying the law, compared to the rigid application of the law written in stone. It also involves awareness of the consequences of obeying or breaking the law including punishments.

In Paul's letters in 1 Cor 8, the word conscience is used eight times in connection with the issue of eating meat offered to an idol. Paul's position was that conscience, properly used, would be fine with eating the meat offered to pagan idols. The reason is that the idols of the pagan gods have no real existence. So, by reason it would be fine to eat the meat offered to an idol. But in the Christian community, the issue of fairness to others arises. In that regard, Paul advised against eating the meat if it would offend the consciences of fellow Christians who don't have the correct judgment of conscience based on reason. Such a person was described to have a weak conscience. Because of a weak conscience, a person may think a right choice is wrong, like eating meat offered to an idol. So, the Christian with a strong conscience would sacrifice the choice of eating such meat to prevent wounding the weak conscience of the brethren. Paul himself was helping people to use reason to raise consciousness and make the right choice. Although Paul did not express another choice besides the self-sacrifice for the Christian with a strong conscience, I think one could educate and strengthen the conscience of the weak brethren and then both could eat the meat with good conscience.

An example in more recent history and close to home is Martin Luther King Jr.'s *Letter from Birmingham Jail*. He was jailed for his nonviolent direct action of civil disobedience. King pointed out that breaking unjust law was in tune with Christian values.[3] The civil disobedience program was done openly, lovingly, and accepting any punishment. When criminals break laws, it is often done secretly, selfishly, and trying to avoid punishment. The approach of civil disobedience was obviously consistent with conscience. King was not only doing the right thing but also explaining his good reasoning behind the movement so that he wouldn't set a wrong example of breaking laws.

The big question is: What kind of inner guides were the segregationists using before King stimulated their consciences? The answer is, it was the unreasonable and unfair superego, or the inner parrot, of the people who were practicing or supporting segregation. Apparently, they were Christians not using their consciences in this regard, probably because of their superego conditioning.

Probably the biggest first step in early Christianity was allowing Gentiles to join the Christian group, and that too without having to practice circumcision or Jewish laws. This inclusiveness was quite in harmony with conscience. Some Christians wanted the newcomers to keep the Jewish practices. In fact, the author of the Book of Revelation disapproved of some Christian leaders who approved Christians eating meat offered to idols and not following Jewish laws. There is a controversy about whether the John who authored the Revelations was the Apostle John or another John of Patmos. The Revelation itself reveals it was written by the author while he was living in Patmos. It appears that John was being critical of Paul. Paul's ideas were consistent with conscience.

In terms of the impact of the Book of Revelation, my experience is that some Christians seem to take it as seriously or more so than the Sermon on the Mount. Speculations and predictions about the sign of the beast, antichrist and end of the world, rapture, and the sufferings of people left behind have grasped the attention of a great many Christians. In my experience, the people who take the Sermon on the Mount to heart seem to live by their conscience much more than the ones who give great importance to the speculations about end times. I know of a Christian man who went around in the city and marked two big houses in the wealthy section of the community, one house for himself and another

---

3. King, "Letter," *Why*, 85–112.

for his dog when he came back to earth after rapture and the people left behind [including the owners of the two houses he marked] would have perished.

ST. PETER AND THE USE OF CONSCIENCE

The three times the word "conscience" is used in 1 Peter is interesting by itself. The first reference is 1 Pet 2:19. "For it is a credit to you if, being aware of God, you endure pain while suffering unjustly." This reminds me how the nonviolent activists endured physical and emotional pain using their consciences without retaliating.

1 Pet 3:16 "Keep your conscience clear, so that, when you are maligned, those who abuse you for your good conduct in Christ may be put to shame." St. Peter is obviously reinforcing the efforts of fellow Christians to live by their consciences in spite of people who abuse them.

1 Pet 3:21 "And baptism, which this prefigured, now saves you–not as a removal of dirt from the body, but as an appeal to God for a good conscience, through the resurrection of Jesus Christ." Baptism as an appeal to God for a good conscience gives a great deal of importance to conscience. It emphasizes living by conscience.

JESUS AND CONSCIENCE

Let us start with perhaps the most memorable example of Jesus, Yeshua, promoting conscience over superego. It is the Beatitudes (the part of the Sermon on the Mount starting with Blessed are . . .) I call it "Blessed are the 'blessed out'."

In the Beatitudes, Jesus gave a list of people with certain features who were blessed: the humble, those who mourn, the gentle, the merciful, the peacemakers, those who hunger and thirst for righteousness, those who are pure in their hearts and those persecuted because of righteousness, and those who are falsely accused of wrongs and persecuted because they follow Jesus. We can see that these were people showing different aspects of living by their consciences. But they lived in the dominating Roman culture which believed in the power of force and looked down on the poor and humble. In such a situation, many good people could have judged themselves with superegos influenced by the culture. So, I feel Jesus was blessing them, teaching them to think well of their good characteristics. In psychiatric practice, I have helped many good people with low self-esteem because they were living by their consciences but judging themselves by their superegos which were affected by a culture admiring success by force and hooks and crooks. I say live by your conscience and judge yourself by your conscience, not by any crooked standard of culture.

Jesus did not use the word conscience, but he exemplified the concept. Therefore, insight into conscience versus superego and PIG is tremendously useful to understand and follow Jesus's teachings and actions. Let us look at many examples. Telling parables, emphasizing and clarifying the purpose of rituals, stating a prevailing idea and then going against it to pursue the deeper meaning of it, are many of the ways Jesus promoted conscience over superego.

Take the example of the parable of the Good Samaritan. Regarding the teaching to love your neighbor as yourself, a lawyer asked Jesus, "who is one's neighbor?" The story is that a traveler was robbed, beaten, and lying half dead on the roadside. A Temple priest and a priest's assistant went by without helping this poor victim. Then a Samaritan came across the scene, and he bound the wounds of the victim, took him to an inn and paid for the man's stay until he recovered. The priest and the priest's assistant were apparently living by their superegos going about their prescribed duties of their profession but not using their consciences and responding to the dire need of a fellow human being. When Jesus asked the lawyer which of those three was a neighbor to the victim, the lawyer answered the Samaritan who showed mercy. And Jesus told the lawyer to follow that example.

Besides the love of the neighbor, Jesus was promoting the ideal of loving the enemy in this parable. Let us explain. After the time of Kings David and Solomon, the Jewish kingdom had split into the Southern kingdom, with its capital in Jerusalem, and the Northern kingdom, with its capital in Samaria. Several political events took place, and from late sixth century BC to the time of Jesus, Jews and Samaritans were enemies. Samaritans were essentially considered half-breeds because they had intermarried with other groups when they lived among the others. It is the human cultural tendency or superego approach to devalue or discount the goodness of members of the enemy group. By making a Samaritan the hero of the story and telling the Jewish lawyer to follow the good example of this Samaritan, Jesus was stimulating the consciences of the audience including the lawyer so that they could judge reasonably and appreciate what is good. Using conscience is essential to love or even to be fair to the enemy. Also, the Good Samaritan did not check the identity of the victim to choose whether to help him or not.

In the story of the Prodigal Son, the younger of the two sons of a father had asked for and got his inheritance. He wasted the inheritance and had to eat with the pigs. He learned his lesson, repented, and returned to the father as a changed person. The father accepted him and celebrated the son's return. But the elder brother did not join the celebration. Celebrating a good transformation reinforces choices consistent with conscience. The older brother's resentment is an example of the emotional constipation caused by his superego. A harsh superego tends to hold on to negative feelings when it is useful to let the feelings go. The father consoled the older brother, again showing his compassion from conscience.

Interestingly, many times Jesus first referred to the prevailing tradition or law (what people's superegos would be saying) before he introduced a very challenging new approach. For example, in Matt 5:43–44: "You have heard that it was said, 'You shalt love your neighbor, and hate your enemy'. But I say to you, 'Love your enemies and pray for those who persecute you, so that you may be children of your Father in heaven; for he makes his sun rise on the evil and the good and sends rain on the righteous and the unrighteous. For if you love those who love you, what reward do you have?'" I will address the love and hate issue in the chapter on love.

Jesus dealt with the matter of rituals in a fascinating way, promoting conscience over superego. He emphasized that the Sabbath is made for people, not people made for the Sabbath. (Mark 2:27) Jesus himself was criticized for healing a man on a Sabbath day. As I write this, social isolation has been implemented to prevent the spread of the coronavirus. A vast majority of Christians complied, but a particular church in my area held services as usual with people congregating in the church. A churchgoer expressed confidence in her safety, saying she is covered by the blood of Jesus. In Matt 5:23, Jesus instructed that before offering a sacrifice, if you remember that your brother has something against you, reconcile with your brother before making the offer. It shows the priority of promoting the fruit of the Spirit which involves using conscience to make good choices. In the psychiatric condition called "Obsessive Compulsive Personality Disorder" or "OCPD," the patient may have the strong need to repeat a ritual for fear of not having done it perfectly because of harsh superego judgment. Also, such people tend to pay too much attention to the details and take excessive time to perform the ritual. In my experience strengthening conscience and shrinking the overgrown superego works in overcoming this imbalance. For example, a female patient had a compulsion to confess repeatedly about a sexual sin she had committed some years back. If she did not confess repeatedly, she stayed worried that she could face damnation. She got over the problem as she learned to use her conscience and balance her superego.

In the Gospel of Matthew, chapter 25, God separates the blessed and the damned. The blessed are the ones who helped those suffering from hunger, thirst, sickness, and incarceration. People of conscience tend to do such acts of love, compassion, and broad empathy. People guided by superego tend to limit helping to their group or those they have a legal obligation to help.

CONSCIENCE AND CHRISTIAN HISTORY

Justin Martyr *(CE 100–165)*

He was a Greek philosopher who converted to Christianity and became a prominent Christian Apologist. He emphasized living by reason or virtue and being a good person. He said that all good people would be saved because God loves goodness. Since people living by conscience make good choices we can consider they would be saved. Justin continued to respect Greek philosophy accepting aspects of Stoic's morality and Plato's concept of God's transcendence and not having a material body (incorporeality).

Clement of Alexandria *(CE 150–215)*

He addressed the philosophical and cultural concerns of the times. He clarified some of the statements in the Bible, (1 Cor 1:20) "Where is the wise? Where is the scribe? Where is the dispute in this world? Hath not God made foolish the wisdom of the world?" which was taken wrongly or literally by some Christians. I have come across people rejecting very useful insights from non-biblical sources with the attitude that it is foolish. Clement explained to people that there are foolish philosophies like epicureanism but there are good philosophies when people use the God-given gift of reason properly. He agreed with using visual arts like pictures of doves and fish to help in worship.

Clement had an Egyptian Christian teacher Pantaenus who had visited India and found local Christians there. This is one of the pieces of evidence for the existence of Christianity in India from the first century. Pantaenus was exposed to Indian wisdom including Buddhism. Clement shared in his interests showing the importance of openness of mind. Regarding wealth and Christian spirituality Clement taught that wealth in itself is not a problem but that being greedy is wrong. This is reminiscent of what the Buddha said to a rich man. Buddha told the man that wealth is fine if he is not attached to it and uses it with diligence and compassion. Justin and Clement showed openness of mind and depth of understanding which are important features of living by conscience. An example of using wealth properly was a wealthy lady who employed seven secretaries to assist Clement's most illustrious student Origen in his elaborate scholarly work. Pantaenus, Clement, Origen, Lucius, and Arius were connected with the famous Catechetical school of Alexandria.

Origen *(CE 184–253)*

Origen is considered the first scientific Christian theologian by a prominent modern theologian Hans Kung. Origen wrote about two thousand treatises. A very dedicated and disciplined man, he had castrated himself, according to historian Eusebius, at age eighteen, apparently based on Jesus's saying about people who have made themselves eunuchs for the Kingdom of God. (Matt 19:12) He did not get stuck at the literal level of interpretation of scripture but elevated interpretation of scripture to allegorical, ethical, and mystical levels. He taught that if we do wrong, we will have consequences which are for transformation, not for condemnation.

He had a theory of eons. "According to this theory, the gradual progression toward the final restoration of all things takes an enormously long time, an incalculably long series of world ages or eons."[4] A soul changes to a different body as it moves from one eon to another eon. This is different from reincarnation where the transfer to another body happens in the same age of the world.

Origen was condemned in CE 400 by a council in Alexandria for teaching that God is incorporeal (has no physical body) against the orthodox teaching that God has a physical body like a human person. Patriarch Theophilus I of Alexandria had preached Origen's view that God

---

4. MacGregor, *Reincarnation*, 59.

is incorporeal and in the *Festal Letter of 399* he had denounced those who believed God has a physical body. It caused riots in the streets by a big mob of monks who believed God had a body. Then the Patriarch changed and turned his view against Origen. The next year he called a church council and condemned Origen and his followers who believed God is incorporeal. The emperor Justinian had made an edict in 543 against Origen. In 553, the Fifth Ecumenical Council condemned his teachings of preexistence of souls as Plato taught. Origen believed that at resurrection, bodies would become ethereal and ultimately all souls, including Satan, would be saved. There is very interesting information about this in Wikipedia.[5]

Constantine

Christianity, which was persecuted by many Roman Emperors, transitioned to the dominant religion of the Roman Empire during the rule of Constantine the Great in AD 306–337. The story is that Constantine was exposed to Christianity by his mother Helena. Sometime before the Battle of the Milvian Bridge in 312 between Constantine and Maxentius, he saw a vision in the midday sky of a cross-shaped trophy over the sun and a text attached to it saying, "By this conquer." That sign was marked on the shields of his soldiers. He succeeded in the battle. In the "Edict of Milan" in 313, he gave freedom for his subjects to follow which religion they choose. He had adopted Christianity in 312 but he got baptized only on his deathbed in 337. The speculation is that he wanted to continue his sinful ways until he was on his deathbed.

Even as Christianity was gaining much freedom and power, a big split was growing within Christianity about the divinity of Jesus. On one side was Arius, a pious and popular priest who considered Jesus as divine but not equal to the Father. Jesus's own statements like "No one is good but God alone," (Mark 10:18) or "I have come down from heaven, not to do my own will, but the will of him who sent me," (John 6:38) seem to support this position. Moreover, church fathers like Dionysus and Origen had taught that Jesus was inferior to God the Father in some ways. But Bishop Alexander and his Deacon Athanasius considered Jesus eternal unlike Arius who believed Jesus was not eternal, that Jesus had a beginning. He had even the two Eusebius's (Bishop Eusebius of Nicomedia and

---

5. Wikipedia, "Origen," paras. 1–7, 52–57.

Bishop Eusebius of Caesarea, the highly regarded church historian) on his side. Arius was an ascetic. It was said that men were impressed by his intellectual superiority and women charmed by his beautiful manners and the poetic rendition of his teachings.

Athanasius later became Bishop of Alexandria. He was a stubborn man who would use any means–lie, cheat, manipulate, threaten, and use violence including torture and murder. He also used his especially Christian weapons to attack his opponents: excommunication and anathematization. He had enemies kidnapped, imprisoned, and exiled. Jesus's statements "I and the Father are one" (John 10:30) and "He who has seen me has seen the Father" (John 14:9) were in his favor. Athanasius had used inflammatory language against Arians calling them crucifiers of Christ. And followers of both sides had street fights. We can guess their superegos often worked against conscience. Dogmatic differences caused dog eat dog divisions.

In 318, Alexander convened a church council in which more than one hundred bishops participated. The majority of them were in favor of Alexander. When the Arian side refused to change their position, they were excommunicated. Arius left Alexandria and met with his friend Eusebius of Nicomedia, a chief leader of the Greek speaking Church. They polished Arius' view as the superiority of the Father over all other beings and the son's role as savior, intermediary and example. A council of bishops in Nicomedia supported Arius. With that support, Arius next approached Eusebius of Caesarea, the great historian. This bishop also held a council and supported Arius.

Constantine wanted Christian unity and peace in his empire, so he sent his closest Christian advisor Hosius to evaluate the conflict and recommend solutions. Richard Rubenstein notes that Constantine considered the arguments between the two factions trivial and pointed out to the Alexandrian Bishop how the Greek philosophers tolerated far more serious differences of opinions without faction fighting.[6] Here we can note that faction fighting is among the evil "works of the flesh" that St. Paul listed. Faction fighting and splitting has been a significant problem in Christian history. I recall some years back a patient reporting that her church which opposed wearing jewelry was splitting because some members wanted to wear a simple wedding ring. Constantine invited bishops from Christianity worldwide for the Council of Nicaea in 325. The

---

6. Rubenstein, *When*, 50.

council started in early June and Constantine participated as "the bishop of the outsiders." More than two hundred and fifty bishops attended.

There were detailed discussions about the Arian and anti-Arian views. Finally, they voted. Arius had only two supporters. Constantine exiled those three. The sessions went on for over a month. The council condemned Arius and incorporated the word *homoousion* (meaning "of the same substance," i.e., that Jesus and the Father are of the same substance) into the Creed. The council condemned lending money at interest by clerics, but they failed to make a canon enforcing celibacy of the clergy. The bishops attended a celebration of the emperor on July 25th before leaving.

Constantine had severe laws against sexual immorality. A girl who eloped and her partner would be executed. Molten lead would be poured into the mouth of any servant who helped them to elope. Men were to be burned alive if convicted of rape. Adulterers would be exiled. Concubinage and pederasty were outlawed, and illegitimacy was penalized. Celibates were allowed to inherit property.

Constantine had ordered the execution of his son Crispus who was from his first wife Minervina, whom he had divorced. The story is that Constantine's second wife, Fausta, had alleged that Crispus had tried to rape her when she rejected his attempts to seduce her. According to Rubenstein, Constantine was a staunch believer in the Roman ideal of the virtuous marriage, and when he became Christian, a dose of fanaticism was added to the belief.[7] The emperor went to Pola, Italy where Crispus was working, tried the case and ordered the execution of Crispus.[8] After the execution, Constantine returned to Rome. It is noteworthy that in the case of another man convicted of adultery, Constantine only exiled him.

In Rome, Constantine's pious Christian mother, Helena, who was mourning her grandson, accused the emperor of executing Crispus on false evidence. Helena provided evidence for Fausta having plotted to get rid of Crispus so that her son would inherit the empire. Then Fausta died in a steam bath, whether killed by Constantine's agents or committed suicide to avoid execution. These incidents raise the question about whether Constantine had just a religious conversion or a spiritual transformation. He had clearly converted to Christianity. As we noted earlier, he participated in the Council of Nicaea as a Christian leader. Many people in

---

7. Rubenstein, *When*, 90.
8. Rubenstein, *When*, 91.

Early Christianity delayed baptism, some even believing like Constantine that getting baptized in deathbed or close to it gives more assurance to salvation since baptism removes all sins. Spiritual transformation goes far beyond accepting a religion; it involves living by conscience, showing the fruit of the Spirit. Maybe he had a spiritual transformation with some imperfections. Extremism about sex has played a significant role in Christian History. Constantine prohibited gladiator games and animal sacrifices. Churches received subsidies of food for distribution to the poor. He made Sunday a holiday.

The Nicene Creed has survived, and Christianity has been the largest religion of the world for centuries. The Nicene Creed did not stop the controversies about the divinity of Jesus and the councils' excommunications; street fights and enmities continued for some decades. Constantine used his soft and hard powers for Christian unity and peace. He made significant progress, but Arianism and Anti-Arianism conflicts continued. In 380, Theodosius made the Nicene orthodoxy the law and made Christianity the official religion of the Roman Empire.

Arius was rehabilitated at the Council of Nicomedia in 328. A gathering of bishops admitted Arius to the communion in 335 and Constantine was on his side. Arius died in 336. In April 337, Constantine became ill. He was in Nicomedia, got baptized by the Arian bishop Eusebius and he died on May 22nd on the Festival of the Pentecost. The Orthodox Church canonized Constantine.

Athanasius was exiled five times by four different emperors. He returned to Alexandria in 366 and reportedly spent the rest of his life repairing the damage he caused in his earlier days. He died in May 373 in Alexandria. He is the first person who identified the twenty-seven books of the New Testament that have been used since then. I wonder whether his earlier personality played a big role in his inclusion of the book of The Revelation in the Bible. Athanasius was canonized and venerated as a saint by the Eastern Orthodox, Roman Catholic, Coptic Orthodox, Anglican and Lutheran churches; Arianism was suppressed by various political forces and faded from the fifth to seventh centuries.

Leo Tolstoy, the champion of conscience and the Sermon on the Mount, complained about churches distracting people from the Sermon on the Mount by their focus on the creed and rituals. In his book, *The Kingdom of God is Within You*, he said: "And what is most important of all–the man who believes in salvation by faith in the redemption or the sacraments, cannot devote all his powers to realizing Christ's moral teaching in his life."[9] Overall, my concern is the low level of importance given to conscience among the church folks and their loss from that. I notice excessive problems with superegos in many church groups. I leave the doctrinal arguments to the doctors of the churches.

In the Semitic religions, belief in the One true supreme being, Yahweh, God, or Allah respectively is crucial. In other religions like Hinduism and Buddhism, it is one's behavior that is crucial. Alcoholics Anonymous' approach "God as you understand him" is insufficient for the requirement of Semitic religions. While I respect the Christian insistence on making the belief about Jesus and God accurate, I find world historian H.G. Well's view interesting: "By the fourth century of the Christian Era, we find all the Christian communities so agitated and exasperated by tortuous and elusive arguments about the nature of God as to be largely negligent of the simpler teachings of charity, service, and brotherhood that Jesus had inculcated."[10]

Both the Greek speaking Orthodox church and the Latin speaking Western church kept their unity under this belief until 1054, but they split in 1054 because the Latin church made a change in the Creed. They changed "Holy Ghost proceeded from the Father" to "Holy Ghost proceeded from the Father and from the Son." That split has not healed. In their final meeting in 1054, they ended up using their sharp religious weapons; the Catholic side excommunicated the Orthodox and the Orthodox retaliated by taking one more step–by anathematizing the Catholic counterpart in the negotiation. We are left wondering about their consciences and their use of extreme religious weapons. (*Excommunication is separation from the communion of the church but the person remains a member of the church, but anathema is complete separation from the church: both are until the person repents.*)[11]

St. Augustine of Hippo

St. Augustine of Hippo (354–430) is a crucially important figure in the whole history of Christianity. He was a theologian, philosopher, bishop of Hippo and originator of several theories which have tremendously influenced Christianity. He was born in a province in present day Algeria.

9. Tolstoy, *Kingdom*, 76.
10. Wells, *Outline*, 457.
11. Boudinhon, "Excommunication," paras. 2–4.

His mother was Catholic, and father was Pagan until he converted on his deathbed.

In his autobiography, he wrote about a big sin he committed in his youth. There was a pear tree with a lot of fruits near his family's vineyard. One night, he, along with some other "wretched youth," shook the tree and took away all the pears they could carry. He did it not because he was hungry or wished to enjoy the fruit. In his judgment, he did it because he enjoyed the theft, the sin, itself. He goes on a long description of this theme including the following: " . . . I became evil for nothing, with no reason for wrongdoing except the wrongdoing itself. The evil was foul, and I loved it; I loved destroying myself; I loved my sin–not the thing for which I had committed the sin but the sin itself."[12] Does this very self-critical judgment seem too harsh? Could the incident have been a youth group testing some limits and enjoying the group activity? How many youngsters who pick some fruits from a neighborhood garden grow up to be a gang of thieves? Or do they grow up to be normal adults? My experience has been the latter. What I wonder is whether Augustine had a tendency to make harsh superego judgment from early in his life.

From the age of seventeen, he had a lover for fifteen years and a son by her. His lover was of a lower class and his mother Monica refused him to marry her. So, he let her go. His son lived with him until he died at age sixteen. The girl Monica chose for Augustine was only ten, two years below the legal age for marriage. By the time she was twelve, he decided to become a Catholic priest and so they did not marry. In the meantime, he had a lover for a while. In his education, he learned Latin and Rhetoric. His writings reflect his mastery of these subjects.

He grew up Catholic, but he lived as a Manichaean for many years. Manichaeism teaches the existence of an evil force equal to the good God, and human evil and sexuality are part of the former. He was attracted to Christianity by bishop Ambrose. And a spiritual experience: he heard the voice of a child in a garden, "take this and read." Taking it as a message from God, he opened Paul's letters and read: "Not in riots and drunken parties, not in eroticism and indecencies, not in strife and rivalry, but put on the Lord Jesus Christ and make no provision for the flesh in its lusts." (Rom 13:13) He chose to pursue asceticism and convert to Christianity. Bishop Ambrose baptized him on Easter Eve 387. He believed conscience

---

12. Warner, *Confessions*, 45.

is God's voice within us and we should take it very seriously and follow it. In 395, he became Bishop of Hippo. He died in 430.

His teachings have been very influential. Let us explore the main ones. The doctrine of original sin was fully formed by Augustine. He was also the first one to use the phrase "original sin," the idea that every child is born with this original sin because of Adam and Eve's sin. It is the doctrine that all human beings inherit sin, as St. Paul had expressed the idea that Adam brought sin into the world. The phrase "original sin" is not mentioned in the Bible. It is also contrary to the ideas of other great world religions which consider human birth a blessing, "the special human birth," in Buddhist terms. When we think of sin, we usually connect it with something wrong or bad we do, something we are responsible for. He also taught that baptism is the only way out of the original sin. So, all people who are unbaptized go to hell. Thus, it is a hell of an issue. As mentioned in the Introduction, many modern Christian thinkers like Matthew Fox have rejected the original sin idea, but the idea is very common among Christians.

The idea "no salvation outside the [Catholic] church" became very firm with Augustine. The idea was that all others were going to hell. The Vatican II Council reforms in the Catholic Church modified the stance saying that those who are not Catholic by no fault of their own and live by their consciences can gain salvation. Augustine believed that conscience is the voice of God within people, but his emphasis was that God's grace is needed for acting by one's conscience. A different view was expressed by the Catholic monk Thomas Merton in the 1960s: " . . . we know that men of goodwill in all religions, who follow an upright conscience, can certainly attain to holiness and union with God because they receive grace from Him to do so."[13]

His emphasis on sex for pleasure as sin, even in marital relationships, had left an unreasonable influence in many Christian groups. Augustine went from actively involved in sex for pleasure for many years outside of marriage to sex only for procreation in marriage. So, he went from one extreme to another extreme rather than having a deeper integration of human needs and conscience. Even if it were a suitable solution for himself in his life situation, this teaching for all seems to be an extreme. I wonder whether what happened was a psychological defense called "reaction formation" –going from one extreme to the opposite

---

13. Johnston, *Mysticism*, xi–xvi.

kind of extreme. The objection to artificial birth control, prohibition of husband ejaculating by oral sex, masturbation, and homosexual sex are connected with the idea against sex for pleasure. The idea that masturbation is against natural law and therefore against God led to the teaching that it is a worse sin than rape which is against another person. This is an example of my statement in another situation: When dogma runs over dharma (right conduct) it creates bad karma.

The Catholic Church's stance is that by the natural law (the divinely ordained goal of something) sex is for procreation. It is unclear why only procreation was considered the goal of sex by the natural law. In human experience, pleasure is clearly a function of sex by nature, lasting beyond menopause in women. The function of a woman's clitoris is pleasure. The Catholic Church is fine with sex for pleasure within marriage so long as nothing is done to preclude conception. Hence, mutual masturbation and oral sex are accepted only for foreplay or female orgasm but not male ejaculation. Of course, we have the responsibility to use sexual pleasure with conscience. In 2016, Pope Francis stated that in matters like contraception the couples must use their own consciences and not just the dogmatic rules of the Church. In October 2020, Pope Francis became the first Pope to endorse same sex civil unions. In December 2023, Pope Francis allowed Catholic priests to bless individuals in same sex relationships, but he did not change the Church's prohibition of them from receiving the sacrament of marriage. Pope Francis' compassionate approach is consistent with conscience. Unlike many other Christian denominations, the Catholic Church has taught for a long time that homosexual *orientation* is not a choice of the person, but homosexuals should restrain from homosexual sexual acts.

Interestingly, the songs of Solomon in the *Old Testament* and the ancient Indian books *Thirukkural* and *Kama Sutra* promote the joy of sex. *Thirukkural* is a highly respected work. *Kama Sutra* was written around the third century AD by a celibate Hindu monk to promote sexual pleasure. Its moral guidelines are rather loose. For example, he discusses situations when men in authority could try to seduce wives of other men. Religious groups can rightfully set their rules and say that if you want to gain the benefits they offer, you have to live by their rules. So, be aware of the rules of your groups and the benefits they offer. In modern times, we come across Christian leaders mostly positive about sex for pleasure in marital relationships. Tony Campolo, a leader in evangelical social action and a former Professor of Sociology observes: "Of course, those sermons that tell us sexual desires are a good part of our humanity are right. God made us so that we want sex. We have to recognize that God deliberately made that whole erotic trip one of the most pleasurable trips we can take. And any form of religion that takes the fun out of sex has to be a bad religion."[14] He considered contraception good and sexual hang-ups as spiritual hang-ups. A well-informed conscience would support the right choice.

Augustine is admired for his teaching that time originated with creation. He explained this insight in the Book XI of his *Confessions*.[15] This insight is consistent with the modern scientific view that time originated with the Big Bang. Stephen M. Barr says: "Bertrand Russell was deeply impressed by what he called St. Augustine's "admirable relativistic theory of time."[16] Francis Collins notes another important contribution of Augustine, who " . . . provided a warning about how interpreters of the Bible might erroneously and unnecessarily set up circumstances of conflict. Writing specifically about Genesis, he said, "In matters that are obscure and far beyond our vision, even in such as we may find in Holy Scripture, different interpretations are sometimes possible without prejudice to the faith we have received. In such a case, we should not rush headlong and so firmly take our stand on one side, that if further progress in the search for truth just undermines this position, we too fall with it." (Augustine of Hippo, "On the Literal Meaning of Genesis," vol.1, ch.18–37)[17] Collins is pointing out the problem of a literal reading of Genesis in many churches conflicting with science because of not heeding the caution Augustine provided.

A big step by Augustine was the just war theory. He developed two guidelines about war: the right to go to war and the right conduct in the war. The following are principles of this theory:

1. It has to be the last resort after all peaceful options are considered.
2. It is waged by a legitimate authority.
3. It needs to be in reaction to an attack suffered.
4. There has to be a probability of success.
5. The intention must be to reestablish peace.

14. Campolo, *Following*, 231.
15. Augustine, *Confessions*, Book XI, 290.
16. Barr, "St. Augustine," para. 9.
17. Collins, *Road*, 147.

6. It has to be proportionate in the use of force.

7. Civilians must not be targeted.

These principles could be used sincerely guided by conscience, but they could be twisted by superego and abused for selfish or hateful reasons. The Crusades are such examples I would discuss next. As I discuss the Crusades next, we can see how Christianity many times pursued not just war but war using justifications.

CRUSADES

Crusades were a series of military expeditions by Western Christians between 1095 and 1291 to free the Holy Land from Muslim domination. The Crusader term derived from the Latin word for cross, "crux," since the crusader had a cross of cloth sewn on the breast of his garment.

Jerusalem was under the rule of Saracens (Arabic Muslims) from 638 until 1085 when the Seljuk Turks gained power there. The change from the liberal and tolerant Saracens to the more restlessly ambitious Turks caused insecurity among Christians. Threatened by the Turks' expansion, the Byzantine emperor appealed for help from the western Christians. In the eleventh century, there was a big increase in the pilgrimage to the Holy Land. There were concerns about the Turks causing problems for the pilgrims.

Pope Gregory VII (1073–1085) had reformed the papacy from corruption and he had made celibacy for priests compulsory so that they could devote more to their vocation. Then came Pope Urban II (1066–1099). He saw an opportunity to bring together the religious forces of Western Europe to get control of the Holy Land and expand the Latin Church over Egypt. Syria and Palestine to put the Byzantine Church aside.

Pope Urban II made a very impressive speech at the Council of Clermont, France in 1095 about the need for and benefits of a Holy War. He dwelt on the attacks on the pilgrims and the plunder and pillage going on in the Holy Land by the infidel Turks. The Pope addressed the military threat to the Christian brethren of Constantinople from the infidels. He promised to all who went for the expedition the remission of sins and immediate entry into paradise for those who died in the expedition. He appealed to the peoples' wish for power and prestige by talking about the opportunities for wealth and he calmed their fears by stating victory would be easy. He also appealed to the spirit of adventure. His audience of several thousands were so excited that when they came out, they shouted "Deus vult" (God wills it) which became the cry of the crusading crowds. This is considered one of the most important speeches in history. For the peasants, an escape from the burdens of the feudal system, even for many months, was quite desirable. The Pope's message was spread to villages and towns by the priests.

In 1096, the first crusade started–the "people's crusade" of huge masses. H.G. Wells remarked that it was the first time in history that such a spectacle of huge masses of almost leaderless people moved by an idea."[18] On their way, they massacred Hungarians and committed excesses on Jews. Thousands were massacred by the Turks. Only half of the half a million crusaders survived. The organized forces of real crusaders led by strong noblemen captured Jerusalem in July 1099. The blood from the slaughter of the conquered ran down the streets. The Christian kingdom of Jerusalem was stable for forty-five years.

I see no benefits for our purpose to explore the specifics of the second, third, fourth, fifth, and seventh crusades. There was much violence, death, and destruction but the crusaders did not achieve their goal. I recommend Henry Treece's book *The Crusades* for details.

The Children's Crusade of 1212 was very tragic. Two shepherd boys, Nicholas of Cologne in Germany and Stephen of Cloyes in France: these two boys were not connected to each other although their stories are similar. Thousands of French and German boys and girls moved south towards the Mediterranean hoping that the sea would part and they could walk over to the Holy Land based on the story of the sea parting for Moses. They believed they could achieve this by the power of faith. It is said that priests and parents were supportive of the movement. So was Pope Innocent III. Their mission was an utter failure. According to Henry Treece, only one out of thirty thousand French children returned home; the rest were enslaved in Cairo or auctioned off in Algiers. And out of the twenty thousand German children, only about two thousand returned.[19]

The Eighth Crusade was by King Louis IX. The king died of dysentery in 1279. There was no significant fighting. The Crusaders and the

---

18. Wells, *Outline*, 563.
19. Treece, *Crusades*, 245.

Hafsid dynasty signed a treaty involving no territory, but Christians got some commercial and political rights.

The Sixth Crusade was one of a kind and it is also called a diplomatic crusade because it did not involve a military battle and involved negotiation. It was Emperor Frederick II of Germany who handled this. Frederick was a highly knowledgeable man who knew six languages, including Arabic. He was well-versed in Christianity and Islam and rather skeptical of religions. He had become emperor with the understanding that he would go for another crusade, and he would give up his possessions in Italy and Sicily, but once he became emperor, he did not do these things. He was evasive and the next pope, Gregory IX, excommunicated him and invaded his possessions. Frederick II went to the Holy Land, discussed with the sultan about the pope, their common threat from the Mongols, and reached an agreement. Then he got Papal armies from his possessions and pressured the Pope to cancel the excommunication.

Frederick II was a very intelligent, open-minded, and inquisitive person. He had Christian, Jewish, and Moslem philosophers in his court. Another person in his court–Michael Scott–translated Aristotle and the Arabic philosopher Averroes. Frederick founded the University of Naples in 1224, expanded the medical school at Salerno University and started a zoological garden. He wrote Italian poetry. He also was a keen observer of bird life. Arabic numerals and Algebra passed through him to students. He had written a memorable letter condemning the pride and religion of the clergy. He died in 1250. No wonder this unique man was called *stupor mundi* [the wonder of the world]. I think of him as a wonderful man of conscience.

Henry Treece, in his book *The Crusades*, agrees with and quotes from Sir Steven Runciman's summation of the Crusades in his book, *The Kingdom of Acre:* "The triumphs of the Crusades were the triumphs of faith. But faith without wisdom is a dangerous thing. . . . There was so much courage and so little honor, so much devotion and so little understanding. High ideals were besmirched by cruelty and greed, enterprise and endurance by a blind and narrow self-righteousness; and the Holy War itself was nothing more than a long act of intolerance in the name of God, which is the sin against the Holy Ghost."[20] The part of the above statement "faith without wisdom is a dangerous thing" can be substituted with "faith without conscience can be a dangerous thing." And it would

---

20. Treece, *Crusades*, xi–xii.

be a clear example of St. Paul's observation that some people destroy faith by rejecting conscience.

"Outbreak of Conscience Against Authority"

According to H.G. Wells, there were two specific examples of the outbreak of conscience against the authority of the church: St. Francis and Waldo. Francis remained friendly with the church and was rewarded. Waldo rebelled and was punished. Francis (1181 or 1182–1226) was the son of an Italian merchant. In 1292, he participated in a war between Assisi and Perugia and was a prisoner for a year. After his release, he was sick for some time and recovered.

Then, on one occasion at a damaged chapel, he heard a voice from a crucifix, a voice telling him to repair his house which was in ruins. Francis sold many clothes from his father's business and gave the money to repair the chapel. His father got angry and took him to a bishop. Francis took off his clothes down to his breeches and gave them to his father. Then, he left wearing a cloak the bishop gave him. In February 1208, he listened to the reading at the Mass, the words from Matt 10:9–11: "Take no gold, nor silver, nor money in your belt, nor bag for your journey, nor two tunics, nor chaplets, nor a staff; for the laborer deserves his food. And whatever town or village you enter, find out who is worthy in it, and stay with him until you depart." Although he was a lay person, he started preaching and he set up a simple rule of life for them. Once he had eleven followers, in 1209 he went to Rome and got permission from the Pope. He tried his best to follow the teachings of Jesus and walk in his footsteps. This was his secret. His Franciscan order grew well. In 1212, he began a second order for women known as the Poor Clares. St. Clare of Assisi was one of these women. He and his followers celebrated poverty. In 1224, he had the vision of a six-winged angel on a cross who gave him the gift of the five wounds of Christ.

Francis loved all creation. He considered the moon his sister and various animals like his family. There is a story that he stopped a wolf from attacking people. A great mystic, Francis lived a life of simplicity, voluntary poverty, love of all, compassion, and service to the poor and sick. He was a great example of conscience. H.G. Wells noted that he was able to preach unmolested by Muslims in Egypt and Palestine.[21] In 1219,

---

21. Wells, *Outline*, 575.

during the Fifth Crusade, he met with Sultan Al Kamal who treated him graciously, but nothing more came out of the visit. When he was away, the Franciscan order was reconstructed with more intense discipline and authority, and he resigned his position as head of the organization. Also, the group started owning properties through trusts. He died in 1226 and was canonized in 1228. Pope Francis took the name "Francis" in honor of St. Francis of Assisi.

Peter Waldo was a successful businessman in Lyons who was spiritually inspired by a traveling minstrel. He gave up his wealth and started a simple life based on the spirit of the Bible. He had many followers. Peter Waldo rejected many things about the Catholic Church: existence of purgatory, authority structure of the Church, participation in war, venerating saints, and the idea that only priests could consecrate the sacramental bread. He was excommunicated in 1184, and his followers were harassed by the Inquisition.[22]

Inquisition

The term Inquisition originated from the Latin "inquiro" meaning inquire into. Inquisition was a papal judicial institution to combat heresy and evil deeds like sorcery and witchcraft. There were four different inquisitions: Medieval, Roman, Spanish, and Portuguese Inquisitions. The inquisitors actively searched for the offenders to catch and punish them, and the punishments included torture and death. Medieval inquisition involved punishing people who committed public denial of Catholic doctrines by baptized Christians. It was mainly focused on the Cathar Christians, a gnostic group whose beliefs differed from Catholic beliefs, and the followers of Peter Waldo. Some of these groups existed in parts of Italy and France in the thirteenth and fourteenth centuries. Devil worship, incest, and adultery were also punished under this Inquisition. In the first three centuries, punishment for heresy was spiritual, usually excommunication. But from the fourth century when Christianity had much power, the punishments included confiscation of property, exile, torture, loss of civil rights, and even death. After 1200, a Grand Inquisitor led every Inquisition. By 1256, Inquisitors were given absolution if they used torture.

Roman Inquisition was a tribunal established by Pope Paul III in 1542 to counter Protestantism. The tribunal had six cardinals. Probably

---

22. Wells, *Outline*, 574–76.

the most famous case tried by this Inquisition was against Galileo Galilei in 1633. As Protestantism became no danger to religious unity in Italy, this tribunal became increasingly an ordinary organ of papal government.

Spanish Inquisitions of papal tribunals were established upon request by Catholic kings to deal with apostates or Catholics with Jewish or Muslim roots returning to Jewish or Muslim faiths. In 1391 in Seville, hundreds of Jews were killed. Similar were the cases in Cordoba and other places. As a consequence, there was mass conversion of Jews to Christianity. In 1492, the Jews were given the choice of conversion to Christianity or exile. In 1592, Islam was proscribed. Protestants were eliminated. Even Ignatius of Loyola who founded the Jesuit Catholic order was arrested twice on suspicion of heresy. The archbishop of Toledo, a Dominican monk, was imprisoned for seventeen years.

The Portuguese Inquisition started in 1536. Many of the Jews who escaped from Spain and were living in Portugal were in trouble with the church again. The Inquisition extended to Portuguese colonies: Brazil, Cape Verde, and Goa (India). Between 1540 and 1794, tribunals in three Spanish centers resulted in the burning of one thousand one hundred and seventy-six people and penance of twenty-nine thousand five hundred and ninety.[23] The extremism in Goa is in sharp contrast to the Christianity in further south in Kerala where St. Thomas the Apostle started Christianity in the first century and from then, the Christians lived in peace and harmony with Hindus, Jews, and Muslims (more in the chapter on Peace).

H.G. Wells' observation is quite pertinent in the context of conscience: "The Inquisition was organized as a standing inquiry under their direction, and with fire and torment, the church set itself, through this instrument, to assail and weaken the human conscience, in which its sole hope of world dominion resided."[24] In this context, Fyodor Dostoyevsky's novel, *The Brothers Karamazov*, is very interesting. In it, Ivan, one of the Karamazov brothers, has a prose poem about "The Grand Inquisitor" who has imprisoned Jesus and interrogates him. Part of the interrogation is: " . . . we have the right to preach to man that what matters is not freedom of choice or love, but a mystery that he must worship blindly, even at the expense of his conscience. And that is exactly what we have done. We have corrected Your work and have now found it on *miracle*,

---

23. Lea, *History*, 231–315.
24. Wells, *Outline*, 577.

mystery, and *authority*. And men rejoice at being led like cattle again . . . "²⁵ I have read that some of the people conducting the Inquisition were merciful. Overall, the system showed a very harsh superego approach, "being led like cattle."

The Inquisition in Venice was abolished in 1806 following the decree of Napoleon in 1797 which dissolved the Republic of Venice. Between 1813 and 1825, Inquisition was abolished in the former Spanish colonies in America. The Portuguese Inquisition was abolished in 1821. The last execution was of a teacher in Spain in 1826 for teaching Deism. The Office of Inquisitions in the Papal states had lost most of its power outside the Papal States and became primarily an advisory committee to the Pope. The Papal States themselves were annexed to the Kingdom of Italy in 1870, marking the end of the Papal States as an independent entity. The Inquisition's role and focus also shifted, eventually becoming the Dicastery for the Doctrine of the Faith, a papal advisory body on theological and disciplinary matters.²⁶

Colonialism and Slavery

The Catholic Church had gained a lot of power gradually and the Popes had much control over religious and political matters and wealth. Pope Alexander VI (1492–1593) was probably the most corrupt pope. He was a prime example of how badly power corrupts. He had held a lucrative position as vice chancellor of the Holy See for many years and had four children by his mistress Vannozza. He became Pope partly by bribing. He drew a line of demarcation between Spain and Portugal, the areas of the new world they could explore and exploit. Spain got South America, and the Portuguese got India, for example. Spain and Portugal had to promote the Catholic Church in return. Once Columbus discovered America and Vasco de Gama discovered India, Europeans started expanding their power to what they considered the New World. Besides Spain and Portugal, England, France, and Holland set up colonies.

European Countries settled their own people into the colonies and enslaved the natives more or less. When the Europeans needed more workers, they started getting them from Africa. The conflict between two prominent Catholic theologians regarding enslaving native population

---

25. Dostoyevsky, *Brothers*, 309.
26. Wikipedia, "Inquisition," paras. 48–50, 65–67, 116–21.

is interesting. One of them was Juan Gines de Sepulveda (1494–1573). He was a philosopher and theologian. He had translated several works of Aristotle into Latin. He had not visited America; however, he was a strong supporter of the Spanish colonization, enslavement, and forced conversion of natives. His main argument was based on Aristotle's view of "natural slaves". He argued that the native Indians were natural slaves. By "natural slaves", Aristotle was talking about individuals who lack the ability to function independently and have to be managed by others. He was not talking about an ethnic group. Sepulveda's idea was used by the Spanish conquerors to enslave the natives.

Sepulveda had a great opponent: Bartolomé de las Casas (1484–1566). Casas was a Spanish landowner, priest, historian, social reformer, and friar. His life story is especially enlightening. He was born in Seville and moved to Hispaniola along with his father in 1502. There, he was a landowner and slave owner. He took part in the slave raids and military expeditions against the natives. In 1510, he became the first ordained priest in Hispaniola. The next year, he was exposed to a Dominican friar who spoke intensely against the exploitation and abuse of the natives by the colonists. Las Casas' view was against the friar and the colonists got the King to remove the Dominicans from the Island. As a chaplain, he took part in the Spaniards' conquest of Cuba. He witnessed many of the atrocities inflicted on the natives.

He was living as a priest and a colonist in 1514. Prior to Pentecost, he was preparing for a sermon. For this purpose, he read the *Book of Sirach. a* book of Jewish ethical teachings written between 299 and 175 BCE. As he pondered on some passage in the book, his mind opened, and his conscience got stimulated. He realized that the Spanish enslavement and abuse of the natives was illegal and immoral. From then on, he changed. He gave up his slaves. He encouraged others to do the same. He became a strong protector of the natives. For the rest of his life, he worked hard against abuse of native people using his powers, preaching, writing, influencing the authorities, including the king in Spain. In 1522, he entered a Dominican monastery as a novice and became a friar in 1523. He was appointed a bishop in 1245. Las Casas had plenty of opposition from slave owners and even some fellow religious leaders. In 1550 he had a famous debate with Sepulveda which did not reach a firm conclusion. He died in July 1566 in Madrid.[27] How his conscience was stimulated,

---

27. Romero and Canales, *Las Casas*, 3, 5, 28.

and he overcame his superego is a great example for us. Now, we will deal with the very important Protestant Reformation and the Catholic Counter Reformation, and then we will get back into colonialism, and how it ended.

Protestant Reformation and Catholic Counter Reformation

The Protestant Reform was a movement in Western Christianity protesting against many of the corruptions and abuses of the Catholic Church. In 1517, Catholic monk Martin Luther in Germany published ninety-five theses against the Church and Papacy, mainly against selling indulgences but also about the policies regarding purgatory and the authority of the pope. Indulgence was a paper certifying reduced time in purgatory for the soul of the person for whom the indulgence was bought. Later, he objected to devotion to saints, compulsory celibacy of priests, excommunication, the theory of the communion bread and wine turning into the body and blood of Jesus (transubstantiation), and the role of secular rulers in church matters. He rejected the Pope's demand for him to recant forty-one sentences drawn from his writings. He refused to recant as it would be against his conscience. The Pope excommunicated him in 1521. From 1510 to 1520, he had lectured on the Psalms and the books of Galatians, Hebrews, and Romans. His study of Romans led him to his idea of salvation by faith alone. Luther had no peace of mind about the fear of eternal damnation until he came to believe in salvation by faith in Jesus as the savior as the key to salvation. Previously he was trying to have salvation by goodness, but it did not heal his uncertainty.

Luther published his translation of the Bible in German in 1522. He married a former nun in 1525. He organized the new church and wrote its rulebook. He had a stroke in 1546, and he died at age sixty-two. Lutherans had persecuted Anabaptists, a pacifist Christian group which practiced adult baptism (no infant baptism) and thousands were killed. Five-hundred years later, the Lutherans apologized to the Anabaptists and the two churches reconciled. Conscience triumphed! Calvinism and many other denominations came into being after Luther split from the Catholic church.

The Catholic Church reacted with the Council of Trent (1545–1563) which denied the Lutheran idea of justification by faith. This Council confirmed the Doctrine of Merit that is salvation by good works and sacraments. The Council affirmed the existence of purgatory, belief in transubstantiation, and the authority of the scriptures as well as the teachings and traditions of the Church. They approved the use of religious images and veneration of saints. A new Catholic order, the Jesuits, promoted intellectual pursuit along with spirituality. These movements stimulated more education, more individual freedom, Protestant ethics, social welfare systems, and music and art. Jesuit educational institutions have been providing great education in various parts of the world. I have personally benefited from their service in India. In 2021, the Jesuits committed one hundred million dollars for reparation of slavery.

The thirty years war (1618–1648) was a tragic result of the religious conflict. It is one of the longest and most severely brutal wars in history. It is estimated to have caused over eight million casualties including deaths in battles and from famine and disease caused by the war. The war ended with the Peace of Westphalia in 1648. The war nurtured suspiciousness among the different groups. Also, the first witch-hunts in Europe started during the war. In these violent conflicts, we can guess the violent superego clashes, and it is hard to see the working of conscience.

The Holy Roman Empire was a confederation of medium and small sized states in Europe from 962. In 1618, Ferdinand II, king of Bohemia and future emperor of the Holy Roman Empire, tried to impose Roman Catholicism in his domain which caused rebellion by the protestant nobles of Bohemia and Austria. After five years of struggle, Ferdinand won. King Christian IV of Denmark tried to get territory in Germany but failed. Denmark lost its role as a European power. There were many fights among different states. One of the main conflicts was between the Catholic and the Protestant states. Cities, towns and villages were plundered by armies on both sides. Finally, there were peace negotiations in the Westphalia region and the Spanish Dutch treaty was signed on January 30, 1648.[28] *The Columbia History of The World* records the following about the war: "When after years of costly campaigning when the rulers run out of money, the mercenaries extracted their wages in the form of plunder, rape, and senseless destruction. Troops of armed men roamed the countryside in search of peaceful towns to loot. They blackmailed entire communities, pillaged churches and monasteries.... For months and for years, armies of from ten thousand to forty thousand men subjected

28. Wikipedia, "Peace," paras. 1–11.

Germany to senseless slaughter and pillage, *all in the name of religion.*"[29] (italics added).

Abolition of Slavery and Decolonization

Emperor Ashoka, in the third century BC, abolished slave trade in his empire and ordered existing slaves to be treated gently. France abolished slavery in 1794 but reinstituted it in 1802 and abolished it the second time in 1848. Great Britain abolished slavery in 1799. In 1807, Britain made slave trade illegal in British territories. Slavery was abolished in the entire British empire in 1833. In the US, slavery was abolished in 1865.

The American Revolution (1765–1783) was the first time any colonies were liberated. Brazil became independent in 1822. Spanish colonies in America became free in the nineteenth century, with the exception of Cuba, which became free in 1902. Colonies of the British Empire became free in the twentieth century including Egypt in 1922 and India in 1947. Colonies of the French Empire, including Vietnam, also gained freedom in the twentieth century. The unique way Gandhi used nonviolent activism stimulated the consciences of followers and a large number of opponents changed the course of history. So, it was not a surprise that British historian Arnold Toynbee said that Gandhi liberated India and also Britain.[30]

Quakers

Quakers have been a significant force promoting abolition of slavery and the promotion of peace. This Christian group started by George Fox in England in the mid-1600s promotes non-violence, simplicity, honesty, equality, humility, and community. They hold quiet meetings, listen to God in silence, and share messages individuals receive with the group. They don't have creeds and priests. Their high ideals, openness of mind, and inwardness all nurture conscience.

---

29. Garraty and Gay, *Columbia*, 588.
30. Ramachandran, "Essence," paras. 1–8.

Second Vatican Council of the Catholic Church (1962-1965)

An important theme was reconciliation. It encouraged friendship with other Christian groups and other religious groups. Catholics could pray with other Christian groups, and local languages could be used during Mass. Representatives of other Christian denominations were included as observers; they were excluded in voting. The Council distanced herself from legalism, clericalism, and triumphalism towards more love, compassion, and humility. There was emphasis on conscience. One of the apparent changes was in the apparel of nuns' strange outfits, which scared some children, to regular moderate dress. Pope Francis genuinely shows the spirit of Vatican II.

The Vatican II document states: "Through loyalty to conscience, Christians are joined with other men in the search for truth and for the right solution to so many moral problems which arise both in the life of individuals and from social relationships. Hence, the more a correct conscience prevails, the more people and groups turn aside from blind choices and try to be guided by the objective standards of moral conduct."[31] This was a great step. There was a big shift from the teaching of no salvation outside the Catholic Church as noted earlier.

Christian Fundamentalism, and Racism in the US

Christian Fundamentalism is a Protestant Christian movement in America that arose in the nineteenth century. It was a negative reaction to enlightenment, biblical criticism, theory of evolution and liberal theology. It was opposing many liberal forces in society in modern times. Between 1910 and 1915, two California businessmen, Lyman Stewart and Milton Stewart, arranged for the free distribution of about three million copies of *The Fundamentals*–a series of twelve pamphlets and ninety articles. These articles promoted the fundamentalistic ideology.[32]

Fundamentalistic beliefs are inerrancy of the Bible, belief in the creation story and Jesus's miracles in the Bible, the virgin birth of Jesus, the bodily resurrection and second coming of Christ, and Jesus's death for the atonement of human sins. Fisher Humphreys (a Former professor of Divinity) and Philip Wise, a pastor, in their book *Fundamentalism,*

---

31. Flannery, *Vatican II*, 916-17.
32. Malone, "Fundamentals," paras 1-6.

observe the attitudes of fundamentalism: suspicion, fear, anger, and separation. Fundamentalists are suspicious of changes and very suspicious of liberals. They are afraid of opening their minds to new information. They might avoid higher education, involving materials that could touch on their faith. They are easily angered as they perceive threats from other peoples' ways and views differing from their own. With the combination of suspicion, fear, and anger they tend to be on edge, and they can easily go off the edge related to religious matters.[33] So, keeping distance from others who are different is needed for their comfort, but they miss the benefit of a broader perspective by exposure. Isn't it tragic that people who consider themselves the true Christians miss the opportunity to live by the crucially important teaching of Jesus: love? We want to mention that there are people who may be connected with a fundamentalistic church or school for various reasons who personally are above the negative features we are talking about. Also, our intention is not condemnation but stimulation of conscience.

With their strong negative feelings and narrow perspective, they are guided by the kind of superego easily prone to hatred, so it was not surprising that fundamentalism and the KKK had a symbiotic relationship in early twentieth century America. In his book, *The Fiery Cross: The Ku Klux Klan,* American historian and clinical psychologist, Wyn Craig Wade wrote: "While fundamentalism would make a controversial, often divisive, contribution to religion in twentieth century America, its most critical impact on our social and political history was that, without it, the Ku Klux Klan could never have enrolled the fantastic numbers nor could it have gained the remarkable power it wielded between 1922 and 1925."[34]

The story of David Curtis Stephenson, called Steve by people, who joined the Klan in 1921 and became Grand Dragon of Indiana in 1924 is interesting and reveals the way fundamentalism can be so destructive. He rose in the ranks because he could attract a great deal of members. He attracted many fundamentalist ministers by making them honorary members, by giving donations and encouraging Klan members to become members of the churches ministered by the Klan friendly ministers. Steve also helped Klan-friendly politicians win power. Steve held impressive rallies. Republican governor Ed Jackson won with his help.

---

33. Humphreys and Wise, *Fundamentalism*, 57–64.
34. Wade, *Fiery*, 169.

Steve, who had married twice and left both wives, was attracted to Madge Oberholtzer, an intelligent attractive young lady who was working as manager of the Young People's Reading Club. The two were introduced at Governor Jackson's inaugural banquet. They had met a couple of times. Then one day he invited her to his house. He and his two companions were drinking, and they persuaded her to drink some and then he pressured her to go with him on a train trip to Chicago although she told him she did not want it.

Steve drank more on the trip, and he brutally attacked her, bit deeply in various parts of her body. When he woke up and she asked him for medical help, he would do it only if she would say she is his wife. She managed to get some mercury pills to commit suicide. She could take only part of the pills as they burned her throat, and she started throwing up. Steve took her back to her home. At home, a doctor saw and did what he could, but the mercury poisoning shut down her kidneys and she died. She made a document about Steve's attack on her before her death. Steve was charged with second degree murder and got life imprisonment. Governor Jackson did not pardon him. He made public the dirty secrets of many politicians probably to spite them. Several went to jail for corruption. This whole episode turned a lot of people away from the Klan. Within a year, the number of Klan members in Indiana fell from three hundred and fifty thousand to fifteen thousand.

Another interesting point historian Wade makes is that the most articulate critic of the KKK was not an American, it was a young Vietnamese man Nguyen Sinh Cung, a correspondent for a Paris publication. He wrote vividly and touchingly about lynching. His analysis of the Klan in 1924 and prediction of the Klan's decline in the future were accurate as per Wyn. Ten years later, he went back to Vietnam, changed his name to Ho Chi Minh and became a leader. We can only wonder what role his experience in the US played in the Vietnam War. Steve was released from prison in 1950, but he spent another six years in prison for failing to report to his parole officer. He was free in 1956. He deserted his wife of thirty years who had stood by him during his incarceration. He was living with another woman in Jonesborough, Tennessee when he had a seizure and died in 1966. Timothy Egan in *A Fever in the Heartland* notes that Stephenson had brought the KKK out of the shadows and got their message endorsed by ministers, prosecutors, judges and political leaders. Eagen's theme is how Madge stopped the Klan's plot to take over America.[35]

Emmett Till

In August 1955, a fourteen-year-old African American boy from Chicago was murdered while visiting family in Mississippi. He was brutally killed for allegedly flirting with or whistling at a white woman. The woman's husband and his half-brother abducted Emmett, mutilated his body, shot him, and sank the body in the river. The mutilated body was recovered and upon his mother's insistence, he had an open casket funeral which exposed to the public the cruelty of the white racists. This incident strengthens the civil rights movement. In January 2022, the Senate passed a bill honoring Emmett and his mother with the Congressional Gold Medal, the highest civilian honor. Obviously, incidents like Till's stimulated a great many consciences and helped the civil rights movement.

The Southern Poverty Law Center

The Southern Poverty Law Center is a nonprofit organization, founded by Morris Dees, Joe Levin, and Julian Bond in 1971. It has played a very significant role in the decline of KKK and other hate groups. They got much financial and emotional support from a lot of people across the country. By winning multi-million-dollar lawsuits against some of the most violent white supremacist groups, the SPLC was able to close down these groups. They have promoted equality for women and minorities and children's rights. Since the 1980s, they have been monitoring the activity of hate groups. And they have been promoting teaching tolerance programs since the 1990s.

Although the Klan declined, racism in politics and in fundamentalist Christianity continued until the civil rights movement succeeded. Then there was a very significant decline. It was in their 1995 convention that the Southern Baptist Convention passed a resolution apologizing to Blacks for one hundred and fifty years of racism. The apology was in tune with conscience, but many people feel Southern Baptists did not use conscience fully in their convention because three years later, they passed a resolution that wives must graciously submit to husbands. The resolution

---

35. Wade, *Fiery*, 204.

also stated men and women are equal in God's eyes. President Jimmy Carter, who is highly regarded for his promotion of peace and goodness, left the denomination because of its rigid views like this and refusing women to become ministers. I wonder why the denomination did not tell couples to have a creative cooperative loving relationship and let them work out the details. It would be wrong to think all Southern Baptists to be fundamentalists and racists. We personally know many who are not. There are various reasons for people to belong to a certain denomination, especially family and social connections. Fundamentalism of any religion mixed with unfair politics creates very harmful results socially, politically, and spiritually.

Because of fundamentalist Christians' attitudes of suspiciousness, fear, anger, and separation that we discussed before, they tend to be attracted to groups like QAnon. QAnon became more prominent in the news after many of its members took part in the attack on the Capitol on January 6, 2021. QAnon beliefs included a belief that there is a global cabal of Democratic satan-worshiping cannibalistic pedophiles. They also believe that former President Donald Trump is a key leader of QAnon who is secretly fighting to expose and defeat the cabal of evildoers.[36] A survey conducted by Professor Paul Djupe and colleagues of Denison University's political science department in October 2020 looked at a representative sample of seventeen hundred Americans. The surveyors found that 50 percent of Evangelical Christians either "strongly agreed" or "agreed" with QAnon beliefs.[37] In January 2021, American Enterprise Institute's Survey center on American Life asked a random sample of over two thousand Americans to rate the accuracy of a number of statements. One of the statements was "Donald Trump has been secretly fighting a group of child sex traffickers that include prominent Democrats and Hollywood elites."[38] Among those statements as "mostly" or "completely" accurate, 27 percent were white evangelical Christians. Obviously, they were using superegos and not consciences to guide them. And we can notice the problem of faith or belief without conscience.

36. Wikipedia, "Qanon," paras. 1–4.
37. Djupe and Burge, "Conspiracy," paras 1–16.
38. Cox, "After," para. 2.

Bryan Stevenson and Equal Justice Initiative

Attorney Bryan Stevenson is the founder of the Equal Justice Initiative (EJI) in Montgomery, Alabama, founded in 1989. EJI is a legal practice dedicated to defending the wrongly condemned especially on death row and the incarcerated poor. In his very inspiring book *Just Mercy* he describes how he worked on the case of an innocent black man Walter McMicken on death row and much legal effort and cooperation of the victim's family and honest witnesses including one who recanted his previous false testimony. The story exposes the unconscionable way several county officials manipulated the system and pushed an innocent man into death row and the local media's report supporting the false story against McMicken. Sadly, this was a reflection on the problem of conscience in the Bible Belt.[39] Stevenson and his staff have saved from execution over one hundred and thirty wrongly convicted death-row prisoners—winning exonerations and freedom for some.

Stevenson has founded three sites in Montgomery, Alabama. The first two, Legacy Museum and National Memorial to Peace and Justice, opened in April 2018. The topic of the museum is the continuation of racial discrimination of African Americans after the end of slavery through Sharecropping, Jim Crow laws, mass incarceration, and lynching. The National Memorial for Peace and Justice has a dark metal column suspended from above in the air. On the metal column, the date of lynching and the name of both the victim and the county are inscribed. From 1877 through 1950, forty-four hundred black people were lynched. The third site, Freedom Monument Sculpture Park, opened in March 2024. The park is in a seventeen-acre area on the Alabama river and there on a one hundred and fifty-five-foot long, forty-five-foot-tall monument was inscribed one hundred and twenty-two surnames adopted by the 4.7 million former slaves based on the 1870 US census. The first census listed them as free people. The park includes sculptures by many artists.[40] These are the kinds of historical visitations that can stimulate conscience.

---

39. Stevenson, *Just*, 48, 59–64.
40. Equal Justice Initiative, "Legacy Sites," paras. 1–7.

Enormous Historical Significance of Conscience in Christianity and Beyond

In *Dominion: How the Christian Revolution Re-made the World*, historian Tom Hollis points out how St. Paul combined Jewish morality and Greek philosophy to a tremendous effect in his insight of the law written on the heart (Rom 2:15). Hollis writes: "Its impact was to render Paul's letters–the correspondence of a bum, without position or reputation in the affairs of the world—the most influential, the most transformative, the most revolutionary ever written."[41]

Famous Christian thinkers like St. Thomas Aquinas, C.S. Lewis, and Paul Tillich gave tremendous importance to conscience. The Catholic Church teaches to always obey the certain judgment of conscience. Pope Francis is a champion of conscience. C.S. Lewis used the existence of conscience as evidence of God. Lewis was an atheist previously. Francis Collins, a prominent US physician, scientist, and former Director of the National Institute of Health, was an atheist who became a Christian by the influence of Lewis' writings. Collins found the arguments of some atheists about conscience as a cultural artifact or an evolutionary by-product unrealistic. Collins shows that one can be a committed scientist and a strong Christian.

Religions show a mystical side and a fanatical side. Mystics tend to use conscience and produce the fruits of the Spirit. Mystics promote peace. Francis Assisi was a lone Christian leader who tried to promote peace by meeting with the Sultan al Kamil of Palestine during the crusades.

On the fanatical side, closer to our own times and not well-known is what happened in Serbia. We can notice the actions against conscience behind the historically terrible actions by the Serb Orthodox Christian militia in 1992 through 1995. One of the top Serb Orthodox Christian leaders was Radovan Karadzic who was a psychiatrist, and therefore, of much interest to me. With the level of knowledge of a psychiatrist, one can imagine how extremely opposite to conscience a person's superego has to be to promote the level of mass destruction and cruelty his militia committed. Especially heinous was their use of raping as a tool for ethnic cleansing to get Muslims to leave Serbia. Ten thousand or more females were raped. More than eight thousand men and boys were killed. Interestingly, Orthodox Christians honor and venerate the Virgin Mary.

---

41. Holland, *Dominion*, 96.

Karadvic was sentenced by the international court of justice for crimes against humanity and died of a heart attack while incarcerated.

We can imagine the people who participated in the Crusades may not have much knowledge to use their conscience and realize the wrongness of their mission. But it is hard to imagine the same kind of ignorance in the case of the Serb Christians.

What I have noticed in many Christian communities is a tendency, more or less, on the part of the flock to follow the authorities like sheep. The more authoritarian the leadership, the worse this tendency. This is an example of people living by their superegos and neglecting their consciences. This is a problem in other religions and ideologies like communism.

As Shakespeare emphasized in Hamlet:

> "This above all: to thine own self be true,
> And it must follow, as the night the day,
> Thou canst not then be false to any man."[42]

Shakespeare also warned us against unbelieving priests. I would say, "Beware of leaders who go against conscience."

Earlier we explored how, inspired by Tolstoy's writings, Jesus's Sermon on the Mount and his own integrated spirituality, Gandhi used his conscience to stimulate the consciences of his followers to participate in the massive nonviolent movement. He was struggling against the colonialism of the very powerful British Empire for India's independence but also working hard to transform the unfair caste system among Hindus. The caste system which discriminated against lower castes and the outcastes had existed for several thousand years. It is a special credit to Gandhi that he tried to transform an entrenched internal problem even as he was engaged in the intense struggle with an extremely powerful external enemy. He was jailed for fifteen years by the British. India got independence in 1947 but divided into India and Pakistan. Gandhi was assassinated in 1948 by a Hindu extremist. Summarizing his greatness historians William Shirer and Vincent Sheen used the moving words of Plato about Socrates: " . . . of all the men of his time I have known, he was the wisest, justest, and best."[43]

As mentioned in the Introduction, American Christian missionary, E. Stanley Jones, was a close friend and admirer of Gandhi. Martin

---

42. Shakespeare, *Hamlet*, Act 1, Scene 3, 44.
43. Plato, *Phaedo*, 117c–118a.

Luther King Jr. had read many books on Gandhi, but it was Jones' book on Gandhi that particularly inspired King to pursue Gandhi's technique of nonviolence in the Civil Rights Movement. The nonviolent struggle works primarily by stimulating people's consciences to make fair and reasonable changes. When it becomes a massive movement, external pressure becomes another force for change. Gandhi told people to follow their own consciences which is the way to be an authentic person. Nonviolent movements have brought about tremendous progress in overcoming various forms of oppression in the human race. Gandhi was strict about keeping them peaceful. In fact, early on in the movement, in 1922 several members of his protest movement attacked a police station and killed twenty-two policemen. In response, he called off the movement, admitted his mistake in court and asked the judge for the maximum sentence he deserves. Sentenced for six years, he was released after two years because of good behavior. It was in December 1931, with much more preparedness for peace, that he decided to restart his noncooperation movement. Having learned from Gandhi's example, King and his close associates were careful to choose people willing to endure the suffering involved without retaliating.

Thomas Ricks describes in *Waging a Good War* the training that volunteers underwent before they participated in the student protests. They role-played how to act and react appropriately. An interesting example of the effect of the training was when an attacker spat on a protester. The protester responded: "Sir, do you have a handkerchief?" The attacker started to reach out to his pocket before he caught himself and said: "Hell, no." For a moment the protester reminded the attacker of their humanity, the protester thought.[44]

The Problem of Irrational Gratification (PIG)

Besides the superego, we deviate from conscience because of the problem of irrational gratification (PIG). Idolatry, sorcery, drunkenness, and orgies are irrational ways of trying to meet the need for power and pleasure. PIG is driven by emotions like the seven deadly sins: pride, greed, envy, wrath, lust, sloth, and gluttony. These emotions could lead to wrong choices. Loose or distorted superego may be involved too. There is a saying that alcohol dissolves conscience. When alcohol or drug abuse or

44. Ricks, *Waging*, 1–36.

other problems are involved in a group the group members develop similar superego judgments. So, Alcoholics Anonymous (AA) and similar support groups advocate addicts to change playmates and playgrounds. The 12 steps of AA therapy promote conscience and the group's ideology becomes part of the participant's superego, although AA doesn't directly talk about it.

Our Great Potential and Hope

The US is the stronghold of Christianity in the world. Genuine democratic process and power sharing are quite in tune with conscience. The Founding Fathers of America must have had a great deal of inner struggle in promoting the changes harmonious with conscience. The phrase "to form a more perfect union" expresses their humility recognizing more or less the imperfections and the hope and motivation to make progress. Superego has been working through Racism, Sexism, Fundamentalism, Militarism, Egoism, or greed and Egotism or pride. Christianity properly perceived with real depth and breadth of human spirituality from the Axial Age through the great innovations over the centuries and sincerely practiced like Martin Luther King Jr. did, could truly be the conscience of the nation.

Since there is much talk about America as a Christian nation, the Pew Research Center's October 2022 report is highly relevant. While 60 percent of respondents thought the founders of America intended for the country to be a "Christian nation" (37 percent thought not), only 45 percent thought the US should be a Christian nation (51 percent said no). Regarding the current situation, 33 percent think the U.S is a Christian nation and 64 percent think otherwise.[45] Another Pew report on March 15, 2024, showed 45 percent of people said they have heard about Christian nationalism and 25 percent had unfavorable and 5 percent favorable views to it. But 54 percent of Americans hadn't heard of it.[46] Theocratic states tend to pollute both religion and politics. Look at Pakistan and Afghanistan. We can remember Voltaire's observation about the Holy Roman Empire: "It was in no way holy, nor Roman, nor an Empire."[47]

---

45. Pew, "Forty-Five," 33.
46. Pew, "8 in 10," 16.
47. Wikipedia, "Succession," para. 12.

American Evangelicals in an Age of Extremism is the subtitle of journalist Tim Alberta's book *The Kingdom, the Power, and the Glory*. Alberta has an intimate knowledge of American Evangelicalism as he grew up in it and his father was a pastor in an evangelical church. In the prologue to his book, he writes: "Truth be told, I *did* see evangelicals divided into two camps—one side faithful to an eternal covenant, the other side seduced by earthly *idols* of nation and influence and exaltation—but I was too scared to say so."[48] This book shows he has overcome that fear. The Evangelicals have played decisive roles in American politics from President Carter's defeat by President Reagan and President Trump's victory in 2016 and, as of this writing, strong support for his candidacy for 2024. Alberta points out the evangelical's spiritual problems from excessive allegiance to American right-wing politics and culture wars. During the COVID-19 pandemic, a genuinely spiritual minister, Winans, who took over Alberta's father's church, lost a lot of parishioners to another church where the minister did not close in-person services and also preached against vaccination.

An interesting idea a Liberty University professor shared with Alberta is that when Jesus was telling the man and woman to leave father and mother and form their union, Jesus meant the couple to make useful changes from what they learned while growing up. One issue for me is that in all the discussions in this lengthy book on a very prominent Christian group, there is no significant discussion on conscience. I don't blame Alberta for the lack of discussion on conscience. I believe it is because of the deficiency of discussion on conscience by churches. An Australian pastor shared the information that conservatives in Australia were happy with universal health care. Alberta has given interesting details of the Christian and political aspects of many prominent American Evangelicals including the scandals of some. I believe understanding and utilizing conscience is the greatest need for Evangelicals to balance their spiritual defects of religion without conscience.

I quote the following observation by Alberta on a Faith and Freedom Coalition gathering in Nashville organized by Ralph Reed, an evangelical leader and Republican activist: "For three days Reed looked on as thousands of believers were told that their children were being groomed; that their communities were under invasion; that their guns were going to be confiscated; that their medical treatments were suspect; that their

---

48. Alberta, *Kingdom*, 3.

newspapers were lying to then; that their elected officials were diabolical; that their government was coming after them; that their faith is being banned from public life; that their leader was being unjustly persecuted; on their behalf, and that their nation was nearing its end."[49] Such extreme views show their problem with various aspects of conscience, especially the respect for truth.

The story of Brian Zahnd, pastor of the Word of Life Church in St. Joseph, Missouri is enlightening for us. Zahnd's father was a prominent attorney and a Republican. Zahnd used to attend church, and he cherished music. One night in his youth he attended a revival service. There, he had an encounter with Jesus and became a "Jesus freak." He joined the Jesus movement. At seventeen, he organized a ministry called Catacombs which was partly a church and partly a music venue. And later he changed the place to the Word of Life church. At age twenty-two, he appointed himself as the head pastor although he had no seminary training. The church expanded and became a megachurch with all its power and influence. It was a Republican culture with a few Bible verses here and there. In his middle age, he seems to have had a midlife crisis. He began to realize he and his church folk had not grown spiritually. In his search for change he discovered the Church Fathers and studying them helped him to transform. He got an invitation to do the invocation when Vice President Dick Cheney visited the city, and he hesitated but finally accepted the offer. He barely did the invocation and then left. Zahnd told Alberta that he heard Jesus asking him why he was politicizing Jesus. I believe this was his conscience. Zahnd told his congregation he was moving in a new direction. Sadly, a large number of his congregants left when he became more spiritual and not political.[50] Hot politics mixed with tasty religion seems to sell like hot cakes among many people who do not use their consciences properly. For the good use of conscience, good information is crucial. People who limit their media source to a channel promoting much propaganda tend to miss reason, the Golden Rule, and the other elements of using conscience. I have seen this problem with many of my patients and helped them to correct it. I think Christians who use their consciences properly would be happy with a balanced life.

In her book *Star-Spangled Jesus,* April Ajoy discusses her unhappy experiences in growing up in a Christian Nationalist family and social

49. Alberta, *Kingdom*, 193.
50. Alberta, *Kingdom*, 279–93.

situation. She has the credibility of being the daughter of an evangelical pastor who had the Christian Nationalistic ideology. Moreover, she worked for the Christian Broadcasting Network for some time. She learned how Christian Nationalism strongly supports white racism. Slavery was minimized and rather justified. It is serious and humorous that she prayed for Jesus to wait for his second coming after she had her marital sex on her wedding night. Her high school geometry teacher, a concerned Christian lady, taught young girls not to go horizontal, stay vertical, with their boyfriends. Many years back I had treated a teenage girl who became pregnant and had an abortion because she had believed that sex in a standing up position won't cause pregnancy. Her father was an anti-abortion activist.

Ajoy had a sociology professor who encouraged using reason and an open mind, but it was an exception in the world of Christian Nationalism. Ajoy says: "My change required years of deep reflection. There is a reason questioning and deconstruction are demonized and belittled from pulpits across the country."[51] Groups promoting conscience would positively enhance reasoning and deep reflection. But groups that want to hold on to some unreasonable or unfair system would try to protect the unfair system by finding ways to block conscience by denying questioning and deep reflection. Also, groups with rigid superegos tend to isolate members who are moving towards using their consciences. Similar to Socrates's teaching that an unexamined life is not worth having, an unexamined faith is not worth having. Moreover, unexamined faith risks problems of religion without conscience that we explored earlier. Having rejected Christian Nationalism's views on homosexuality and gender roles, Ajoy handled in spiritually healthy loving ways her brother's homosexuality and the nontraditional gender roles in her marriage. Ajoy provides an example of spiritual liberation from religious extremism.

Another book I find useful to mention here is *Circle of Hope: A Reckoning with Love, Power and Justice in an American Church* by Eliza Griswold, daughter of Frank Griswold, Episcopal bishop who consecrated the first openly gay bishop in 2003. Griswold observes that around sixty million Americans consider themselves "evangelical." She points out that besides the majority of evangelicals aligned with the religious right, there is a minority of radical or left-wing evangelicals who follow Jesus's Sermon on the Mount. The book portrays the lives of several real people

---

51. Ajoy, *Star-Spangled*, 219.

living by their authentic faith through the vicissitudes of life. Towards the end of the book Griswold depicts how her father, who was seriously sick, asked her to read aloud the story of the adulterous woman in the Bible. She felt the point of the story her father wanted to tell her was that God is love and mercy. Her father died during the Lent of 2023.[52]

Views of Two Pastors, an Action of Pope Francis, and a Good Step by the Southern Baptists

I find many of Atlanta-based Andy Stanley's views in his 2022 book *Not In It To Win It* quite useful to discuss regarding conscience. The subtitle of the book, *Why Choosing Sides Sidelines The Church*, reveals his objection to churches aligning with political parties because it prevents them from also ministering to people of the other party. Being divided over masks and vaccines, and with many evangelical leaders considering COVID vaccines as the mark of the beast (signs of a destructive beast described in Revelation in the Bible) has not promoted Jesus's message. He objects to reducing Christianity to faith and reducing faith to belief. He emphasizes doing good as Jesus taught and showed by example.

Stanley himself had experienced some families leaving his church as he had suspended in-person service at his church to protect people from the spread of COVID. Interestingly, he had the full support of the church members who were part of the medical community. Stanley was criticized by a long-standing friend and church member for giving an interview on CNN in July 2020 about him suspending in-person services. He was excited to talk about Jesus on CNN as their audience is less religious and more progressive than Fox News. As he points out, Jesus was not concerned about guilt by association. Guilt by association is often a superficial superego approach. Conscience would view the reason for the association, the extent and the effect of the association to judge whether it is right or wrong. Stanley has received many attacks of the cancel culture, usually from fellow Christians. Culture wars tend to justify demonizing members of the other party. He says Christians should not participate in the culture wars where you are not to love your enemy and there is no space for compromise or common ground.

---

52. Griswold, *Circle*, 331.

He says: "Both Old Testament and end-times warfare imagery and language are incompatible with the new covenant mandate of Jesus."[53] A lot of Christians are confused about Jesus's teaching of peace because of the "onward Christian soldiers" view promoted by many Christian groups. Stanley emphasizes what he calls "the law of Christ" that is Jesus's statement, "My commandment is this: Love each other as I have loved you." (John 15:12) Jesus also taught to be compassionate to each other and to get rid of anger, rage, bitterness, slander, and various forms of malice. But we can easily notice many Christians following, and many others, including several high-level media personalities and political leaders, not following these standards, especially when dealing with conflicts such as political differences, culture wars, and real wars. Everything is really not fair in love and war. Stanley says that if we really care about America and Americans, we must do two things: (1) apply our faith as directed by Jesus, and (2) we should vote our law-of-Christ-informed-conscience every chance we get."[54]

Let me quote two important points from pastor George A. Mason's article "Applying Christian Wisdom":

> (1) "Despite the prominence of the word as revelation, the Bible is a book of wisdom–less a rulebook than a guidebook. And even when it seems to be a rulebook, those rules are intended to be a guide to what 1 Timothy calls "the life that really is life." (2) "It is past time for religion to join science in partnership for the preservation of the planet. Theology has to join anthropology with ecology in a more holistic approach."[55]

Pope Francis visited the native Americans of Canada in July 2022 and asked them for forgiveness for the Church's role in the cultural genocide of thousands of Indigenous children.

Beginning in the 1880s and including much of the twentieth century, over one hundred and fifty thousand children were forcibly taken from their families and sent to so-called Residential Schools where they were prevented from speaking their language or practicing any of their traditions. They were forcibly Christianized. Thousands of them were physically and sexually abused and several thousand died. In the twenty-first century, many decades of sexual abuse were exposed in different parts of

---

53. Stanley, *Not in It*, 126.
54. Stanley, *Not in It*, 191.
55. Mason, "Applying," paras. 18–22.

the world. It caused a sharp decline in church attendance in countries like Ireland. After decades of hiding the problem, the church has taken steps to punish abusers and prevent abuse.

In May 2022, Southern Baptist Convention published a report by an independent investigation by a company named Guidepost about sexual abuse by the pastors or church affiliated personnel. They released a database of men who abused a total of seven hundred victims over the past twenty years. The database was previously kept secret. Activism by victims and their supporters has been very useful to heal the hurts and take steps to prevent abuse.[56] Such steps side with conscience rather than the earlier superego approach.

Besides the usual diseases, disorders, violence, and other forms of suffering, the human race has faced a fierce pandemic in recent years and a worsening climate crisis. We live in the information age with vast scientific, cultural, religious, and other information, as well as disinformation and false propaganda. Right wing and left-wing superego clashes are damaging conscience. Christians have the opportunity and responsibility to use our consciences and promote the fruit of the Spirit which we will explore in the coming chapters. And it is crucial to understand better the problems from the superego and the PIG in order to use conscience properly.

Pierre Teilhard de Chardin's Combining of Science and Christianity

Chardin (1881–1955) was a highly respected French Paleontologist and a Jesuit priest and philosopher. In his book *The Phenomenon of Man*, he explained his theory that human evolution involves increasing complexity and with it, increasing consciousness. This evolution is moving towards an "Omega Point" when the whole universe reaches a point of ultimate complexity, consciousness and unity. He wrote: "Evolution = Rise of consciousness. Rise of consciousness = Union affected." [57]

---

56 Guidepost Solutions, "Southern," 1–288.

57. Chardin, *Phenomenon*, 243.

My Hope

Former President James Earl Carter (1924–2024) passed away on December 29, 2024. He has been acclaimed for many achievements of his one term presidency and even more for his four decades of humanitarian work post-presidency promoting healthcare, democracy, housing and peace. He showed his strong Christian commitment by the good fruits of the Spirit he exhibited. As I write this in early 2025, President Donald Trump is making rapid radical changes in the US governmental agencies and making efforts for peace in Ukraine and in the Israel–Palestine conflict. I hope Christians and others would recognize the importance of conscience, make choices by that guide, and produce great levels of the fruits of the Spirit. Let us promote the spirit of the Axial Age.

Part II

Conscience and Fruit of the Spirit

THE WORKS OF THE FLESH

"Live by the Spirit, I say, and do not gratify the desires of the flesh. For what the flesh desires is opposed to the Spirit, and what the Spirit desires is opposed to the flesh; for these are opposed to each other, to prevent you from doing what you want. But if you are led by the Spirit, you are not subject to the law. Now, the works of the flesh are obvious; fornication, impurity, licentiousness, idolatry, sorcery, enmities, strife, jealousy, anger, quarrels, dissensions, factions, envy, drunkenness, carousing, and things like these. I am warning you, as I warned you before; those who do such things will not inherit the kingdom of God." Gal 5:16–21

THE FRUIT OF THE SPIRIT

"By contrast, the fruit of the Spirit is love, joy, peace, patience, kindness, generosity, faithfulness, gentleness, and self-control. There is no law against such things. And those who belong to Christ Jesus have crucified the flesh with its passions and desires." Gal 5:22–24

CONSCIENCE PROMOTES THE FRUITS of the Spirit. It is said we can judge a tree by its fruits. Works of the flesh are a result of not using conscience properly as we make choices. Religion without conscience tends to produce "works of the flesh." So much anger, hate, destructiveness, judgmentalism, and exclusion has been going on in the world, including in a religious context, especially in a religious context. Conscience is an essential part of spirituality. Right-wing and left-wing extremism in religion, politics, and media also reflect the deficiency of conscience. If the masses used their consciences better, the extremist leaders would have much less support and power.

Chapter Four

Love

"Love is patient; love is kind; love is not envious or arrogant or rude. It does not insist on its own way; it is not irritable or resentful; it does not rejoice in wrongdoing but rejoices in the truth." 1 Cor 13:4–6

Being deeply loved by someone gives you strength, while loving someone deeply gives you courage. — attributed to Lao Tzu

LOVE IS SO IMPORTANT that 1 John 4:16 says: "God is love, and whoever abides in love abides in God and God in him." St. Paul stated that love is the most important among the great virtues of Faith, Hope, and Love. And Paul said even if he has so much faith that he could move a mountain, he is nothing if he did not have love.

Patience, kindness, and rejoicing in truth are the positive features of love in Paul's quote above. I will be discussing patience and kindness in upcoming chapters. We can rejoice in truth every time. It is particularly with rejoicing at a time when truth is damaged by various forms of half-truths, white lies, spins, b.s., and bold lies. We have even heard that "truth is not truth." Somebody said the truth might make you "pissed" at first, but it would make you free later. Partners in various relationships can rejoice in truth because it helps them to cooperate in creatively dealing with whatever issues they are facing. Practice of psychiatry has made me aware of how difficult it could be to deal with truth.

Awareness of the true situation and choices are crucial to use conscience in choosing what is right. We can experience different levels of pleasure in exercising our various skills. Skillfully utilizing conscience with true awareness, especially in dealing with difficult issues, provides the inner joy from conscience, and thus, our search for truth gets reinforced.

According to Paul's quote above, love is not envious, arrogant, rude, stubborn, irritable, or resentful and it doesn't rejoice in wrongdoing. These are features of a good person, a loving and lovable individual. But what do we make of people who show the features opposite of love? How about people who support and follow political leaders or media personalities or other prominent individuals who are arrogant, rude, stubborn, irritable, and relish wrongdoing? I know people who themselves don't have these features, at least not much, but follow and support leaders who show such features. This is a significant problem with many Christian and other groups and individuals. Such followers are not following their own consciences. Often, group ideology and identity seems to be a major factor in people going against conscience and following wrong leaders. That is a clear example of superego overtaking conscience.

There may be situations where a rude, arrogant, and irritable leader is promoting a cause very dear to a Christian group. In that case, the Christian group would put persistent strong pressure on the leader to change for the better if the group uses conscience to guide its choice. Moreover, the group has to consider whether they are setting a good example for other groups.

Of course, anybody may be irritable or resentful at times. Like the old saying, "One swallow doesn't make a spring." it could be out of character. All kinds of feelings may cross our minds and we could let them flee away. But persistent negative feelings would require our attention and effort to root them out. We have to find the emotional reasons for the feeling and a way to deal with it. People who are rude, stubborn, arrogant, and the like are not quite lovable and so they diminish or block love both in giving and taking.

DEFINING LOVE

I found the following two good definitions of love.

> "Love is the active concern for the life and the growth of that which we love." Psychoanalyst Erich Fromm in his acclaimed work *The Art of Loving*. (p. 22)[1]
>
> "I define love thus: The will to extend one's self for the purpose of nurturing one's own or another's spiritual growth." M. Scott Peck, psychiatrist and author of *The Road Less Traveled*, a book which has sold more than seven million copies. (p. 81)[2]

Both authors emphasize the active nature of love and its purpose of growth. We will explore the various aspects of love.

PROTECTING AND NURTURING

Love involves protecting and nurturing of self and others and accepting protection and nurturing from others. For this wonderful circle of life to work well, we need to love and be lovable.

During the COVID-19 epidemic, protection involved taking the measures recommended by the official medical scientists. That would be consistent with conscience. I notice many people using unreasonable superego judgment based on wrong information or unhealthy social influences.

The angle of argument that wearing a mask limits freedom and so it is undesirable goes against the broad perspective of reasonable sacrifice and healthy self-discipline. Unreasonable superego influences by unhealthy sources seem to be a major factor behind this deficiency of love for self and others. Scientists like former NIH Director Francis Collins have expressed their disappointment about many people in the US apparently taking mask wearing or not as a political statement. Group influence is a clear factor in this issue. Collins is also a practicing Christian, and his recommendation should appeal to the conscience of Christians. But apparently in a lot of cases it did not work, if we consider the low vaccination rate among some Christian groups.

Group affiliation is important for us, but it shouldn't be at the expense of one's conscience. In an interesting case, Kelly's (not her real name) group of girlfriends were getting into shoplifting some not very costly things, and Kelly did not want to join that activity. Her girlfriends tried to rationalize what they were doing and persuaded her to join them.

---

1. Fromm, *Art*, 22.
2. Peck, *Road*, 81.

Kelly kept resisting until her friends kept calling her a "chicken." Then, she gave in one time. She was getting therapy for depression during those days. In therapy, it came out that she had a weakness for shame because her family used shame to manipulate her and it had become part of her superego's response (along with the external demand causing the shame). She was told the difference between superego and conscience. After that, she used her conscience and refused to join her friends for stealing, and she felt good about her stance. She protected herself by distancing herself from the group, and later she became part of another group which was a healthy choice.

BALANCING PROTECTION AND NURTURING

Protecting and nurturing are the two ways we exercise our love. Our energies of love get channeled in these two directions. Isn't it wonderful to see people and animals protect and nurture their young ones! Balance and harmony between these two channels of energy are very important for the functioning of healthy love.

Excessive energy or resources going into protection causes overall weakness of the system. I find an analogy to fruits interesting here. Fruits have skins for their protection. It is amazing to consider the wide variety of skins. So much variation in color, texture and thickness. And how they change as they grow and ripen and become rotten if the fruit is not picked when it is ripe. Nature seems to have shaped the skin of different fruits to suit the level of protection they need. Coconut fruit which grows on tall palms needs strong protection as it falls to the ground. And nature has gifted it with a fibrous husk and a hard shell containing the meat, or the flesh, which is edible and the coconut water which is delicious to drink. In recent years, coconut water has become a popular drink.

What is particularly interesting is that there are mature coconut fruits which look normal in size and shape but are much lighter in weight. If we cut it we could see that it has very little or no meat inside. We call it the empty nut! The resources of the fruit have gone into protecting but really protecting nothing or almost nothing inserted of producing a small fruit with meat inside.

There is an interesting sacred ritual among Hindus: breaking coconut in the temple or at home is part of a sacred function. It is symbolic of cutting through our superficial attachments and defenses and reaching the spiritual core inside. People try to choose coconuts with good flesh inside by lifting them to make sure they weigh normally. In an unusual spirit of religious harmony, there is a mosque in Kerala, India, where there is a place designed for Hindus to perform this ritual. I joke that it could be an opening ceremony for psychotherapy as we deal with nutty issues and thick defenses.

While empty coconuts are quite rare in nature, excessive defensiveness is not quite uncommon among people. Almost like empty nuts! It is a superego problem based on experience of rejection or some other hurt and fear of similar problems. The rejection or hurt could be from a Church. A Church-connected social group could create the same type of hurt. Excommunication from a Church could be a terribly painful humiliation. Requiring public confession of sins causes some people to withdraw. Rejection from Church leaders or from a denomination because of race or sexual orientation or divorce could lead to giving up on Christianity by many. This rejection leads others to simply join a more accepting Christian group. The case is similar within other religions.

I have heard from Gandhi's grandson Arun Gandhi about his grandfather's experience in South Africa. The elder Gandhi was taking a walk one Sunday morning when he noticed many people going into a church building. As a spiritual person he thought he would join the prayer. So, he went in. The minister who was in the middle of his sermon broke from his speech. He came down to where Gandhi was standing and pushed him out saying the church was not for colored people. Gandhi took it in his stride, still loving Jesus but cautious about Christians.

Fear of God works negatively in many cases making them less loving. Many sensitive children who were exposed to the idea of a wrathful God couldn't get past it to love themselves and love God until they could overcome their scared superegos and follow their consciences. About their childhood experience of church several people have said: "They scared the hell out of me."

Prov 9:10 is quite insightful: "The fear of the Lord is the beginning of wisdom; and the knowledge of the Holy One is understanding." The fear of the Lord which is the beginning of wisdom becomes the end of further progress into knowledge of the holy if the fear is too intense. It really backfires. Hate is another very important force that damages love and I will explore it next.

HATE

"Darkness cannot drive out darkness; only light can do that. Hate cannot drive out hate; only love can do that."[3] Martin Luther King Jr.

Hate involves self-hate and hate of others. I will deal with self-hate first.

There are several common features of hate. Let us say Sam hates Mary. Sam would find all kinds of faults with her, some would be imaginary faults and others some minor real faults that are grossly exaggerated. Sam would overlook and tend to forget or minimize the good things about Mary. He would avoid listening to others praising her and he would use chances to gossip or express negative impressions about her. He would try to damage her. He would avoid opportunities to reconcile.

Aristotle discusses anger and hate in the *Rhetoric Book II*. According to him, anger results from an offense against us but hatred may occur even without any such offense.[4] For instance, somebody may hate another person for being a member of another race or another party. Anger is aimed at returning pain to the offender. But hatred may be directed against a group of people. Anger has accompanying pain but hatred may not have such pain. The angry person can pity the offender, but the hater does not pity. The angry individual is satisfied with the suffering of the offender whereas the hater wants the destruction of his or her enemies. Time tends to cure anger but hate stays on.

SELF-HATE

I have heard the real story that when the Dalai Lama was out of Tibet and the first time he heard about self-hate, he could not believe it. He had not heard of somebody hating himself or herself. It is a strange thing in one way but given our superego it is quite understandable.

Self-hate has a spectrum from various levels of self-criticism to self-injury and suicide. While the severe forms of self-hate are rather rare, the milder forms are not uncommon. It is not a matter of constructive self-criticism to learn from one's mistakes to do better and feel better. It is repeated self-punishment without learning anything new and making no progress. The person tends to feel stuck.

---

3. King, *Strength*, 37.
4. Aristotle, *Rhetoric*, 66–68.

Those who seek relief from the suffering of self-hate by substance abuse or unhealthy relationships make their lives more complicated and unhappy. Such was the case with Anny who hated herself. Her mother had addiction problems and had left home when Anny was in her early teens. Her father was caring but he had unrealistically high expectations of her. Her superego ideal was to be clean, unlike her mother, do well in her studies, and excel socially. She got into a romantic relationship with a teenage boy who introduced her to sex and substance abuse.

She hated herself and started cutting herself. That led to her psychiatric admission and treatment for depression. Subsequently, she had outpatient treatment for depression and substance abuse. She made progress for some time but then relapsed, cut on herself and was hospitalized. Upon discharge, she started seeing me and continuing with a 12-step program for addiction. We focused on her self-hate and step four–taking a fearless moral inventory. She had previously resisted working deeply on the 12 steps for recovery from addiction. She found step four, that is, taking a fearless moral inventory of the 12 steps particularly difficult because it stirred up too much guilt. So, we worked on the healthy and unhealthy kinds of guilt.

I explained to her the way conscience and superego work and how superego stimulates unhealthy or excessive guilt or shame, causing more depressed and anxious feelings and sometimes self-mutilation to relieve the negative feelings. We went over it many times how it applies to her–how her harsh superego was behind her self-hate and self-punishment, including cutting on herself. And we discussed how conscience stimulates therapeutic levels of guilt or shame to make useful changes. She also read my book *Fulfillment Using Real Conscience* dealing with these matters and was excited to tell me how she was applying it in her life.

Treatment in such cases is complicated. She has had some brief relapses under an unhealthy relationship which she broke off later. She even scratched her wrist superficially after a close family member criticized her. Beyond such minor incidents she has maintained her highly remarkable progress. She was only superficially connected with her family's church until her early teens and then she had stopped her connection. She gradually developed an authentic spirituality as she lived by her conscience and had a healthy connection to a church.

I have tried other approaches like identifying triggers, challenging negative thoughts, pointing out their worth, pointing out that feelings are not facts (for example, if you feel you are a loser doesn't mean you are really a loser) to deal with self-hate. These approaches have a certain level of benefits, but the conscience approach is far superior because it utilizes the deepest guide of human beings. People feel good when they consciously use their conscience, giving it the importance it deserves. Symptoms such as distorted thinking fall into place when people use conscience properly.

Psychiatrist Theodore Isaac Rubin recounts in his book *Compassion and Self-hate* how he became severely depressed as a result of what he considered a great failure and hurt pride. He says: "The measure of my *right to be* was unfortunately based solely on accomplishment. One seeming failure was enough to upset this fragile, tenuous arrangement and to produce an almost incapacitating depression. One night, after his [his analyst's] uncompromising compassionate outlook touched me deeply, and, I am sure, stirred my own dormant fund of compassion, a radical change took place."[5]

About the difference between compassion and self-hate, Rubin says: "Compassion is the strongest human therapeutic agent in existence. Its potential for constructive growth and human creative possibility is almost limitless. Self-hate is the strongest anti-therapeutic agent in existence. Its potential for destructive possibility is almost limitless."[6]

With compassion, Rubin overcame his depression. In his case, I notice the superego's harsh judgment, which caused the depression, and conscience behind compassion did the healing. Unrealistic and rigid ideals picked up from society tend to cause self-hate. Rubin says: "The greatest, the best, the worst, the finest, absolutely right, absolutely wrong, all contribute to a world and a self which does not exist and which is, therefore, antithetical to the actual self in the actual world."[7]

HATING OTHERS

I was shocked by the news coverage of the white supremacists' marching and one of them attacking a peaceful group with his car, killing a young lady in Charlottesville, Virginia on August 11–12, 2017. It was so unlike the peaceful town where the University of Virginia is located with so many enlightened people. That is where I did my psychiatric training and

---

5. Rubin, *Compassion*, 3–4.
6. Rubin, *Compassion*, 4–5.
7. Rubin, *Compassion*, 113.

deepened my spiritual interests. When I was interviewing for the training program, one of the professors joked that they were so cosmopolitan that they even had some Americans too. There were several groups involved in the protest. The prominent hate group, the KKK, has been closely connected with Christianity especially in the first half of last century.

Here in Birmingham in 1921, a KKK member who was also a Methodist minister shot and killed a Catholic priest James Edwin Coyle because the priest had officiated at the marriage of the minister's daughter to a Puerto Rican American. The minister was acquitted. The minister's attorney was Hugo Black who later became Supreme Court Justice.

As social animals, we human beings tend to be part of groups. Loyalty to one's group is more or less very important. So-called hate groups give special importance to hating the group they oppose. Right-wing and left-wing extremists hate each other. Having a common enemy facilitates the closeness of members in a group. Hatred based on difference in race has been a significant issue in the US for centuries. In spite of significant progress towards fairness, there is still room for improvement. Unfortunately, there has been more racial tension in the last few years.

Christianity has been a part of the problem and part of the solution. A great many white Christians in the South had rationalized their practice of segregation finding some angle of argument to soothe their inner conflict. When a particular system had gone on for long, many people may not have felt even any inner conflict. There was a kind of unhealthy calm in the social order. So, one can understand why many whites considered the people promoting the civil rights movement as "troublemakers." Interestingly, Congressman John Lewis used to tell people to make "good trouble."

Martin Luther King Jr. explained that the nonviolent direct action was meant to cause a crisis—a nonviolent constructive tension—for the purpose of growth. It reminds us of the saying that a crisis is an opportunity for growth. In psychiatry, we see it often especially in cases of personality disorders. By using the Gandhian technique of nonviolence and the spirit of Jesus's Sermon on the Mount, King was able to stimulate people's consciences to promote civil rights. He gained great support from black Christians and many white Christians. Here is a clear and crucial distinction between superego and conscience. When Christians were practicing segregation, they were not using conscience, at least in their relationship to Blacks.

We can also understand how difficult it is to swim against the strong current of a society. It is easy for individuals to miss the longstanding wrong direction of their community. Even those who transcend their superegos and want to act by their conscience would find it practically difficult because of the bad reaction from society. Recall the way Socrates had to drink poison and die for stimulating the people to use reason.

On May 14, 1961, in Anniston, Alabama, twelve-year-old Janie Forsyth (later McKinney) gave water to the Freedom Riders (a group of civil rights activists who were traveling from Washington, D.C. to New Orleans). In Anniston, a violent mob led by the KKK attacked the bus in front of Janie's house and her father's grocery store after their bus was firebombed by the KKK. Janie noticed their suffering and responded to their request for water because of her Christian spirit. She first took the bucket of water to an elderly black woman who reminded her of her nanny. The KKK considered trying her as an adult but finally decided that she is mentally deficient and did not proceed. But the incident left a black mark on her family, and she was ostracized in school. Later in life, she became a communications specialist at UCLA.[8]

Janie took the message of love and compassion in the New Testament seriously to heart even in her teenage years. One of her favorite passages was: "Whatever you do to the least of my brothers, you do it to me."

Some people with hate act aggressively trying to damage the person they hate. Others express their hate passively by distancing themselves from the person and friends of that individual. All hatreds are connected with superegos, but the contents of the superegos vary. For example, in some cases the superego may be hating another person based on racial differences. In another case, the superego may be rejecting another based-on difference in political affiliation. In a third case, the difference may be in religion. In all cases, the solution is utilizing conscience.

NURTURING SELF AND OTHERS

Rabbi Hillel (110 BCE–10 CE) reportedly had a saying: "If I am not for myself, who will be for me? And if I am only for myself, what am I?"[9]

Nurturing involves meeting our human needs. Relationships are a crucial part of our needs. So, we have to understand and deal with our

---

8. McKinney, "Twelve-year-old," paras. 1–14.
9. Rabbi Hillel, *Pirkei Avot*, 1:14.

own needs as well as the needs of others, at least others in our close relationship to sustain happiness. Much unhappiness is caused by unmet needs. Difference in the priority of different needs of partners in a relationship, especially in marriage, could cause intense conflict. For example, if the husband's number one need is power and the wife's priority is for affection and sex, they would have an unhappy relationship if they don't understand and compromise.

The intensity of needs could vary greatly and that causes a lot of misunderstanding. Sexual need could vary from needing daily to once in a few weeks or more or less. And the way individuals deal with needs differs, from very active to quite passively.

People may be partly or even fully unaware of the underlying unfairness they perpetuate to cause unhappy relationships. In one case, let us call her Lilly, her husband was frequently frustrated, and they had silly arguments. As to the days when their relationship was peaceful and happy and whether it had anything to do with sex or anything special she cooked or anything to do with his sense of power, Lilly thought about it and said: "Sex, once we have sex, he is fine for two or three days. He shows sexual interest, but he wouldn't make a big fuss about it. He would fuss about something else." As to why she didn't respond to his desire, she said: "I don't have the urge that often." Regarding whether she could enjoy sex more often if she got into it although she didn't have the urge, she said she thinks she could.

Discussing human needs, Lilly's strongest need was for security and power. She had more than the same need in her girlfriends. The reason was that when she grew up, she experienced insecurity and powerlessness in her family. As to whether her husband met her extra need, she answered yes. After explaining about conscience and how she could try to apply the spirit of the Golden Rule, she said she would try to have sex more often. When she returned for the next session, she was excited to say it worked well and she too was enjoying the more frequent sex. Their relationship became happy. In a later session, Lilly said she helped some of her girlfriends to use conscience in conflicts from differences in needs. Interestingly, she felt more of a sense of power too, which was so much her cup of tea. Previously she had a little sense of power in not having sex when she didn't have the urge for it. Her assertiveness to say "yes" became much more satisfying than her assertiveness to say "no."

Physical needs like air, food, shelter, sleep, and elimination are obviously crucial for survival. Conscience prompts us to take care of ourselves and do what we can to help those who are not able to meet these needs. Many religious organizations promote charity. Promoting peace and justice and dealing realistically to do one's best against global warming are crucial steps conscientious people are taking. On the other hand, many religious people support political leaders or follow media personalities who are on the opposite side consistent with their superego judgment. Those who damage peace movements by violent actions also are acting against conscience.

We have a strong need for esteem from ourselves and from others, especially people close to us. Since we know best our intentions, efforts, and struggles, we have the most materials to judge ourselves. And we know the outcome of our effort which is also important to consider. Gandhi had said that perfect effort is perfect victory. Accordingly, we could give an A for strong and sincere effort. But, in the marketing world, what matters is the level of sales or material success in legally defensible ways, whether ethically right or wrong.

Remember the slogans: "Nothing succeeds like success" and "Nothing succeeds like the appearance of success." We have to evaluate feedback from others and utilize them for our benefit. If we are too sensitive about any negative points, then others would hesitate to give feedback. So, it is important for people to know we are taking their feedback properly. The difference between Conscience and superego is particularly important in handling this need.

Power, security, and freedom are very important since we need power to meet other needs too. We can try to have physical, financial, emotional, and spiritual strengths. Emotional and spiritual strengths involve love and wisdom. Physical exercises, meditation, and prayer are important to maintain our power. The distorted view of some Christians about meditation (that it is some foreign religious practice which would pollute Christians) has become much less but still happens. People can focus on their breath to meditate. I give Christian sacred words for Christians to use in meditation. The distorted view is from superego and overcoming it with conscience adds to one's wisdom. Knowledge is power and it is useful to know a good deal about one's own religion and some realistic things about the major world religions.

We have the need for identity—a sense of our individuality and our belonging to different groups. Age, gender, race, nationality, religious, and political affiliation, occupation, sexual orientation, and belonging to any special groups. Regarding our individuality, body image has become a major factor in society and so in people's superego. Conscience would emphasize health and keep matters of appearance in perspective. A significant part of our identity is our social roles. In work and in business relationships, the roles may be clear and well-defined. In that case, the choice may be to follow the expected line or go against it. Men and women have become more flexible in their roles in marriage in recent times.

Discussing the issue of the individual identity of an emotionally and spiritually healthy adult beyond a body, a name, and an address, Thomas Merton wrote: "It means having a belief one stands by; it means certain definite ways of responding to life, of meeting its demands, of loving other people, and in the last analysis, loving God. In this sense, identity is one's witness to truth in one's life. This does not mean merely the capacity to cling with conviction to official or external standards, to values one does not personally experience good but which one accepts in order to experience security, in order to please authority and so on."[10] If we reflect on it and the way many Christian denominations function, we could understand why many church members resist authentic individuality and go along with the group.

Merton admitted serious resistance to developing authentic identity even in the spiritually oriented monastic life. Here, Merton must be talking based on his personal experience as a monk besides his knowledge from other sources. In my experience, it is an exception to find Christian ministers, priests, and other leaders who promote authentic individuality. In this connection, we have to admit that many people may be unable to develop an authentic individuality. It is crucial for such people to get guidance from authentic leaders. The tragedy is that such dependent individuals often depend on immature religious leaders who manipulate them against their own best interests. It becomes a superego bond between the leader and the follower.

We are "selfish and groupish" in the words of Jonathan Haidt. Group identity is important for us as social animals. Social, political, and religious groups can show a spectrum of closeness from very loose connected to tightly knit. People in tightly knit groups may feel some loss of personal freedom. But some people enjoy losing some freedom because they feel less responsibility. I have heard many times people give the reason for certain choices as "we are conservatives" or "we are liberals." When one spouse is in a tight group and the other spouse is not, it can

10. Merton, *Contemplation*, 78.

cause much conflict. Cults meet the need for believing and belonging. The big questions about cults are whether the activities of the cult are good or bad and whether members can have more freedom gradually.

I treated two ladies whose husbands were in a relatively new religious cult. Both ladies did not share their husbands' interests and activities with the cult. The men put pressure on their wives to conform, in one case more than the other. The men were resistant to change, resistant to loving influences. It is sad to see the unhappiness people cause by not using their conscience by letting others twist their reasoning. The theories the group was promoting were unbelievable to the wives. Even as a psychiatrist, I find it hard to believe the extent to which sane people's beliefs can get twisted. Beware of what you believe!

Moving on to the need for pleasure, pleasure is not an icing on the cake of life but very much an important human need. Healthy pleasures nurture us physically, psychologically, and spiritually. And it protects us physically with a better immune system, emotionally relieves tension, and promotes enthusiasm. Intellectual and spiritual pleasures reinforce our deeper humanity. In general religions do not prohibit pleasures, especially in moderation, though some Islamic traditions prohibit music, and pleasure from intoxicants and sex run into a great deal of restrictions by Christian denominations as well as other religions.

Southern Baptists, Brethrens, and members of the Assemblies of God reject drinking alcohol. The Mormon church prohibits drinking coffee and tea. These are denominational rules, not matters of conscience based on reason, moderation, or the Golden Rule. If somebody has an addiction to alcohol or caffeine, then they should abstain by reason of conscience. When it is just a matter of a denomination's objection, I think members need to consider whether they will lose the benefits the denomination offers if they break the denomination's rule. Many people's superegos are significantly influenced by their religious group, and so they might have inner conflict about breaking the group's rule, even if the choice is right by conscience.

Intellectual pleasures are our special gifts as humans, connected to our intellect with its reason and imagination. Socrates considered intellectual pleasure as higher and physical pleasure as lower. According to utilitarianism, actions are right depending on how much happiness they produce and how much unhappiness they relieve, and actions are wrong to the degree they cause the opposite result. A prominent Utilitarian, John Stuart Mill argued that pleasures that are especially human are the higher pleasures and the pleasures we share with animals as lower pleasures. Mill stated: "It is better to be a human being dissatisfied than a pig satisfied; better to be Socrates dissatisfied than a fool satisfied."

Intellectual pursuits and humor give us intellectual pleasure. Intellectually stimulating information from reading or listening to programs in the media is very useful for us. There are many subjects which can enlighten us about life and enrich our lives that we could pursue. Thus, we can gain several benefits at the same time.

According to Aristotle, good humor is a virtue. Like all virtues, it is the middle ground of two extremes. So, good humor is the golden mean between buffoonery on the excess side and boorishness on the deficient side. It is pleasant, gentle; not hurting anybody. It can make people feel calm and close. Wit can be used to gently expose something wrong or bad. The situation where the humor is expressed has to be appropriate.

Sarcasm is not good humor. The word "sarcasm" derived from a Greek word meaning tearing flesh. It is tainted with hostility. Sarcastic communications about opponents in politics and ideologies seems to be rather common. People say social media has made the tendency worse. Many people feel a sense of power in attacking others with bad humor. Even the sugar-coated bitter pill leaves a bad taste in the mouth or causes one to throw up.

As human beings with long term memories, we have to deal with the ongoing issues of the past. We need to learn useful lessons from past experiences and move forward with the wisdom from the experiences. We have to be mindful to prevent strings from the past from pulling our legs and hinder our moving forward. That is where forgiveness and reconciliation become major factors. I think of forgiveness somewhat like relieving emotional constipation. If we experience hurt from somebody, it's natural to feel anger and want to retaliate and keep a distance from the person who hurt oneself. The intensity of hurt depends on the level of hurt and the sensitivity of the victim, such as hurt from a close family member or friend. In psychiatric practice, I could notice the intense hurt when one's spouse and best friend get involved in an affair most intensely if the victim had been hurt before, especially if it was not resolved satisfactorily. The strong push for forgiveness in the Lord's prayer, "forgive us our debts as we also have forgiven our debtors," clearly promotes conscience while many cultural superego forces promote holding grudges and taking revenge. Of course, victims being cautious to prevent getting hurt again is understandable.

While one can forgive even without cooperation from the offender, reconciliation needs cooperation from both. A broader and deeper understanding of the human condition helps greatly in promoting reconciliation. Conscience promotes reconciliation; superego demotes reconciliation. The spirit of Jesus's teaching has prompted many people to try reconciliation. After reconciliation, it is important to be cautious about not overreacting to any actions from the other person that may have some semblance to a previous problem. Caution but not overreaction is the proper choice. Similarly, we have to be cautious of what Sigmund Freud called "repetition compulsion," our tendency to repeat old patterns.

Present balance and future direction are important human needs, especially when we are in a transitional stage. Prioritizing our different needs and limiting what we juggle at any time are important to be effective in living by conscience. Practice of meditation is very useful in strengthening the ability to focus the mind on what is important and tune out unimportant thoughts and feelings. Future direction takes into account what we learned from the past and what needs and how we plan to pursue them in tune with conscience.

Our special human need for meaning is also at the heart of religions. They deal with all the so-called existential issues: freedom and responsibility, isolation, death, and meaning. Meaninglessness can cause significant depression and anxiety. Many people just live by secular meaning, not dealing with life hereafter. Most religions provide deep meaning for life here and hereafter.

St. Paul said: "When I was a child, I spoke as a child, I understood as a child, I thought as a child, but when I became a man, I put away childish things." (1 Cor 13:11) As we grow up, we have to transcend the childish pattern of being nice and not naughty so that we can get the toys we wish from Santa Claus. We have to explore the deeper meaning of life. As grown-ups in our times, we have the potential and responsibility to use our consciences with a great deal of information about Christianity and other world religions. In our experience, a lot of Christians don't know the real historical origin of their particular denominations.

According to the *World Christian Encyclopedia* by Barrett, Kurian, and Johnson published by Oxford University Press in 2001, there are more than thirty-three thousand total Christian denominations[11]. They

---

11. Barrett, et al., *World*, Table 1–5, 16.

define a Christian denomination as an organized Christian group within a specific country. Many Christian denominations teach that members of other Christian denominations would go to hell. What a Hell of a situation!

According to a Pew Research Center study in November 2021, 73 percent of the US population believed in heaven and 62 percent believe in hell. Among Christians, 92 percent believe in heaven and 79 percent believe in hell.[12] I come across very few Christians who know that there have been a couple of great Christian Thinkers (Origen and Bishop John Shelby Spong, as far as I know) who did not believe in eternal damnation. Many Christians express a belief that without the fear of eternal damnation people won't behave well. But we can notice Buddhists and Hindus behaving well with the concerns about karma or moral consequence, and without fear of eternal damnation.

Mahatma Gandhi said: "I hold that it is the duty of every cultured man and woman to read sympathetically the scriptures of the world. We are to respect other religions as we would have them to respect our own. A friendly study of the world's religions is a sacred duty."[13]

Understanding other groups is a crucial part of applying the Golden Rule. In the spirit of this idea, we have another suggestion. To have a fair understanding of the major world religions, reading a book like *The World's Religions* by Huston Smith and *The Varieties of Religious Experience* by William James could be quite useful. Understanding the other people's meaning system is a significant part of our empathy for them. On the other hand, publications taking unfair and unreasonable angles of arguments about other religions reflect the unfair superego and not conscience in action. Also, eternal damnation is taught mostly by Christianity. Ecumenical movements among Christian groups and interfaith activities with other religions help promote cooperation with others. It is consistent with conscience. Living by conscience is living at our best. And so, it provides us with the deepest satisfaction. It is our ripeness. And in the words of Shakespeare, "Ripeness is all."

---

12. Pew, "Republicans," para. 3.
13. Gandhi, *Young*, 308.

ROMANTIC LOVE

There can be no realistic discussion of love without dealing with romantic love. The high level of emotional and physiological excitement makes romantic love so special. Falling in love is an exceptionally enjoyable fall. Even in arranged marriages, there is the hope of falling in love after marriage. As they say in India, "we marry somebody compatible and then we fall in love." In that situation, it is not "falling in love" but it is more like "jumping in love" after looking before you leap. In any case, romantic love is a specially interesting and enlightening experience. Deep sharing of each other's thinking and feeling and physical intimacy of pleasing each other makes romantic love exceptional. What is very important is to make the best of it with conscience, not letting superego or the PIG ruin it and cause unnecessary suffering.

Unrealistic expectations by one or both partners in a romantic relationship is not uncommon. Compared to the meeting of prospective young men and women arranged by families or supervised by families long back, people enjoy total freedom from restrictions by anybody except themselves. With so much freedom comes the greater level of responsibility. Nobody else to blame. Not having any generally accepted social norms about dating and cohabitation leaves many people who want a committed relationship unhappy. The superego standard for many people seems to be "do whatever you like." This kind of situation makes conscience all the more important for people to guide their choices to be fair and reasonable. Christianity could play a very important role in promoting conscience and thereby helping to guide people caught in a situation with no guidance except their own feelings.

One of the common problems with romantic love is the unrealistic expectation of it lasting automatically forever in the couple's relationship–in the "then they lived happily ever after" story ending. Interestingly, Vatsyayana, author of *Kama Sutra*, probably the oldest book on sex, stated: "Thus if men and women act according to each other's liking, their love for each other will not be lessened even in one hundred years."[14] To be realistic, there would be difficulties in doing what each other likes because of differences in human needs and attitudes. Moreover, the ups and downs of life would have its effect on individuals. Even the level of sex hormones and dopamine involved in pleasure fluctuates. So, a basic

---

14. Vātsyāyana, *Complete*, 77.

level of commitment is crucial to maintain a good relationship through the thick and thin in life.

In earlier ages in human history, external forces such as family, religious groups, and society had heavy influences on couples to keep their relationship. In our own times, those external forces are so weak or nonexistent that the responsibility for commitment falls on the individual. Conscience plays a crucial role in keeping a commitment especially when many social forces—and therefore superegos—promote opportunism. Commitment involves voluntarily giving up the freedom to have other romantic relationships. Some people's fear of commitment is almost like fear of death. This is understandable if we think of death as the end of further possibility.

DIVORCE RATE AS A REFLECTION ON THE PROBLEM WITH LASTING LOVE

The divorce rate per thousand population in the US was 6.5 in 2018 compared to 8.2 in 2000 according to the CDC. The following divorce statistics are based on "Divorce statistics: over 115 studies, facts and rates for 2022," published on the Internet by David Wilkinson and Finkbeiner LLP law firm.

An estimated 41 percent of first marriages, 60 percent of second marriages, and 73 percent of third marriages end up in divorce. The US has the sixth highest divorce rate in the world. The average length of first marriages is males 7.8 years and females 7.9 years and in second marriages ending in divorce is males 7.3 years and females 6.8 years. The most common reasons for divorce are lack of commitment, 73 percent, too much argument, 56 percent, and infidelity, 55 percent. Other reasons below 59 percent are: married too young, unrealistic expectations, inequality, lack of preparation for marriage, and, in 25 percent of cases, violence or abuse. Those who marry after age twenty-five have a 24 percent less likelihood of divorce.

High School dropouts are 13 percent more likely to divorce. Political affiliation and divorce rate: conservatives 28 percent, liberals 37 percent, and moderates 33 percent. Living together before marriage increases the divorce rate by about 40 percent. Women with six or more premarital sexual partners are about three times less likely to be in a stable marriage. Pornography addiction was reported as a factor in 56 percent of divorce in one study. The likelihood of divorce goes up to 147 percent if a close friend gets divorced and 33 percent if a friend's friend is divorced and 75 percent if a coworker is going through a divorce. Living together before marriage increases the chance of divorce by 40 percent. Divorce rates among US Navy Seals is 90 percent. Divorce rates among ages fifty and above doubled in the past twenty years. If both partners had a previous divorce, the chance of divorce is 90 percent. The risk of divorce is 14 percent less for a strong religious believer. Somebody with no religious affiliation has 14 percent more chance of divorce. Among Christians, the percentage of divorce is: Evangelicals, 26 percent, Catholics, 28 percent, and 38 percent for non-Christians. Couples with children have a 40 percent lower divorce rate compared to couples without children. People with a college education have an 18 percent lower risk of divorce.[15]

The very high divorce rate in cases of friends and coworkers who divorce indicates superego influence. This is my impression based on clinical experience, too. Lower divorce among people who marry after age twenty-five and ones with college education show the benefit of a more stable or mature personality. And probably making better choices consistent with conscience, using better reasoning. Selfishness and hate are major causes destructive to love.

ABUSE OF INTIMATE PARTNERS

The Economist, October 12–18, 2024 reported the following: "According to the World Bank, almost one-third of women around the world have been physically, psychologically, or sexually assaulted at least once during their life-tine (the share is around a fifth in rich countries). The vast majority of assaults are committed by current or former intimate partners. In Mexico and Honduras, nearly six women per one hundred thousand are murdered every year. The global average hovers around two per one hundred thousand."[16] According to the National Library of Medicine report in April 2023, as much as 15 percent of cases of domestic abuse victims are men.[17] Isn't all this abuse a clear indication of humanity's tremendous need for transformation?

---

15 Wilkinson & Finkbeiner, "*Divorce Statistics*," 1–3.
16. The Economist, "Beating," paras. 3–5.
17. Huecker et al., *Domestic.* §6, para. 5.

SELFISHNESS

"For where your treasure is, there will be your heart also." Matt 6:21

Selfishness has two parts: greed and excessive pride (conceit or egotism). Often, the two are connected because many people are conceited based on their wealth. The cultural ideal of material success goes with the idea that greed is good. Although greed and pride are listed in the seven deadly sins, that does not seem to be taken as seriously in recent times as it used to be. The superego values promote greed and egotism. Fair and reasonable material well-being and self-esteem are good and in tune with conscience. The problem is, when we handle our needs at the expense of others or in ways that damage our own balance. We hear statements like, "I am a good person, so what?" by good people whose self-esteem is low because they lack wealth and fame. That is a superego problem. Judging by conscience, good people deserve to feel good. Manipulative marketing is rather widespread. Many people have told me that they tend to feel low from unhealthy exposure on social media.

In a democratic country like the US, Christians who use conscience would naturally support policies that would help to promote love, peace and the other elements of the fruit of the Spirit. In fact, Christianity could play a significant role in promoting conscience in the culture, and many Christians do so. But many other Christians reinforce unhealthy superego approaches in society, maybe unconsciously.

GREED OR AVARICE

Greed is an uncontrolled desire for possession or use of material gain. By the word "uncontrolled," I refer to its meaning, "unbalanced," and being unbalanced involves something being too much, at the expense of, or the deficiency of, something else. If greed is successful, it gives the person a sense of power and with it, a sense of pride. The deficiency may be in relationships, spirituality, and in the overall meaning to life. The person may be somewhat aware of or unaware of the imbalance because of heavy defenses. Full awareness of the imbalance may happen when facing a crisis. In dealing with the issues of mortality, many people reorient their lives, but it may be too late for some. The saying "better late than never" is quite applicable. Jesus's statement that one cannot have two masters—God and Mammon—is well-known. We can have a reasonable priority for our financial and spiritual needs. The four goals of life in Hinduism are interesting: wealth, pleasure, ethical living, and ultimate liberation.

ROLE OF LOVE IN OUR BEING FULLY HUMAN

Thomas Merton says about love: "Love is, in fact, an intensification of life, a completeness, a fullness, a wholeness of life."[18] And Merton further states: "We will never be fully real until we let ourselves fall in love—either with another human person or with God."[19] He had himself experienced both kinds of love. Religious devotion is a form of love. The quality of our love and devotion would be best if we are guided by conscience.

LOVE OF OUR PLANET AND ALL THE BEINGS IN IT

Hurricane Ian, which hit Florida on September 28, 2022, has caused more than one hundred deaths and an estimated loss of one hundred and ninety-nine billion dollars. The last seven years have been the hottest years recorded. Wildfires and floods have been causing so much damage in different parts of the world. Pakistan's monsoon flood in 2022 has damaged more than 1.7 million homes and killed more than fourteen hundred people. A third of the country was affected. The climate is in crisis.

When a loved one is in a crisis, we pay more attention and try to do what we can to help. We need to have a similar spirit in dealing with the climate crisis. The Biden Administration's "The Inflation Reduction Act" included three hundred and seventy billion dollars for clean energy was a very commendable step.

DIVINE FIGURES AS THE ULTIMATE INSPIRATION FOR LOVE

For a lot of Christians, the unique example of Jesus's love in his life and death and ongoing love for all is the ultimate inspiration. And, as they love Jesus, they could love others and be lovable and accept love from

---

18. Merton, *Love*, 24.
19. Merton, *Love*, 25.

others. Similarly, love of Allah and Prophet Muhammad for a lot of Muslims and so on. Such love provides joy which we will explore in the next chapter.

Chapter Five

Joy

A thing of beauty is a joy forever. —John Keats[1]

"Never, never, even in their moments of richest and wildest happiness, were they unaware of a sublime joy in the total design of the universe, a feeling that they themselves were a part of the whole, an element in the beauty of the cosmos. This unity with the whole was the breath of life to them. —Boris Pasternak in Doctor Zhivago[2]

To rejoice at another person's joy is like being in heaven. —Meister Eckhart[3]

THE ABOVE INTENSELY BEAUTIFUL and deeply meaningful description by Boris Pasternak touches on so many vital aspects of joy: the *awareness* of a sublime joy in the total design of the universe, the identification of oneself as part of the wonderful whole, deeper meaning in life, and the intimate sharing of love. The dictionary definition of joy is "a very glad feeling, happiness, great pleasure, or delight." Joy is connected with a deep experience of goodness, truth, beauty, pleasure, love, identity, and meaning. Deep experience is a common feature in the joy related to every need and that is connected to conscience rather than superego. Naturally,

---

1. Keats, *Endymion*, 1.
2. Pasternak, *Doctor*, 34.
3. Eckhart, *Selected*, 12.

when several sources of joy join together in an experience, the more joyful the experience would be.

GOODNESS IS A GREAT source of joy. And the joy is a compensation in a way for the stress and strains of doing good in many situations. Over the years of my work as a physician, I have noticed many people who go well beyond their call of duty and experience joy in their effort. I have seen many patients with addiction and/or personality disorders who were in the habit of making bad choices, causing suffering on others, but became healthy and good people who experience the joy of goodness. Chapter nine will deal with goodness in more depth.

EUREKA!

The Archimedes story is an exciting incident of the joy from discovering an important truth. Archimedes was a great scientist who lived in Syracuse, Sicily in the first century BCE. He was ordered by his king to find out whether a new crown made for the king was of real gold as the goldsmith claimed. Archimedes was trying hard to find a solution but was failing. Then, one day he filled his bathtub to bathe. When he got in the water, he realized that the volume of the water displaced was equal to the volume of his body part submerged. So, he realized he could measure the volume of irregular objects like a crown. (Since pure gold is heavier than other metals, once the volume and weight of the crown is known he could easily answer the king's question.) With this realization, he ran down the street naked to the king shouting "Eureka!" meaning "I have it!"[4] The intensity of his joyful reaction is understandable. Scientific discoveries are joyful for the scientists involved in the work and others who are interested in the field of inquiry. The vast number of exciting astronomical explorations and discoveries in recent years has produced a great deal of joy for millions of people. As physicians, when we deal with complex cases when the diagnosis is obscure and, after much effort, we find it, we feel joy. As psychiatrists, we experience joy when we gain psychological insight into complex human issues and problems.

4. Bellarmine, "About," paras. 1–6.

MYSTICISM AND FANATICISM

Mystical experiences like the one Thomas Merton had that we discussed in chapter two were profoundly joyful to them. By reading and reflecting on it, we could get vicarious joy. I have come across people who had less dramatic spiritual experiences and they cherished the memory of the experience. In my work, in the rare cases where the patients had such experiences, they gained significant benefit clinically from the experience. In this connection, Albert Einstein's view of religion is relevant. He wrote about three stages of religion: first stage, religion of fear; second stage, religion of morality; and third stage, the cosmic religious feeling. He added that the cosmic religious feeling appeared in its early development and in some prophets in many of the Psalms of David and a much stronger element of it is contained in Buddhism. Einstein claimed that "the cosmic religious feeling is the strongest motive for scientific research."[5] I believe conscience promotes such broad-based spirituality.

Religious songs, chanting, and music with spiritual meaning can evoke joy. Such activities as part of religious functions attract a lot of people to religious functions. Secular music which could also evoke joy a lot of times. Religious fanatic groups like the Taliban prohibit music except the religious music approved by them. That is part of their extremism which stifles people's humanity and spirituality. The Taliban's explanation is that they are preventing improper thoughts. *The Economist Magazine* in January 2023 reported that an Iranian mullah warned women against peeling aubergines (eggplants) because it might stimulate improper thoughts.[6] Of course, prohibiting sources of hate, violence, and addiction would be useful but that is not the extremists do. They get bent out of shape about temptations, especially about sexuality, and come up with extremely unreasonable steps. It reminds us of the protest going on in Iran following the death of a lady under morality police custody on September 13, 2022, for not covering her hair properly and died under detention. Several people have been punished to death for protesting. This is the problem of extremism, when people don't understand and pursue moderation.

5. Einstein, *World*, 20–2.
6. The Economist, "Women," 14.

JOY FROM BEAUTY AND PLEASURE

Quite opposed to the ascetic approach of renunciation the Indian poet, philosopher and social reformer Rabindranath Tagore expresses his objection to renunciation in a poem in the collection of poems for which he received the Nobel Prize for literature in 1913. In this poem, Tagore asserted that renunciation is not a tool for deliverance for him. He would enjoy the various colors and fragrances that the divine source pours into the vessel of his life. He would light a hundred lamps with divine flame and place it on the altar of his temple. He would not close the doors of his senses, and the joys of sight, sound and touch would bear divine delight. He would let his illusions transform into joyful illuminations and his desires mature into fruits of love. Incidentally, it was Tagore who called Gandhi Mahatma (great soul).

While conscience delights in finding the truth and communicating the truth, the superego tends to twist the truth if that serves the superego's agenda. With the expansion of information sources and rather explosion of propaganda, it has become increasingly difficult to find the truth in many situations. Political polarization, authoritarian rulers pressuring the media to slant in their favor, extremisms in politics and religion, conspiracy theories and the like are taking away a huge share from truth and the potential for joy. That is sad but we can hope the human race will wise up and be guided by conscience.

Let us now turn again to John Keats and this time take up another quote "Beauty is truth, truth beauty," and reflect on the joy from beauty.[7] The harmonious mingling of component parts, beautiful in themselves, touches our hearts, and delights our souls. Watching the beauty of nature, the landscapes, gardens, and varieties of flowers promotes joy in us. What is healthy is more beautiful and conscience promotes what is healthy. Superego may or may not care about the damage and destruction of nature from the climate crisis depending on their selfish interests. Photographs and paintings of beautiful landscapes, trees, flowers, birds, and bees stimulate joy within us. And for those who believe in a Higher Power, the experience of beauty raises the appreciation of the Spiritual Power.

---

7. Keats, "Ode," lines 49–50.

SPIRITUALITY AND JOY

Festivals and various celebrations, whether religious or secular, are special occasions for joy. As are pilgrimages. Joy in relationship with God is a very strong theme in the Bible. See the following examples.

"When the cares of my heart are many,

Your consolations cheer my soul." Ps 94:19

"For the Lord takes pleasure in his people;
He adores the humble with victory." Ps 149:4

"I will be glad and exult in you;
I will sing praise in your name, O Most High." Ps 9:2

"Rejoice in the Lord always: again I will say, Rejoice." Phil 4:4
Jesus's statement "Just so, I tell you there will be more joy in heaven over one sinner who repents than over ninety-nine righteous persons who need no repentance." (Luke 15:7) Jesus said this after telling the parable of the lost sheep. In the parable, a man who has a hundred sheep, but one sheep gets lost, and he leaves the other sheep and goes after the lost sheep. When he finds the sheep, he rejoices, and he calls his friends and neighbors to celebrate with him. Such is the joy of spiritual transformation. The intensity of the joy is related to the difficulty of transformation.

Loving relationships are a great source of joy and living by conscience makes a person loving and lovable as discussed in chapter four. We are at our best when we love deeply and honestly. We are automatically guided by conscience. Even in spite of many difficulties, love can make life fulfilling just with the bare basics. The eleventh century Persian poet Omar Khayyam wrote how the desert becomes paradise with a piece of bread, some wine, and the beloved singing.[8] Healthy spirituality of various kinds promotes joy. While the concept of God differs in different religious groups, we can notice the joy when people sing devotional songs.

Conscience promotes a healthy identity and the joy that goes with it. It means a good sense of one's individuality and the sense of belonging to the whole. People who had Near Death Experience tend to have such a sense of the universe. Superego tends to focus on narrow sources of

---

8. Khayyam, *Rubaiyat*, 15.

identity and if it becomes too big a part of the person's identity, it becomes a problem. For example, if gender identity is overgrown in a man, he would think and act as a macho male and have problems in relationships with people, especially with women.

Psychoanalyst Erich Fromm connected joy with the "being" mode of human life as opposed to the "having" mode. He wrote: "While having is based on something that is diminished by use, being grows by practice." (The "burning bush" that is not consumed is the biblical symbol for paradox.) "The powers of reason, of love, of artistic and intellectual creation; all essential powers grow through the process of being expressed. What is spent is not lost, but, on the contrary, what is kept is lost. The only threat in my being lies in myself: in lack of faith in life and my productive powers; in regressive tendencies; inner laziness and in the willingness to have others take over my life. But these dangers are not inherent in being, as the danger of losing is inherent in having."[9] Being mode tends to follow conscience and having mode tends to be guided by superego.

Spiritual meaning is at the heart of religion and spirituality. It involves life here and hereafter. Religions have very different teachings about their dogmas and what happens hereafter. But on the whole the spiritual and ethical principles of conscience–the Golden Rule, reason, moderation, and respect for truth–are more commonly emphasized.

The Book of Joy by the Dalai Lama, Archbishop Desmund Tutu, and writer Douglas Abrams provides the interesting discussion on joy by the two great spiritual leaders, two Nobel Peace Prize winners. The Dalai Lama transcends his Buddhist background and the archbishop transcends his Christian background in their joyful interaction and discussion. The Dalai Lama explains that sense pleasures last only for a short time, but the deeper level of happiness or joy is longer lasting. So, he advises people to promote a mental level of happiness and joy. He suggests even ten or thirty minutes of meditation on compassion could give joyous feelings all day.

The obstacles to joy are fear, stress, and anxiety; frustration and anger; sadness and grief; despair, loneliness, envy, suffering, and adversity; illness and fear of death. Superego tends to make these problems worse by harsh judgements, obsessive focus on the problem and unhealthy feelings and difficulty in handling feelings.

---

9. Fromm, *To Have*, 97.

Conscience would help to deal with each of these problems. Regarding life after death, the Dalai Lama joked he would prefer to go to hell because he could help some people there to handle their problem. The Dalai Lama said that he meditated five times a day on death, intermediate state and rebirth. He expressed his hope that this practice would help him when his real death would come. *(I caution readers to evaluate seriously whether this approach would be beneficial or harmful for them, personally.)* They joked about the Chinese government's reported plans to choose the next reincarnation of the Dalai Lama.

They also discussed the eight pillars of Joy: perspective, humility, humor, acceptance, forgiveness, gratitude, compassion, and generosity. These are all in tune with conscience. It is significant to note that the archbishop lovingly offered the Dalai Lama Holy Communion, and the latter graciously accepted it. This is significant because in many Christian denominations, the Communion is only for Christians, and that too, only for members of the particular Christian denomination. These two men are great examples of people of conscience. Guided by conscience, people of different religions can joyfully promote the various elements of the fruit of the Spirit. [10]

One of the greatest importance given to joy or bliss is in the Hindu description of God as Satchidananda. The word has three parts: *sat* means truth, *cit* means consciousness, and *Ananda* means joy or bliss. So, God is described as "Truth consciousness bliss." We can experience joy in enhancing each one of the nine parts of the fruit of the Spirit and the next one is peace which we will discuss in the next chapter.

---

10. Dalai Lama and Desmond Tutu, *Book of Joy*, ix–355.

Chapter Six

Peace

"Peace is the only battle worth fighting." —Albert Camus[1]

"Nothing can bring you peace but yourself. Nothing can bring you peace but the triumph of principles." —Ralph Waldo Emerson[2]

VARIOUS RELIGIONS AND SPIRITUAL traditions emphasize peace. The word peace appears over three hundred to four hundred times in the different versions of the Bible. Here, I will discuss many aspects of conflict or war and peace, including religious harmony and non-violent conflict resolution in the context of conscience promoting this fruit of the Spirit. Let us start with the exceptional story of Ashoka.

EMPEROR ASHOKA

Over two centuries before Jesus the Prince of Peace, promoted peace and conscience, Ashoka ruled a large empire from Afghanistan to parts of Southern India from 273 to 232 BCE. His personal transformation after conquering a neighboring kingdom is one of the most remarkable stories in the history of the world. One of Ashoka's brothers had become a Buddhist monk. Ashoka came to power after killing his other brothers.[3]

---

1. Camus, "Peace," para. 1.
2. Emerson, *Self-Reliance*, 73.
3. Armstrong, *Great Transformation*, 357.

One of his wives supported a Buddhist group and Ashoka had some superficial exposure to Buddhism.

He wanted to expand his empire. In the eighth year of his reign, he invaded the neighboring kingdom of Kalinga (present day Orissa). Unlike the usual conquerors who would have celebrated victory, he dwelt on the suffering he caused. He thought of the one hundred thousand Kalingan soldiers who were killed in the war, many times more who were injured, and one hundred and fifty thousand people who were displaced. The awareness of the immense suffering and his responsibility for it weighed heavily on his mind. He got his reaction recorded in an edict saying the "slaughter, death, and destruction were extremely grievous" to him and "it weighs heavily on his mind."[4] Armstrong views that the edict was meant to warn other kings against pursuing conquest. But I believe it had a larger purpose too as a public confession based on his deep grief and guilt, and possibly as a model of transformation for others.

The sorrow about the immense suffering he caused stimulated his conscience and strong motivation to transform his life. The spiritual transformation he made is absolutely remarkable. A unique emperor with a good conscience!

Ashoka became a dedicated Buddhist, champion of peace and promoter of dharma: compassion, benevolence, and goodness. He maintained a large standing army. For the wellness of his people, he opened schools and hospitals, undertook digging of wells, he made provisions for the education of women and the care of the aborigines. He promoted planting of trees for shade, public gardens, and gardens growing medicinal plants. He prohibited animal sacrifices and setting fires in forests. Some people call him the first environmentalist. He sent missionaries to spread Buddhist teachings. At the same time, he was respectful of other religions and opposed to religious extremism. In one of his edicts, Ashoka made clear that those who disparage other religions are doing a disservice to their own religion. Interestingly, he even encouraged people of different religions and sects to learn about each other's religion and promote concord. He didn't discuss Buddhist doctrines except among Buddhists. All religions were welcome. He promoted dhamma to all. Dhamma in Pali or Dharma in Sanskrit includes much goodness, kindness, truthfulness, generosity, and purity. This reminds me of the fruit of the Spirit.

---

4. Armstrong, *Great Transformation*, 357–58.

Ashoka set up inscriptions on rocks and pillars promoting dharma and peace, communicating the common values of the religions of his time. Since literacy was uncommon in those days, gatherings of people were held at the sites of the inscriptions and the inscriptions were read to the people. Robert N. Bellah contrasts Ashoka's inscriptions to Persian king Darius' (549–486 BCE) inscriptions which glorified himself as the great king, King of kings and gave a long list of his conquests and violent destruction of revolts. Bellah remarks: "Ashoka's inscriptions are as devoted to peace as Darius' were to war."[5] We can notice Ashoka's conscience and Darius' superego! What is called "Ashoka's wheel" is part of an Ashoka's pillar. The wheel's twenty-four spokes represent twenty-four virtues; it became popular in India as a symbol in the Indian national flag.

Ashoka's grandfather, Chandragupta Maurya, had established the first empire in India covering most of the Indian subcontinent. His mentor Chanakya or Kautilya had written a manual of statecraft, *Arthasastra*, which taught that one of the duties of a king is conquering neighboring territories.[6] Chandragupta and his son, Ashoka's father Bindusara, had expanded the kingdom. I believe Ashoka's superego prompted him to invade Kalinga. So, his reaction with conscience is quite remarkable. According to H.G. Wells, Ashoka was the lone military monarch who rejected warfare after victory and the greatest of kings.

Relating to Ashoka, I had an interesting and sad experience some years ago. A bright young lady, a drug sales rep, was telling me about her recent exciting visit to Japan. Since she mentioned Buddhism, I told her about the great history of Ashoka. Her reaction was: "So bad he ended up in hell!" This was based on her belief that all non-Christians are destined to hell.

Now, the Russian attack on Ukraine is going on, showing the tragedy of inhumanity by the Russian President Putin and support by the Russian Orthodox Church leader Patriarch Kirill, apparently guided by their superegos. One time the news showed Pope Francis crying as he spoke of the Ukrainians' suffering. I think of his tears as a sign of conscience, not a sign of weakness, as some people think; strong men won't cry. In this situation, I think of Victor Hugo's words: "A dry eye goes with a dead soul."[7] Different spirituality in the same religion!

5. Bellah, *Religion*, 547.
6. Armstrong, *Great Transformation*, 358.
7. Hugo, *Les Misérables*, 93.

Beyond any theories about religious harmony, there is a concrete example of two thousand years of interfaith harmony that I will discuss next. Also, all the four world religions there overcame extremism, peacefully utilizing conscience.

A UNIQUE EXAMPLE OF RELIGIOUS HARMONY IN HISTORY

In a region of the Southwestern state of Kerala, India, Hindus, Christians, and Jews have lived harmoniously from the first century CE. Islam joined the group from the seventh century. This area includes Kochi or Cochin, the port city and commercial center of the state, Kodungallur, the ancient port, and a couple of towns and a village, all nearby. Around Kodungallur was Muziris, an international port famous for selling spices like black pepper. There was an ancient civilization from around 1000 BCE there. Pliny the Elder, the first century encyclopedist, described it as a place of rich merchandise.

There was trade between the Middle East and Kerala for many centuries before Christ, and there were Jewish settlements around Kodungallur. The Jewish settlements were probably a special attraction for the Apostle Thomas to travel to Kodungallur in 52 CE. Thomas emphasized Jesus's teaching of love. His followers were called St. Thomas Christians, or Nazranis (followers of Jesus of Nazareth). These Christians were isolated from the other Christians in the world until another Thomas, from Cana in Persia, came with seventy-two families and settled in Kodungallur with the help of the local king. This group called Knānāya Christians belonged to the East Syrian church, and through their friendship, the Nazranis joined the east Syrian Church, and came to be called Syrian Christians. Both these groups were friendly with the Jews and Hindus.

In the seventh century, Islam spread to Kodungallur. A Hindu king gave them a building to use as a mosque. Moslem women dressed modestly without covering their faces. The Muslims also got along well with the other religious groups. And all of them were grateful to the Hindu Kings who were good to them. In fact, the Cheraman Dynasty which ruled the state for about eight hundred years, is historically unique in having supported four world religions without using them for politics.

Among Hindus of Kerala, the caste system came gradually from northern states from the fifth century CE, and it became strong by the eighth century. According to the system, the priestly caste was at the top, royal caste next lower, and the labor caste as the lowest. There were also outcasts who cleaned human waste, sweeping, and the like. The upper castes discriminated against the lower castes, and especially the outcasts. The usual caste system in India involves a trading caste below the royals but not in Kerala, so Christians, Jews, and Muslims filled the gap as traders, and it further helped religious harmony. The caste system was unfair to the low castes and the outcasts who could not enter the temples, and they had to keep physical distance from the upper caste.

The greatest Hindu thinker Shankara grew up in Kalady, in Kerala, in the eighth century CE. He brought together six different groups of Hindus who worshiped six different gods. He clarified that these gods are partial manifestations of the one and only God or Brahman. He became the most important proponent of Vedanta doctrine which identifies the individual self or Atman with the ground of reality or Brahman. It means the innermost essence of each being (Atman) and the essence of the Brahman is the same: consciousness. Shankara advised people to identify deeply with the Atman rather than the temporary aspects of life.

SHANKARACHARYA AND QUANTUM PHYSICS

Quantum Physicist Erwin Schrödinger had supported Advaita philosophy. Shankaracharya had asserted "first, that Brahman, as chitta, or undifferentiated consciousness, pervades the entire universe: and two, that that consciousness is the ground from which the empirical, either physical objects, or the subtle mind, arises."[8] Max Planck, one of the founders of quantum physics, speaking on "The Nature of Matter" in Florence, Italy a few years before his death said: "All matter originates and exists only by virtue of a force which brings the particle of an atom to vibrate and holds this minute solar system of the atom together. We must assume behind this force the existence of a conscious and intelligent mind. The mind is the matrix of all matter."[9]

There have been conflicts about science among religious people who believe in creationism (literal belief in the Genesis description in the Bible) which contradicts evolution and the age of the universe that science teaches. Fundamentalists among Christians, Muslims, and Jews

8. Varma, *Adi Shankaracharya*, 175.
9. Varma, *Adi Shankaracharya*, 178.

tend to have distrust for science. Disbelief in science has crucial practical implications such as people who rejected COVID-19 vaccination and died from the disease. Conscience promotes deeper understanding in the spiritual and the scientific fields. The kind of concordance found in Shankara's and Max Planck's views about the ultimate reality is wonderful.

In the twentieth century, Hindu reformers like Sree Narayana Guru brought about a good transformation of the caste system through educating people about the unfairness, peaceful protests and setting up good examples like temples where anyone could pray. In one of the temples, he installed a mirror in the place of a deity signifying the crucial importance of developing one's inner self. The guru set up a social welfare organization which did play a great role in the uplift of the low social strata. He promoted education and agricultural reform. The guru's statement that, whichever one's religion, it suffices if the person is good, became famous. We can see that the guru attempted to stimulate the consciences of all, fostering reform and peaceful transformation of extremism of the caste system.

There is a living Hindu mystic Sri Mata Amritanandamayi, commonly known as Amma (mother), who has an ashram in Kodungallur and another in Kochi. She is known as the "hugging sage" and the "hugging saint" for hugging her devotees, an unusual practice for Hindu ascetics, especially for a woman. Amma has been doing a great deal of charitable work and spreading spirituality of love and compassion globally.

Nazranis (St. Thomas Christians) had good relationships with the other religious groups. As the Hindu caste system became strong by the eighth century, Nazranis were considered equal to the Brahmins. In fact, a Nazrani could undo the pollution caused to a Brahmin by an untouchable. Nazranis used to get their bishops from the East Syrian Church in Persia. These bishops only managed the religious duties; a Keralite Archdeacon was the Nazrani leader running the socio-political aspects. Local communities had representatives dealing with finances and social affairs.

In the sixteenth century, Portuguese Catholics came to India and established power in Kerala and Goa. They gained influence and power among the Nazranis. Within a few decades, they were able to bring the Nazranis under the Roman Catholic fold. The Catholic hierarchy pushed their dogmas and ideologies on the Nazranis. In 1599, the Catholic Archbishop of Goa, Menezes (a Portuguese man who was also second in civil authority under the Portuguese King) conducted a Synod to force Nazranis to follow Roman Catholic teachings. Menezes manipulated the synod to impose various changes on the Nazranis. These changes included compulsory celibacy of priests, condemnation of the Nazrani's belief that all good people could achieve heaven, insistence on belief in original sin and Catholic baptism as the only way to avoid hell, prohibition of priests eating with any non-Catholics, and the decree to observe holy festivals only among themselves. The Synod decreed against acknowledging the Patriarch of Babylon, who was previously the spiritual leader of the Nazranis. Matters came to a head when it was believed that Portuguese authorities prevented a bishop from Babylon from landing in Kochi in 1653.

A large group of Nazranis gathered, and, holding on to a rope tied to a cross, they swore they would not follow the Portuguese. Many participants of that oath subsequently formed a new church: the Malankara Syrian Orthodox Church. This church had further splits. The Roman Catholic Church gradually became more culturally sensitive, and, in 1896, the Pope gave the Nazrani Catholics their own bishops from local priests. That group has been called the Syro-Malabar rite of the Catholic Church. When the Second Vatican Council proclaimed that those who are not Catholics by no fault of their own and live by their consciences could be saved, it was a great relief for many Nazrani Catholics who had good non-Catholic friends. In 1953, when a memorial for St. Thomas was opened in Kodungallur, Muslims who were the majority in the area played a leading role in the celebrations. It is indicative of the religious harmony here. The Syro-Malabar church has branches in the US, UK and many other countries. Four members of this church have been canonized.

A unique way the Nazranis fought the Portuguese was by damaging Portuguese Spice trade by diverting the sale of black pepper to others instead of the Portuguese. Nazranis were the main producers of black pepper. Gandhi had used salt in his rebellion against the British. Even salt and pepper were used in nonviolent protests!

After the fall of the Second Temple in Jerusalem in 70 CE, a huge number of Jews (ten thousand according to Cochin Jews) migrated to Kodungallur. A Hindu king gave them some special privileges recorded on copper plates. Jews were treated well by the rulers, and they got along well with the other communities for centuries. It changed when the Portuguese Catholics, with their religious fanaticism and antisemitism, came to Kerala. The Portuguese attacked the Jewish settlements in 1504 and destroyed them completely in 1565. The Jews escaped to Cochin where the Hindu King gave them land to settle. Here, the Jew Town was built in 1567, and it still exists. And a synagogue was built the next year. The

Dutch defeated the Portuguese in 1663. The Dutch were tolerant of Jews and Jews got the opportunity to connect with Jews in Holland. The Portuguese had set fire to the Cochin synagogue and caused some damage, but it was repaired later.

There was an interesting Jewish mystic and poet who lived in Cochin, Nehemiah Mota, whose tomb indicates he died in 1516, and he was a Kabbalist. His tomb is a pilgrimage place for some Jews, Christians, Hindus, and Muslims. Pilgrims light candles and request help for their intentions. In recent times, a Christian family has been taking care of the tomb with support from a Jewish man in Israel. Malabari Jews,[10] (Jews who have been in Kerala or Malabar for centuries) celebrate his death anniversary on the first day of Hanukkah, the Festival of Lights. The Christian family told us that when they light a candle in front of Jesus's picture, they light one at Mota's tomb too. Note: Malabari Jews (Cochin) are the Jews who have been in Kerala earlier than the Paradesi (meaning foreign) Jews who migrated to Kerala from Europe escaping religious persecution in the sixteenth century.

Another illustrious Jewish person was Ezekiel Rahabi, a highly successful international shipping magnate in the eighteenth century. He was a diplomat for the Dutch, a friend of the Cochin kings, a religious man who supported the Jews and was friendly with the Christians, Hindus, and Muslims. He built synagogues and provided prayer books for his community. In 1766, he worked as a middleman and delivered several gifts from the Cochin king to Hyder Ali, a Muslim king of a neighboring state which prevented Ali from attacking Cochin. Appeasement may have its place.

There was some racism among the Jewish groups based on skin color. The Malabari Jews with darker skins were considered inferior by the Paradesi Jews who came from Europe in the sixteenth century escaping persecution. Malabari Jews had their own synagogues. The Paradesi Jews who attended the Paradesi synagogue of Cochin had white and brown members. The white ones discriminated against the brown ones who were supposed to have descended from former slaves. At the Paradesi synagogue there was an attorney, a brown Jew, Abraham Barak Salem, who had participated in the Gandhian freedom movement in India. He used the Gandhian approach of educating people about the unfairness and using protests to stimulate the conscience of the synagogue members

---

10. Wikipedia, "Cochin," paras. 1–33.

and overcome the discrimination. Salem was honored as the Jewish Gandhi. A street nearby is named after him.

When Israel was formed in 1948, most of the Jews moved to Israel, not because of any local discrimination but to join a large Jewish community. Jews from Kerala have built a Kerala style synagogue with two pulpits in Israel. Prayers are recited from the lower pulpit. The upper pulpit in front of the women's gallery is used for reading the weekly Torah portion on the Sabbath and holy days. A Kerala synagogue was reconstructed in the Israeli museum in Jerusalem. The two pulpits indicated the high status of women in the community. For Jews Kerala provided the longest happy experience anywhere.

Islam spread to Kodungallur through traders and later through Sufi teachers. Many Muslim traders married Kerala women which shows the freedom the women had. The Cheraman mosque of Kodungallur is the first mosque in the Indian subcontinent. As the caste system among Hindus became more intense, conversion to Islam became more attractive to low caste Hindus. In 2005, when Indian President Dr. Abdul Kalam, a Muslim, visited the Cheraman mosque; the authorities of the mosque invited the descendant of the ancient king who gifted the original building to formally receive the President. A great show of ongoing gratitude and religious harmony!

Kerala Muslims had Sufi influences from early on. In the thirteenth century, a Sufi missionary Shayk Farid came from Afghanistan and established a mosque in Kanjiramattom, twenty-five kilometers from Kochi. He emphasized education and charitable works. An annual festival is held at the mosque in January which attracts thousands of people, who receive a sweet porridge. There is provision at the mosque to practice the Hindu ritual of breaking coconut which is symbolic of breaking through the superficiality and defensiveness to reach the deeper nourishing spiritual core. Just consider the spiritual beauty, harmony and spiritual nourishment of a Hindu ritual practiced at a mosque. It was at this shrine that the sage Vavar received ultimate knowledge and was spiritually transformed. Vavar was a friend of the Hindu Lord Ayyappa. There is a mosque in Erumeli about one hundred and two kilometers from Kochi built in honor of Vavar. Thousands of Hindu pilgrims on their way to Iyyappa's shrine in Sabarimala (one hundred and five kilometers from Kochi) travel through Erumeli and pay respect to Vavar. A lot of them practice the ritual of breaking coconuts. This mosque has a permanent location for the practice of this ritual (the only such mosque in the world, I think).

Muslims in Kerala used to learn Arabic but there was resistance to promote secular education and education of women. In these matters, they were behind the other communities. There were conservative forces with their superegos holding on to tradition. But there were enlightened members who organized a group in the early twentieth century to stimulate people's consciences and spread secular education and women's rights. They gradually succeeded. Again, conscience overcame superego problems.

I believe that the influence of the mystics I have discussed has been an important reason for the unique harmony here. There is no Christian recognized as a mystic here. But I think St. Thomas was probably a mystic. He had emphasized love and goodness and was quite inclusive. His followers believed all good people could reach heaven. The view of S. Radhakrishnan on mysticism is: "While the different religions in their historical forms bind us to limited groups and militate against the development of loyalty to the world community, the mystics have always stood for the fellowship of humanity. They transcend the tyranny of names and the rivalry of creeds as well as the conflict of races and the strife of nations. *As the religion of spirit, mysticism avoids the two extremes of dogmatic affirmation and dogmatic denial.*"[11] (Italics added).

Regarding the religious harmony here, Prof. George Menachery, historian and the editor of the *Encyclopedia of the St. Thomas Christians of India*, observed the influence of Thirukkural ("Sacred couplets" originally in the South Indian language Tamil). Tamil is one of the classical languages of the world and it has existed from around 600 BCE. Thirukkural written by the sage Thiruvalluvar, probably in the early first century CE, is considered the greatest work of Tamil literature. In the introduction of the book in the translation by M. Rajaram, it is said that Leo Tolstoy took the concept of nonviolence from a German translation of this book. Mahatma Gandhi, who learned about it from Tolstoy, called it "a textbook of indispensable authority on moral life."[12] It consists of one thousand three hundred and thirty couplets arranged in three parts–Virtue, Wealth, and Love. Thiruvalluvar promoted conscience. He even used the word "conscience" in Tamil. The example of Kerala shows interfaith harmony and interfaith transformation using conscience.

---

11. Radhakrishnan, *Eastern*, ix.
12. Rajaram, *Thirukkural*, introduction.

A WAR SITUATION AND LESSONS FROM A HINDU EPIC

In the Hindu epic, *Mahabharata*, there are two sets of cousins–five good brothers (Pandavas) and one hundred bad brothers (Kauravas). The oldest of the Pandava brothers had a compulsion to play dice. He lost in the game, and, as a result, the Pandavas had to give their kingdom to the Kauravas to rule for thirteen years. After thirteen years, the Pandavas returned but the Kauravas refused to give the kingdom back.

Learning about this conflict, Lord Krishna, an incarnation of God, offered to mediate for a resolution to prevent war. The Pandavas offered to settle for five districts. When it was rejected, they offered for five villages and upon rejection, they even offered for five plots of land, but the Kauravas refused to give any land. The good brothers were willing to make sacrifices for peace instead of the sacrifices involved in going to war, but the stubborn superegos of the bad brothers disagreed. Then Lord Krishna himself tried to dissuade a strong fighter Karna (who was biologically a Pandava but grew up with the Kauravas) from his plan to fight for the Kauravas by revealing his real identity, but Karna refused to change. Karna had another reason for his support for Kauravas because he wished to compete with Arjuna, the best archer of the Pandavas. This indicates how some people make the wrong choice from loyalty to a group or a person and for personal ambition disregarding their consciences.

After such intense efforts for peace failed, the Pandavas declared war. Even then, as the battle was about to start, Arjuna hesitated to fight his kith and kin. Krishna provided Arjuna a perspective on life, death, reincarnation, the individual Self, and the supreme Self, as well as Self-realization through meditation, or pursuit of wisdom or selfless work or devotion (love) to God. Krishna discussed duty and karma. And finally, Krishna shows Arjuna a vision of the universe and Krishna as God. Then Arjuna was encouraged to do his duty as a warrior unselfishly keeping God in mind.[13]

Religious support of war reminds us of Mark Twain's *The War Prayer* in which he describes the actions of an old man at a church during a war time. The excitement of war and the holy fire of patriotism were energizing people. Young volunteers in uniforms were marching daily and the proud families cheered them on. The Sunday before the battalion would leave for the front, the young men with their dreams of military adventure and their families sat proudly at Church. There was a reading

---

13. Krishnamacharya, *Mahabharata*, 31–39.

from a war chapter from the Old Testament, then some music followed by a prayer by the minister asking God's help to protect the soldiers and give them victory. As the minister was speaking, an older man walked up and replaced the minister. The old man said he is bringing them a message from God for them to consider the broad implications of their prayer for causing immense suffering to the enemy. The people thought the man was a lunatic.[14] Superego over conscience!

BEWARE OF AND BE AWARE OF WAR

Historian Margaret MacMillan ends her book, *War: How Conflict Shaped Us*, with the advice: "We must, more than ever, think about war."[15] Before the advice she gives the reason: "With new and terrifying weapons, the growing importance of artificial intelligence, automated killing machines and cyber war, we face the prospect of the end of humanity itself. It is not the time to avert our eyes from something we may find abhorrent."[16] Earlier, she observes: "And the factors that produce war—greed, fear, ideology—will continue to work among us as they always have."[17] An estimated two million people have died from war between 1989 and 2017 and fifty-two million have been displaced from 1945.

MacMillan discusses the so-called "Thucydides Trap", named after the Greek historian Thucydides who wrote a classic work on the Peloponnesian War. He had said: "The strong do what they can and the weak suffer what they must." Thucydides had written about how the growth of Athens' power caused a lot of fear in Sparta which led to war. A rule based on it states that when an established power is threatened by the rising of another power, war is likely the Thucydides Trap. Experts differ on this idea. There is speculation that the rise of Chinese power might cause a war to occur between China and the US.

What is needed is not obsessing about war or finding thrilling war stories or looking for partisan arguments. What we need is to have a broad and balanced perspective on the important factors causing wars and ways to prevent them. Being guided by conscience would help tremendously.

---

14. Wikipedia, "War Prayer," para. 1.
15. Macmillan, *War*, 272.
16. Macmillan, *War*, 272.
17. Macmillan, *War*, 267.

War is a form of organized superego extremism at least on one side or many sides. The underlying factor can be any human need or many needs.

THE AVOIDABLE WAR BY KEVIN RUDD

In this very insightful and pragmatic book, Kevin Rudd explores the dangers of catastrophic conflict between the US and Xi Jinping's China and ways to avoid it. Rudd is uniquely qualified to write such a book because he was foreign minister and prime minister of Australia and also, he has lived in many Chinese cities as a diplomat and lived in the US for many years. Moreover, he had studied Mandarin Chinese and classical and modern Chinese history, and he is well versed in American history. His theme is that …"our best chance of avoiding war is to better understand the other side's strategic thinking and to conceptualize a world where both the US and China are able to competitively coexist, even if in a state of continuing rivalry reinforced by mutual deterrence."[18] Rudd says that Xi changed China's worldview by enhancing the party's Marxist-Leninist foundations and Chinese nationalism and national ambitions.

In understanding Xi Jinping's worldview, Rudd gives ten concentric circles of interest: from maintaining the power of Xi and the Communist Party, economic prosperity and sustainability to the Belt and Road initiative, increasing influence over developing countries, modifying the rule-based world order, and securing China's maritime periphery in the Western pacific.

Rudd provides "managed strategic competition" as the way to prevent war between the US and China. He points out that the US and the Soviet Union put mechanisms and procedures to prevent war after the Cuban Missile Crisis. What Rudd proposes is for the US and China to have a mutually agreed framework of their diplomatic and military activities to maximize stability and avoid escalation of tensions leading to crisis. Within agreed parameters both countries would have freedom for competition and collaboration. The two countries could compete to win the hearts and minds of people to their differing ideologies. Rudd observes: "The reality is that in this new age of strategic competition between China and the United States, there are, as a matter of logic, only two alternatives: managed competition, with some rules of the road and some prospect of perceiving the peace, or unmanaged competition, with

---

18. Rudd, *Avoidable*, 18.

the loss of all strategic guardrails and the growing risk of crisis, conflict, or war."[19] Discussing the consequences of a regional war between the US and China, Rudd quotes the wise words of Sun Tzu in *The Art of War*. "The art of war is of vital importance to the State. It is a matter of life and death, a road either to safety or ruin." With all the weapons of mass destruction the two countries possess, a war between them could lead to the ruin not only of both of the countries but to the ultimate ruin of the human race itself.

NONVIOLENT CONFLICT RESOLUTION

In *Why Civil Resistance Works*, Erica Chenoweth and Maria J. Stephan analyze three hundred and twenty-three campaigns between 1900 and 2006, and they compare and contrast the various aspects of nonviolent and violent campaigns. They write: "The most striking finding is that between 1900 and 2006, nonviolent resistance campaigns were nearly twice as likely to achieve full or partial success as their violent counterparts."[20] They found that the frequency and the rate of success of nonviolent campaigns have increased over the time from 1900.

Their findings showed participation in nonviolent campaigns was much easier because it involved much less physical risk and it lacked worries whether the methods used justify the ends. Nonviolent campaigns can have a festive spirit too. The large numbers and varieties of people that nonviolent campaigns can attract help them to be more successful. Violent campaigns require people physically able and willing to fight. But nonviolent campaigns can involve various age groups and people who are not physically strong or unwilling to engage in physical fights. And the larger the group, the bigger their supporters. There is power in numbers. Also, nonviolent campaign success leads to long term benefits for societies involved. Even where violent insurgencies succeed, it is much less likely that they will become peaceful democracies. I think nonviolence is the way of conscience in general.

In an article "The Future of Nonviolent Resistance" in *The Journal of Democracy* in July 2020, Chenoweth observes that in the past one hundred and twenty years, about 26 percent of violent and 51 percent nonviolent campaigns have succeeded. She points out that the widespread view that

---

19. Rudd, *Avoidable*, 395.
20. Chenoweth and Stephan, *Why*, 7.

only violent action is strong is a very mistaken notion. Success rates for nonviolent campaigns had been above 40 percent up to 65 percent in the 1960s. Since 2010, the rate has declined to 34 percent for nonviolent and a poor 8 percent for violent campaigns. There are several reasons for the decline: (1) less people participating. The average nonviolent campaign in the 1980s was 2 percent of the population of the country where it was happening. And in 1990, the rate was up to 2.7 percent. But since 2010, the rate has been 1.3 percent at peak. (2) Excessive dependence on mass demonstrations and neglecting civil disobedience techniques like strikes which could put more pressure on the powers who need to be changed. (3) While digital organizing is easier to do, it is also easier for the ones in power on the opposite side to monitor. (4) Embracing or tolerating violent fringes has become increasingly problematic. The share of nonviolent movements with violent fringes was 30–35 percent from 1970–2010 but it has grown to over 50 percent since then. This causes confusion and gives opponents of the movement the opportunity to claim that the movement is basically violent, a false image.[21]

Gandhi's nonviolent freedom movement was going strong in 1922 until a very violent incident occurred in a place called Chauri Chaura. A clash between protesters and police resulted in a crowd setting fire to a police station causing the death of twenty-two policemen. It took two days for the news to reach Gandhi. He stopped the mass movement in spite of objections by many of his associates. When the government held a case against many who caused the attack, Gandhi was also tried. Gandhi asked the judge to give him the maximum sentence he deserved. He blamed himself for not training his followers sufficiently. He was sentenced for six years but was freed after two years for good behavior. Gandhi wrote his *Autobiography* during his jail term. Then, in 1930, Gandhi restarted the civil disobedience movement for the salt march. Although a lot of people wanted to join the march, he selected people he knew to be disciplined, knowing them personally or people sent by reliable organizations from different states. He was vigilant about keeping the movement nonviolent.

In *Waging a Good War,* Thomas E. Ricks addresses how Martin Luther King Jr. and his associates took care to keep the civil rights movement peaceful and well-disciplined. They used the ideas in Gandhi's disciple, Richard Gregg's book on training for nonviolent activism. James Lawson,

---

21. Chenoweth, "Future," 69–84.

who had spent time in India learning Gandhi's philosophy and techniques, joined King's movement and became an effective trainer. Ricks compares the civil rights movement to military training and identifying potential new leaders. Lawson held workshops explaining the theory and practice of nonviolence, giving an overview of religion and philosophy connected with justice, and specific resistance movements like the ones by American Abolitionists, resistance against Nazis, and Gandhi's movement. In the end, he would emphasize Jesus's teaching to turn the other cheek. The training for nonviolent campaigns included role playing, rehearsing, and observers watching the volunteers' performances. Role-playing helped to control the fight or flight response. The observers would report to leaders like Lawson so that the leaders could refine the campaigns. Congressman John Lewis wrote demonstration rules to be followed, including "don't strike back" and "be always courteous." Apart from the tactics, being truthful was very important. After each action, the participants would gather and discuss how the action went and what could be done better. The volunteers sang freedom songs, and they had marshals to check whether the activities were going well.[22]

Information in Wikipedia shows that a series of protests and unrest after George Floyd was killed by a police officer were mostly peaceful. An estimated 93 percent–96.3 percent of demonstrations were peaceful, not causing property damage or injury to people or vandalism. But police had made arrests in 5 percent of the protest events. Protest events associated with vandalism or property damage were 3.7 percent. And real protesters or bystanders injured or killed were 1.6 percent.[23] But the impression given by some media personalities has been that the movements were far more destructive. Such distortion is a tragedy and a shame, showing the lack of conscience. So, it is crucial for peace movements to be tightly disciplined and try hard to provide the public with the true picture. Harassing opponents in restaurants or protesting in front of their homes causes anger or even hate rather than stimulating conscience.

LOVE OR WAR—LESSONS FROM OUR COUSINS

Our closest animal relatives, chimpanzees and bonobos, could stimulate our reflections on relationships. We humans share ninety-nine percent

22. Ricks, *Waging*, 1–36.
23. Wikipedia, "George," paras. 1–5.

of our DNA with chimpanzees and baboons. Chimpanzees live in male dominated groups, and these groups are very attached to their territories, and tend to wage organized conflict on other chimpanzee groups. In raiding others, they kill males, females, and infants. They even eat the infants of other groups. They cooperate to hunt monkeys. Also, they tend to use tools. Bonobos are female dominated. They are much more peaceful and sexually active than chimpanzees. They have sex with the opposite sex as well as same sex. When strange bonobos meet, they watch for a while then move towards each other slowly and socialize, embracing, sharing food, grooming, and pleasuring. When they find new sources of food, they celebrate by communal sexual activity. They use sex for conflict resolution and celebration of the resolution. The clitoris of the female bonobo is thrice the size of its human equivalent, and the females practice genital rubbing with other females. Occasionally, bonobos engage in sex face-to-face. Bonobos live in the south side of the river Congo where food is abundant, but the chimpanzees live in the northern part of the same river where food is rather scarce. One theory is that adaptation to this difference in food source may have led to the difference between bonobos and chimpanzees.

I have noticed cultural conditioning working through superego making people aggressive and using the guidance of conscience making people more peaceful. Religious influence can enhance aggression or peace depending on whether the religion promotes aggressive ideals through superego or peaceful choices by conscience. Since frustration could stimulate aggression, peaceful release of frustration is quite useful. Relaxation techniques and exercises are very useful. So is humor. Sexual release guided by conscience and human standards, not bonobo standards, could be a strong source of stress release.

AN ANTHROPOLOGICAL VIEW BEYOND WAR

Opposed to the idea that there have always been wars, Anthropologist Professor Douglas Fry in his book, *Beyond War,* says: "The earliest unambiguous evidence of warfare dates from less than ten thousand years ago, and war becomes more common with the rise of the state several millennia later. After reviewing the archeological record, Leslie Sponsel reaches the conclusion that "during the hunter-gatherer stage of cultural evolution, which dominated ninety-nine percent of human existence on the planet...lack of archeological evidence for warfare suggests that it *was rare or absent for most of human history*."[24]

Fry discusses conflict management among the Aboriginals in Australia. Among the Aboriginals, the most serious individual disputes were caused by "corpse trouble" or woman trouble." They believe that most deaths were caused by sorcery, and the death has to be avenged; hence the term "corpse trouble." Woman trouble is caused by jealousy, adultery, elopement, and the like. Instead of revenge killing, the Aboriginals have found better alternatives to deal with these troubles. Conflict management measures, such as meetings involving accusers and defenders with elders to find solutions, compensation for damages, public venting of feelings, participation in joint ceremonies or rituals, and punishing wrongdoers with a nonlethal wound with a spear to the thigh. In an interesting approach Fry calls "a wife for a life" the accused murderer's clan give a woman from their clan as a wife to a man in the dead person's clan, thus avoiding a revenge expedition. Another alternative for revenge killing is a member of the dead person's clan circumcising a youth from the accused killer's clan. (A boy had to have an initiation including circumcision to become a man.) Notice the various ways different people meet the cultural ideal of revenge without violence.

Fry emphasizes peace-enhancing values, beliefs, attitudes and actions. Interdependence, cross cutting ties of different groups and working together to deal with the climate crisis and other problems faced by humanity. The COVID-19 pandemic has shown the interdependence of humanity and the need for cooperation among all groups.

PEACE PROMOTION: TWO CHRISTIAN EXAMPLES

One of the very memorable incidents at the 2023 Parliament of the World's Religions in Chicago was Shane Claiborne showing a trowel made from the metal melted down from a gun—a powerful reminder of the biblical teaching to beat swords into plowshares! Claiborne is co-founder of Red Letter Christians alongside Pastor Tony Campolo, and their premise is to focus on following Jesus's teachings. Claiborne, in his book *Rethinking Life: Embracing the Sacredness of Every Person*, emphasizes deep reflection on important Christian teachings such as love and peace. Life with its innumerable varieties is good and wonderful, and the creator God is

---

24. Fry, *Beyond*, 63.

glorious. Working with Mother Teresa in the 1990s impressed on him the understanding that every person is made in the image of God, Jesus is the great and wonderful champion of life, and Jesus is the lens through which we can understand the Bible. Jesus came to expand the law with love. Jesus promoted nonviolence. For example, when Jesus was with the high priest and Peter drew his sword and cut off the right ear of the priest's slave, Jesus told Peter to put back his sword in the sheath (John 18:10–11). In the first three hundred years, Christianity built a strong foundation of a force for life. It was nonviolent.

Claiborne had tried hard, in vain, to find any Christian writing before Constantine which supported killing under any circumstance. He quotes many great Christian thinkers who taught against killing any person. Even Christians serving in the military could not kill; they could do other activities like infrastructure work. Then there were cracks in the foundation slowly with Constantine adopting Christianity, and just war theory and so on that I have discussed in chapter four. Claiborne approaches repairing the foundation by being a truth teller, practicing proximity, being a force for life, protestifying, and being part of giving birth to a better world.

Claiborne gives many sad examples of violence by Christians in power. Theodosius who became emperor after Constantine made Christianity the official religion of the Roman Empire. He incited mob violence against pagans. A brutal man, he slaughtered thousands of people including seven thousand people in three hours on one occasion. Francis of Assisi had pleaded with Cardinal Pelagius Galvani, a crusader, to stop fighting but Pelagius continued killing Muslims in the name of Christ. Regarding hate, Claiborne says: "Over the course of history, and into the present, the church has actually theologized prejudice and hatred, sometimes even to the point of supporting genocide, which is what happened in Nazi Germany."[25] Towards the end of his book, he says: "Even as the age in which we live is filled with death, anxiety, and grief, it is also a time that is pregnant with hope and the promise of new life."[26] I would add, beware of superego; use conscience. Christians who violate the spirit of Jesus's teaching against killing are also acting against the nonviolent spirit of the Axial Age. As the title of Claiborne's book, *Rethinking Life*,

---

25. Claiborne, *Rethinking*, 126.
26. Claiborne, *Rethinking*, 275.

suggests, rethink life, reflect, use conscience (act using reason, respect for truth, the Golden Rule, and moderation).

Jim Wallis, Georgetown University's Bishop Desmond Tutu Chair in Faith and Justice, addresses three big concerns in the US: rejecting Christian Nationalism, reclaiming true faith and re-founding democracy. In his book *The False White Christian Gospel,* Wallis recounts how he grew up in a racially divided Detroit and he crossed the color lines from his younger days and experienced the problems of white supremacy that the black community was experiencing. He says: "Crossing the color line for democracy is the beginning of the journey to repent, repair, and redeem America's original sin for white people, and especially for White Christians."[27] I would add that it would be the way to use conscience. He also says: "When we see a *civic promotion of fear, hate, and violence as the trajectory of our* politics, we need a *civic faith of love, healing, and hope* to defeat it."[28] And he observes: *"Bad religion provides easy and self-serving certainty; good religion leads us to deeper reflection. And that is where our freedom lies."* [29] He calls white Christian nationalism a fake Christianity. Jesus was a universalist. From the beginning of this nation white nationalism had co-opted Christianity. A very important meeting of younger and older evangelical leaders in Chicago in 1973 had authored a declaration which admitted social and political injustices evangelicals were committing and called for repentance and reform. But many evangelicals went in a different direction and by 1980, the religious right was shaped by the far-right Republican political operatives.

Wallis argues that the US is at a "Kairos time," a Biblical term meaning a perfect time to promote a multiracial democracy. He warns that democracy could die at the ballot box. Wallis is one of the founders of a new network, Faiths United to Save Democracy (FUSD) which is multiracial, multifaith, and multigenerational. I believe this group would find information about conscience and the Axial Age very useful for reinforcing their identity and ideology. White supremacy is a superego problem.

---

27. Wallis, *False,* 11.
28. Wallis, *False,* 15.
29. Wallis, *False,* 114.

INNER PEACE AND PEACE WITH OTHERS

Inner peace depends on harmony among conscience, superego, and human needs. When each of these parts does its part well, there is harmony. When the superego is too critical in relationship to oneself, it causes unhealthy guilt or shame and anxiety from the inner conflict. In one such case, the man in his thirties used to have much anxiety and low self-esteem from harsh judgment of himself although he was really doing what he could in his work and relationships. The anxiety and low self-esteem had caused limitations in functioning and harsh criticism of it caused the vicious cycle of his problems to keep going. Medications for anxiety had some benefits but the overall problems continued until he gained insight into his harsh superego and learned to balance it with his conscience.

On the other side of the harsh and rigid superego—in the case of a loose superego and weak conscience—the people showed low interest and effort in making better use of their potential to function in life. An example is Chip (fake name), a high-school graduate in his twenties who was shy and socially isolated. He worked in a store thirty hours a week just enough to keep health insurance. His parents had many conflicts, and they did not put any significant effort into actively encouraging him to change, probably because they themselves were rather passive and isolated. When he sought help for anxiety, three things were done which made a big difference in his life. One, he was actively encouraged to reflect on his human needs and the changes he could make to meet the needs better. Two, he was taught a meditation technique and encouraged to join a meditation group. Three, he was taught about conscience and superego and how to use these guides to make good choices actively. As he followed these, his anxiety cleared, and he worked more and started socializing and pursuing higher education. He developed a sense of responsibility to utilize his potential and some healthy guilt if he acted irresponsibly.

Forgiveness and reconciliation are very important in human relationships. Conflicts and hurts are part of human lives. Conscience promotes forgiveness and reconciliation. Forgiveness is somewhat like relieving constipation—in this case, emotional constipation. Holding on to all the negative feelings about the hurt is common but it does not help. But the one who feels victimized may want an apology or compensation from the other party and if the other party would do it, then matters could be solved. Harsh and rigid superego judgment of others on the part of either or both parties would make negative reactions worse. Many people hold on to the negative feelings as a protection against getting hurt by the other person again. Such protection is at the expense of love and growth especially if the unforgiving person does not keep open the possibility of change on the part of the other. Understanding the human condition, the method in our madness, the fluctuation of our needs and the way we go about dealing with our needs. With this kind of understanding, parents help the first-born child to deal with jealousy and rivalry when a second child is born. Conscience also would prompt cooperation with third parties trying to negotiate or reduce the conflicts between two parties. So, peace is missing that otherwise could facilitate personal and relational growth.

Mary hurt her friend Sally and their friendship ended. Sally built her emotional wall against Mary. Mary was going through a rough time in her life when she hurt Sally. Mary had shown a lot of regret about the broken relationship and wished to heal the relationship. Sally's husband was a very defensive person who reinforced Sally's defensiveness. The two old friends would have benefitted business-wise and family relationship wise. In therapy for depression, Sally realized that Mary's deep regret about the break-up and strong wish to reconcile were strong signs of her change. So, Sally could feel reasonable confidence to try reconciliation. Her husband was skeptical, but he went along with their reconciliation, and it worked.

While forgiveness can be done by the person who is hurt by himself or herself, reconciliation needs both parties to work on this solution. Psychological and spiritual perspectives help tremendously in understanding conflicts and use conscience to deal with it realistically and compassionately. Psychological and spiritual perspectives take into account the human condition. With such a perspective, one could give some slack for somebody's weak point. Somebody with a harsh superego could take even a small hurt very seriously and hold on to it. It is important to cooperate with a third party such as a professional or a family member or a common friend attempting to bring about reconciliation. Attacking the third party is unconscionable.

As we work on reconciliation, doing our best, we can apply the spirit of the serenity prayer by focusing on changing what can be changed, accepting what cannot be changed and experiencing peace. But it is crucial to recognize that so long as a person is alive and functioning, the person is capable of changing. Forgiving and forgetting can be complex and complicated. A book I often recommend is *Forgive and Forget* by Lewis B. Smedes.[30] In my experience, instead of forgetting, what happens when we forgive is a transformed memory.

In general, people of conscience strive for cooperative and creative attitudes and approaches. Depending on the particular superego conditioning people guided by superego may have an adversarial or even antagonistic spirit and approach. It is very useful to notice this tendency in oneself and others so that one can adjust to be the best in oneself and effective with others. One or the greatest examples of Gandhi and King in their nonviolent struggles was the use of creative approach in highly adversarial and even antagonistic situations. That was the triumph of conscience. I believe communities which are genuinely spiritually oriented would promote a cooperative and creative spirit rather than an adversarial and antagonist spirit. This would reflect in high levels of litigation and violence, rather than peaceful and mutually respectful resolution.

COSTA RICA, A COUNTRY WITHOUT MILITARY

I recall a joke about Pakistan as a military with a country. It is not a joke but an exciting truth that the beautiful country Costa Rica has been without a military since October 11, 1949. Immediately after an armed conflict, Costa Rica became the first country in the world to abolish the army. This admirable country has put the savings from not having a military into education, healthcare, and social safety net and so, Costa Rica ranks high in these aspects. According to the World Happiness index, it ranked twelfth in the world and first in Latin America. I have found the ecotourism of the country very impressive. I have personally experienced the wonderful beauty of nature and the harmony of people. There are thirty-six countries listed as countries without a military. Costa Rica's police force monitors borders and handles drug trafficking issues. And the country has alliances with countries like the US for assistance if and when needed.

"Peace through strength" is a nice saying but what is strength? Is Costa Rica stronger or weaker than its neighbors? When a country spends resources on education, healthcare, environmental protection, economic vitality, and internal unity, isn't it promoting physical, emotional and spiritual strength? Isn't it consistent with conscience? Is Pax

30. Smedes, *Forgive*, 1–194.

Romana, which depended largely on military force, an ideal for a country in our modern times?

The total military spending in the world in 2022 was two thousand two hundred and forty billion dollars. The US expense was eighty hundred and seventy-seven billion dollars.[31] I view these as a reflection of the spiritual poverty in the human race. Costa Rica is a great example, an inspiration for peace, prosperity and health. While most other countries at this stage in history may be unable to abandon the military, I wonder when and how humanity would utilize the blessings of the Axial Age and overcome the pre-Axial Age type of barbarism, wickedness and spiritual poverty.

PARLIAMENT OF THE WORLD'S RELIGIONS

I recall the words of Catholic theologian Hans Kung at the Parliament of the World's Religions in 1993 in Chicago: "No peace among the nations without peace among the religions." Kung was the leader of the religious experts who formulated the "Global Ethic," which was declared at the 1993 Parliament. Kung chose the word ethic to indicate "ethos," a way of life guided by moral principles which could promote harmonious living together. He based it on the Golden Rule and the principle of humane treatment of all people. The Global Ethic has been reinforced at each of the subsequent Conventions of the Parliament of the World's Religions.

The world's premier interfaith convening organization promotes interreligious harmony. They show a commitment to peace, justice, and sustainability. They are inclusive and respectful of the different beliefs, traditions, and values of various religious groups. Having participated in many Parliaments, I have experienced the wonderful diversity and deep harmony at the conferences. I could listen to highly intellectual panels on spiritually important issues, scholarly lectures by very respected speakers, enchanting music, amazing rituals like Sufi dance, opportunities to personally meet many leading figures in the religious and related fields, share interests with a vast variety of fellow participants, and share in the free vegetarian lunch provided by the Sikhs. The atmosphere of seven to nine thousand or so people belonging to various seventy or so countries has been exciting.

---

31. Stockholm International Peace Research Institute, "World," 1–12.

In 1893, the city of Chicago held a World's Fair, World Columbian Exposition. In connection with the fair, several smaller conferences were held. And one such conference was the World's Parliament of Religions. It ran from September 11 through September 27 and was the first interfaith gathering. Representatives of many religions participated. The participation of the Hindu monk Swami Vivekananda has been well-known in India.

The second Parliament was in 1993 in Chicago. Around eight thousand people from different parts of the world took part. Hans Kung presented the document "Towards a Global Ethic: An Initial Declaration" and it was endorsed by many religious and spiritual leaders. A memorial was held in honor of Bede Griffiths and Raimon Panikkar spoke of Griffiths as a trailblazer of interfaith spirituality. Panikkar, a Catholic priest and religious scholar whose father was a Hindu from India and his mother a Catholic from Spain, was a great religious scholar and promoter of Interfaith understanding and harmony. I recall a pithy quote from Panikkar in his obituary: "When I left Europe for India, I left as a Christian. In India, I realized I am a Hindu, and I returned to Europe as a Buddhist, never ceasing to be a Christian."[32] The Dalai Lama spoke on the closing day. With his gentle sense of humor, he encouraged limiting the number of children we bring into the world, saying every birth is precious according to Buddhism but we already have too many precious people. So, it is okay to limit births non-violently.

The Declaration of a Global Ethic states the world is in agony and it need not be. It declares the interdependence of the community of living beings, the individual responsibility for our actions, living by the Golden Rule, commitment to non-violence, justice and peace, and nature-friendly lives. We must avoid prejudice and hatred. We must move beyond the greed for power, prestige and consumption. These are the ways of living by one's conscience.

There have been seven additional Parliaments. The 2021 gathering was online because of the pandemic. Most of them were held in different cities: 1999 in Cape Town, 2004 in Barcelona, 2009 in Melbourne, 2015 in Salt Lake City, Utah, and 2018 in Toronto. The latest Parliament was held in August 2023 in Chicago. Rev. Ray Wade, Rev. Kevin Higgs, and I gave a presentation on Christian Nonviolence. Besides these elaborate

---

32. Fredericks, "At the Limits," 1–10.

international conferences, they encourage interfaith activities frequently in various parts of different countries.

During the 2015 Parliament, my son and I showed my documentary *The World's Most Enlightening Region,* about religious harmony in Kerala, India which can be viewed on YouTube. I have felt very good about the parliaments I attended. Rev. Kevin Higgs, Rev. Ray Wade and I gave a presentation on Christian Nonviolence at the 2023 Parliament in Chicago.

UNITED NATIONS

The United Nations, which was founded in 1945 in the aftermath of World War II, has provided life-saving help to millions of people affected by natural disasters, political conflicts, and diseases. The United Nations Children's Fund, World Food Program, World Health Organization, and the U.N. Refugee Agency have been providing vital assistance to millions. It helped to keep the cold war cold. The U.N. has been a vital forum for diplomatic efforts among various countries in dealing with the climate crisis and issues of food insecurity. The Universal Declaration of Human Rights by the U.N. has been one of the most significant codifications of human rights. Many of the U.N. agencies like the International Atomic Energy Agency are doing crucial work for safety. The U.N. has one hundred and ninety-three member countries now. Conscience would support the efforts to promote peace and help the needy but selfish superegos would oppose what doesn't suit their selfishness.

MEDIATIONS AND PEACE TREATIES

Historically the first peace treaty, the Kadesh Peace Treaty in 1269 BCE, was signed by Harrusi III, King of the Hittites and Ramses, an Egyptian Pharaoh after over two centuries of fighting. The treaty of Paris was signed in 1815 after the defeat of Napoleon. The treaty of Versailles ended the First World War in 1919. The Paris Peace treaties in 1947 were between the Allied Powers and the five defeated European countries. The Treaty of San Francisco in 1962 ended WWII between Japan and the Allied Powers.

A HIGHLY INSTRUCTIVE STORY OF PRESIDENT JIMMY CARTER'S LIFE

In 1978, President Jimmy Carter had a long discussion at Camp David separately with Anwar Sadat of Egypt and Menachem Begin of Israel. On day eleven, they had a breakdown connected with a Jewish settlement in the Sinai desert. Begin and Sadat had decided to leave. Begin had asked Carter to give him some signed photographs of the three of them for his grandchildren. Carter's secretary had brought him eight photographs. He wrote "with Love" to each of Begin's three grandchildren and gave it to Begin. As Begin noticed the names of his grandchildren, he became tearful and seeing it Carter cried too. Then Begin agreed to try the peace effort one more time and they were able to reach an agreement.[33] A genuinely Christian Carter, a man of conscience, was able to touch Begin's heart and, I believe, his conscience.

THE ABRAHAMIC ACCORDS IN 2020

These are the accords between Israel and several other countries (UAE, Bahrain, Sudan, and Morocco) under the mediation of President Donald Trump. Hopefully, his mediation efforts for peace between Ukraine and Russia and between Israel and Hamas will succeed.

A Google search about the major religions of the world and their populations showed the following:

(1) Christianity with estimated 31.6 percent population, (2) Islam with estimated 25.8 percent, (3) Hinduism with estimated 15 percent, and estimated 14.4 percent are religiously unaffiliated. If billions of religious people and their leaders use their consciences to promote peace, this world would be a far better place with much more peace and happiness. There is plenty of religion. What is lacking is authentic spirituality with conscience.

---

33. CNBC, "Photographs," paras. 1–7.

Chapter Seven

Patience

Adopt the pace of nature: her secret is patience. – Ralph Waldo Emerson[34]

I think and think for months and years. Ninety-nine times, the conclusion is false. The hundredth time I am right. –Albert Einstein[35]

THE DICTIONARY DEFINITION OF patience is "the capacity to accept or tolerate delay, trouble, or suffering without getting angry or upset." In this chapter, I will discuss how I learned patience, and we will explore several religious teachings on patience, issues of impatience and the role of conscience and superego in relation to patience. Patience and persistence go hand in hand and applying them in our choices guided by conscience in life makes us strong and happy. But superegos can misguide us, and we have to watch against it.

As a child, I learned patience from growing crotons (decorative tropical plants with colorful leaves). I had noticed my older cousin growing a new croton plant by cutting a branch, putting it in soil and watering it every couple of days. He had told me that new roots would come on the branch in the soil and that is how it becomes a new plant. I followed my cousin's instructions except I added another step. I pulled up the plant to see if the roots were coming. While my cousin's plants grew, mine died. I

---

34. Emerson, *Nature*, 1.
35. Einstein, "Theory," 16.

learned from him that I should have patiently waited and not pulled out the branch and in time saw new leaves coming, leaving the roots alone. In my next attempt to grow croton, I was patient, and it worked.

Emerson's advice to adopt the pace of nature is wise. The beautiful fruit ackee which grows well in Jamaica is poisonous when it is unripe. Knowing how long it takes fruits to ripen helps growers to wait patiently. There is a saying in South India about cooked elephant yam: can't you wait until it has cooled to eat this yam which was under the ground for six months? The quality of fruits and vegetables harvested prematurely is low. At the same time, fruits and vegetables are not their best if they are overripe. We can remember Shakespeare's dictum: "ripeness is all."

Several statements in the Bible are very relevant regarding patience. See the following examples.

> "Whenever you face trials of any kind, consider it nothing but joy, because you know that the testing of your faith produces endurance; and let endurance have its full effect, so that you may be mature and complete, lacking in nothing." (Jas 1:2–4)

> "Blessed is anyone who endures temptation. Such a one has stood the test and will receive the crown of life that the Lord has promised to those who love him. No one, when tempted, should say, "I am being tempted by God"; for God cannot be tempted by evil and he himself tempts no one. But one is tempted by one's own desire, being lured and enticed by it; then, when that desire has conceived, it gives birth to sin, and that sin, when it is fully grown, gives birth to death."
> (Jas 1:12–15)

> "... knowing that suffering produces endurance, and endurance produces character, and character produces hope. And hope does not disappoint us, because God's love has been poured into our hearts through the Holy Spirit that has been given to us." (Rom 5:3–5)

In the Parable of the Sower, Jesus talked about a sower who went out and sowed the seeds. Some seeds fell on the path and were trampled on, and birds ate them. Some fell on the rock and as they grew withered for lack of moisture. Some fell among thorns, and as they grew the thorns also grew and choked them. Some fell into good soil, and they grew and produced a hundred-fold. The seed is the word of God. The seeds which fell on the path represent those who have heard the words, but they let the devil come and take away the seeds. The seeds which fell on the rock stand for people who believe only for a short time and they fall away when they are tested because they don't develop roots. Those which fell among thorns are people who hear the word but as they go on they are choked by the cares and ways of the world and their fruits do not mature. "But as for those in the good soil, these are the ones who, when they hear the word, hold it in an honest and good heart, and bear fruit with patient endurance." (Luke 8:15)

We have to choose good ideas and ideals and nurture them.

VIEWS ON PATIENCE IN NON-CHRISTIAN RELIGIONS

Patience is a great virtue in Buddhism. The Jataka Tales are ancient stories to teach children morality. One such story is about patience. Once upon a time, the Buddha was born as a buffalo. The buffalo lived peacefully in the forest taking care of himself, being compassionate not to hurt any creatures. But there was a selfish and naughty monkey who enjoyed playing tricks on the buffalo. Trying to irritate the buffalo, the monkey did things like jump on his back, pull his tail and throw nuts and fruits at his head. The buffalo patiently and calmly went along with his life. The monkey was bothering the other animals, and they were angry and irritated with him and surprised by the buffalo's calmness. One day, an elephant asked the buffalo how come the buffalo is calmly taking the monkey's abuse. The buffalo replied that he accepted the monkey's misbehavior because it taught the buffalo patience which is a great blessing. The monkey was listening to this conversation and felt ashamed of his misdeeds, and he stopped his wrongdoing. And so, there was peace in the forest.

The sacred book, *Thirukkural*, has a chapter promoting patience. It teaches us to always practice patience. It points out that the world respects those who tolerate rather than those who retaliate. The sage recommends people to be patient like mother earth tolerates the diggers. A similar expression is used in the most highly regarded play "Shakuntala" in the ancient Indian language Sanskrit. The sage who raised the heroine Sakunthala advises her to be patient like earth when she goes to her husband's house. These indicate the importance given to patience.

Sufi master Hazrat Inayat Khan points out in *Mastery Through Accomplishment* that we need more patience the more important the object we pursue. If we rush the steps, we risk failing in our effort. He says: " . . .

There are three chief things in the path of attainment: steadiness of concentration in holding the object of concentration firmly before oneself; at the same time, noticing with open eyes the many steps that one must climb to reach to the object; and the third thing is patient perseverance."[36] He further notes that single mindedness is the main secret of concentration. Those who are easily discouraged and quit halfway tend to fail to achieve their goal. In the spiritual path, those who move forward with hope and move backward with doubt do not progress. The Sufi master cautioned that excessive self-confidence might cause some negligence and lead to failure. Similarly, unhealthy pride causes some people to fail after doing well initially and gloating over it and failing to finish the work well.

Patience is very important in Taoism. There are three meanings of Tao: (1) it is the way of the ultimate reality, (2) it is the way or norm or the rhythm of the universe, and (3) it is the way of human life when it is harmonious with the Tao of the universe. Patience helps with this harmony. Patience is particularly important in practicing what Taoists call wu-wei or non-action. The idea is doing more by doing less. A Japanese story illustrates this point. A local ruler with three sons was trying to choose one of his sons to inherit his position. So, he devised a test. He placed a pillow on the door to his room. Then he called his first son who came in and attacked the pillow with his sword and destroyed it. Then he called the second son who drew his sword but seeing the pillow in midair he caught it. Finally, he called his third son who noticed the pillow on the door, picked it up and put it under his arm and entered the room. The youngest son paid clear attention and did not even draw his sword. And he inherited his father's position.

SOME OF THE BIG PROBLEMS FROM IMPATIENCE

In Sophocles' *Antigone*, this heroine disobeyed King Creon's unreasonable order not to bury her brother's dead body. Antigone was sentenced to death and put in a cave by the king's order. In spite of the pleading by his son Hemon, who was also Antigone's betrothed, and the persuasion by a famous visionary, Creon refused to free her. But after listening to the chorus, Creon allowed her to be released, and Hemon was on his way to get her. But Antigone had hung herself to death before Hemon reached

36. Khan, *Mastery*, 29.

her and he killed himself from grief. Also, Hemon's mother committed suicide from losing her son.[37] I imagine Antigone's patience and hope must have run out.

In many cases of suicide attempts I have dealt with, loss of hope and patience have been major factors behind the desperate act. Excessive guilt and shame from superego were often present. Conscience, faith and hope can go hand in hand to strengthen us against many of the human tragedies whenever our own choices are involved. This is very important for patients, their families, and caregivers to keep in mind. Impatience causes frustration and anger which could lead to many problems like verbal or physical violence, obesity, hypertension, relationship problems and increase negative feelings. Intense anger can even cause heart attack and death. Those who relieve impatience by using alcohol or drugs risk addiction.

HOW TO DEVELOP PATIENCE

Impatience may be connected with unrealistic demands such as perfectionism. Or impatience may be connected with the problem of irrational gratification such as addiction or something along that line. So, people working to gain patience are at the same time developing their conscience, and they can feel especially good about it. Like changing any problem, first, one has to become more conscious of the nature and extent of the problem and when it is better and worse. Become aware of underlying feelings such as anger, hate, frustration, anxiety, tension, or craving for something. Recognize which direction the feeling is pushing you and think well of yourself for resisting it. Then, shift your mind to some relaxing mental image of being at a beach or garden or listening to soothing music. If you are physically tense, taking deep breaths ten times or tensing and relaxing hand muscles ten times could help.

Practicing meditation daily is very useful to maintain patience.

Practicing physical exercises daily is useful physically, mentally, and spiritually.

I believe it is useful to recite the serenity prayer regularly and apply the principle of it in practice. *[see the Serenity Prayer in a footnote in the Introduction].* What I mean is that we must try to change or do what we can for our good purpose and accept our real limits. Our wisdom would

---

37. Sophocles, *Antigone*, 56–60.

help us recognize our real limits. As the saying goes, there is no point in beating a dead horse.

Spiritual exercises like prayer and fasting are also very useful to promote patience.

We have to be patient with others and ourselves. But patience has healthy limits. Like Gandhi and King realized, they couldn't wait too long to suit their opponents. Moderation here too. Patience can patiently nurture the other factors in the fruit of the Spirit. So, now we move on to the next factor in the Fruit of the Spirit, namely, Kindness, in chapter eight.

Chapter Eight

Kindness

When I was young, I admired clever people. Now that I am old, I admire kind people.

— Abraham Joshua Heschel[1]

The ideals which have lighted my way, and time after time given me new courage to face life cheerfully, have been kindness, beauty, and truth. — Albert Einstein[2]

SOME BIBLE QUOTES ON KINDNESS

Let no evil talk come out of your mouths, but only what is useful for building up, as there is need, so that your words may give grace to those who hear. — Eph 4:29

So that in the ages to come he might show the immeasurable riches of his grace in kindness toward us in Christ Jesus. — Eph 2:7

Or do you despise the riches of his kindness and forbearance and patience? Do you not realize that God's kindness is meant to lead you to repentance? — Rom 2:4

---

1. Kushner, *When*, 36.
2. Einstein, *World*, 6.

THE STORY OF JESUS's kindness to Zacchaeus (Luke 19:1–10) depicts how kindness stimulates repentance and reform. Jesus was passing through Jericho. Zacchaeus was a chief tax collector, a rich man. He wanted to see Jesus but, being short, he knew it would be impractical if he stayed in the crowd. So, he went ahead and climbed a sycamore tree on the way that Jesus would pass. When Jesus came to the place, he looked up and called Zacchaeus to come down. Jesus told him he would stay at Zacchaeus' house that day. Zacchaeus was delighted but some others in the crowd grumbled that Jesus had gone to be the guest of a sinner. Zacchaeus promised Jesus that he would give half of his possessions to the poor and he would compensate four times anybody he had overtaxed. Obviously, the kindness of Jesus had touched his conscience, caused repentance and attempts to repair damage. Jesus said to him: "Today salvation has come to this house, because he too is a son of Abraham. For the Son of Man came to seek out and save the lost."

Empathy is a crucial element of kindness. We speculate that Jesus, the healer, empathetically recognized Zacchaeus' need for healing in two aspects of his life: social and spiritual as a sinner who had probably gained wealth exploiting fellow members of the community. Zacchaeus did not need physical healing like the blind man and the lepers Jesus healed. Often it is easier to empathize with the suffering of somebody with an obvious physical illness, but it takes stronger empathy and deeper understanding, usually, to act with kindness when the suffering is hidden or less obvious. As a psychiatrist, I frequently notice this problem with the families of some patients.

Kindness and compassion have much in common. Both involve empathetic feeling and helpful action. Kindness is more action oriented, and compassion involves more feeling, more positive passion. In chapter Four, I discussed self-hate and Theodore Rubin's views and his own personal case. Self-hate tends to involve many negative feelings and harsh judgments about oneself which often causes depression and anxiety. Self-destructive actions are less of a problem than the negative feelings in these cases.

If we know somebody is kind, it makes it easier to approach that person. Jesus's kindness made him easily approachable for the sick and the ones known as sinners or outcasts of society. It is possible that Jesus rather invited himself to be Zacchaeus's guest than let the tax collector invite him. I think Jesus did so because Zacchaeus could have been too shy to ask Jesus to be his guest.

An old story in Islam is that when the prophet Muhammad lived in Mecca, there was an old lady who used to throw garbage at him when he would pass by her house on his way to pray. He would simply walk on. One day, as he passed by the woman's house, the woman did not throw garbage at him. He looked around but did not find her. So, concerned about her, he knocked at her door. With her permission, he entered the house. The woman was lying in bed apparently scared that he would punish her for throwing garbage at him. To her surprise, he realized she was sick, and he cleaned her house and made sure she was comfortable. Since then, she stopped throwing garbage at him and gradually became a follower of Prophet Muhammad.[3]

Moderation and caution are applicable to kindness too. In the Hindu epic *Mahabharata,* one character tells another a cautious tale about kindness. Once upon a time a rishi (a holy man) lived in a hut in a forest and a dog lived close to him. The rishi could change an animal to a different one. One day a panther approached the hut. The scared dog requested the rishi to make him a bigger panther. And the rishi answered the request out of his kindness. The bigger panther fought off the small panther. So, the dog's idea worked. Then came a tiger and the rishi out of kindness turned the dog-panther into a tiger. Likewise, the rishi changed the tiger into an elephant and then into a lion.

When the original dog became a lion, he thought, "The rishi is a very kind person. He might change another animal to a bigger lion than me and that lion might fight me and kill me. So, to prevent that outcome I have to kill Rishi." The Rishi knew the dog-lion's plan and converted him back to a dog. The Rishi expressed his disappointment about the dog's ingratitude and the decision by the Rishi that the dog doesn't deserve his kindness anymore.[4]

I have seen compassion fatigue with some families of patients with severe personality disorders or addiction who resist change in spite of devoted efforts from family for many years. Although it may seem to be indifference, if you don't know the history; and it may be considered benign indifference with some underlying very disappointed love. It is not malignant indifference which covers up hate. The element of sadness on the family's part is a reflection of their love. In the case of malignant

---

3. Bharakda, "Greatness," paras. 7–16.
4. Krishnamacharya, *Mahabharata,* 31–39.

indifference, the underlying hate might be manifested by enjoyment in the suffering of the sick members.

About the multitude of problems human beings face, the Dalai Lama said some problems are caused by external causes like natural disasters, but a lot of problems result from our own mental defects. He says: "Often they are due to differences in ideology, and unfortunately different religious faiths are also sometimes involved. Hence it is very important that we have the right attitude. There are many different philosophies. But what is of basic importance is compassion, love for others, concern for others' suffering, and reduction of suffering."[5]

Dr. Deepak Chopra observes an important point about kindness: "We can have the best intentions to do to others as we would have them do to us, but somehow self-interest keeps postponing the day when it actually happens. I think the only answer is to find a level of consciousness that goes beyond self-interest."[6] Conscience provides the level of consciousness Chopra talks about as it transcends the superego standing for narrow self-interest and unfair group interest.

---

5. Dalai Lama, *Kindness*, 11.
6. Santomero, *Radical*, xiii–xix.

Chapter Nine

Goodness

*[A Wise person] is good to people who are good.
She is also good to people who
Are not good.
This is true goodness.* — Lao Tzu[1]
"There is within human nature an amazing potential for goodness."
— Martin Luther King Jr.[2]

GOODNESS MEANS BEING GOOD or virtuous and doing good. In chapter two I discussed how the sages of the Axial Age stimulated people's consciences and brought out their potential for goodness. They promoted goodness by their teachings and examples. Starting with Zoroaster, who promoted good thoughts, good words, and good deeds, goodness was a prominent feature of the Axial transformation. During Zoroaster's time and before, there was much suffering caused by the aggressive cattle raiders who stole cattle, attacked and killed people, raped women, and caused tremendous fear and anxiety.

In the Introduction and chapter three, I gave wonderful examples of how Jesus stimulated people's consciences to make good choices. Closer to our own times, Gandhi and King have shown us the way to follow in nurturing goodness.

1. Lao Tzu, *Tao Te Ching*, 49.
2. Smith and Zepp, *Search*, 48.

John Wesley's rule focuses on goodness:
Do all the good you can, By all the means you can,
In all the ways you can, In all the places you can,
At all the times you can, To all the people you can,
As Long as ever you can.[3]

Acts 10:38 says: "How God anointed Jesus of Nazareth with the Holy Spirit and with power; how he went about doing good and healing all who were oppressed by the devil, for God was with him." Even as Jesus was dying on the cross, he prayed to God the Father to forgive the people persecuting him, for they did not know what they were doing. And Jesus comforted the thief on the right who asked for Jesus's help telling him he would be with Jesus in Paradise.

The Buddha worked hard for forty-five years traveling across the Ganges plains of India spreading his teachings. Even in his last days, in spite of suffering from food poisoning, he consoled the man who had given Buddha the food which caused the poisoning, let the people in the area visit him and pay their respects, told the monks to ask any questions they had, and even allowed a cranky old man who was not a follower come and ask about his doubts. Buddha's answers helped the old man so much he became a Buddhist. Buddha's trusted cousin Ananda had functioned like Buddha's chief-of-staff for years. Buddha had overheard Ananda refusing the cranky man to visit Buddha, and Buddha told Ananda to let the man visit.[4]

The sages of the Axial Age were committed to promoting goodness in their own way, or we may say, they were promoting the particular aspects of goodness they focused on. The Spirit of the Axial Age was the spirit of goodness. A wonderful leap in the advancement of humanity!

Religions which believe in God emphasize the supreme goodness of God and God's goodness to all. Ps 145:9 says: "The Lord is good to all, and His tender mercies are over all His works."

Good and evil are big subjects for religions. Jesus said: "No good tree bears bad fruit, nor again does a bad tree produce good fruit; for each tree is known for its own fruit." (Luke 6:43) And again Jesus said: "The good person out of the good treasure of the heart produces good, and the evil person out of evil treasure produces evil; for it is out of the abundance of the heart that the mouth speaks." (Luke 6:45) We can notice how

---

3. Wesley, *Sermons*, 675.
4. Scott, *Like a Shadow*, 85.

conscience keeps good treasure in the heart and superego going against conscience keeps more or less evil treasure in the heart.

The ascetic side of religion with the tendency to crucify the flesh is not healthy. Jewish philosopher Martin Buber taught that passion is important for creativity and productivity. He advocated uniting the urges of passion and good direction. "To unite the two urges implies: equip the absolute potency of passion with the one direction that renders it capable of great love and great service. Thus, and not otherwise, can man become whole."[5] We discussed earlier how Buddha tried the ascetic approaches for six years and abandoned it because it did not help.

St. Justin Martyr, the most important Greek Christian apologist of the second century, emphasized goodness regarding salvation of people who were not baptized. He said: "Since they who did those things which are universally, naturally, and eternally good are pleasing to God, they shall be saved in the resurrection…"[6] The followers of St. Thomas, the Apostle, in India believed that all good people would be saved.

The Bible has many warnings about the danger of relating to bad company. For example, I Cor 15:33, "Do not be deceived: Bad company ruins good morals." We have previously discussed the Alcoholics Anonymous's recommendations to change playmates and playgrounds. Close relationships with bad people can turn good people into bad people. We have all seen it happen. On the other hand, good influences tend to promote good transformation.

INSTANCES OF GOOD TRANSFORMATION

In chapter one, we discussed several cases of people who became extremists under the influence of extremists. Equally interesting is how the good influences from good people helped the extremists to transform into good people. In the French classic *Les Misérables,* author Victor Hugo depicts the transformation of a criminal Jean Valjean by the good influence of a bishop who stimulated the criminal's conscience. He had lost his parents in childhood, and he was raised by his sister. He worked to support the family after his sister's husband passed away. During a winter when there was no work and no food for the family, he stole some bread. He was caught and sentenced to five years in prison. Hugo emphasizes

---

5. Buber, *Good*, 97.
6. Sullivan, *Salvation*, 15.

that Jean Valjean was not born evil, and he was still good when he arrived in prison.

At this point, Hugo's reflections are quite worth our reflection: "There, he condemned society and felt himself becoming wicked; he condemned Providence and felt himself becoming impious. ...Can human nature be so entirely transformed inside and out? Can man created good by God, be made wicked by man? Can the soul be completely changed by its destiny, and turn evil when its fate is evil? . . . Is there not in every human soul–was there not particularly in Jean Valjean's soul—a primitive spark, a divine element, incorruptible in this world and immortal in the next, which can be developed by goodness, kindled, lit up, and made to radiate, and which evil can never entirely extinguish."[7]

Jean Valjean spent nineteen years in prison because of five attempts to escape. With the harsh treatments of prison life and the lack of tender human connections, he became full of hatred of humanity. After his release from prison, one evening he approached a bishop for help. The bishop provided him with a meal and a place to sleep. After a few hours of sleep, he woke up. He stole the silver place settings of the bishop and left. The next day police brought him to the bishop. The bishop pretended like he had given the silver things to him and gave silver candlesticks. So, the police freed him. Then the bishop told Jean Valjean that he was giving the silver to him for him to become an honest man. Like a spiritual therapist giving a powerful suggestion, the bishop said: "Jean Valjean, my brother, you no longer belong to evil, but to good. It is your soul I am buying for you...and I give it to God!!"[8]

After leaving the bishop, Jean Valjean stole a coin accidentally dropped by a poor boy. Then he felt guilty and tried hard to return the coin, but he couldn't find the boy. Burdened with guilt and sadness, he cried for the first time in nineteen years. He had been transformed by the bishop's influence on his conscience. Subsequently he lived as a very good person. Quite interestingly, this story was based on a real incident of the transformation of a criminal by a bishop.

The role of goodness in Near Death Experiences (NDE) is fascinating. In his first book published in 1975, Raymond Moody had described the experience of many NDE'rs going through a tunnel, seeing a bright light which reviews the person's life. The being of light emphasizes

---

7. Hugo, *Les Misérables*, 89–90.
8. Hugo, *Les Misérables*, 106.

two things in life: learning to love others and acquiring knowledge. In Moody's book *The Light Beyond,* published in 1988, he states: "You have to understand that the being of light isn't telling them that they have to change. My summation, after hearing hundreds of these cases, is that the people change willingly because they are in the presence of the *standard of goodness*, which makes them want to change their behavior radically."[9] (Italics added) Moody added the case of one NDE'r who was a "fire and brimstone" minister who used to preach eternal damnation if people did not believe the Bible in a particular way. During his NDE, the being of light implied that he needed to change and promote a message of love, and he made that change.

In the fruit of the Spirit, goodness is connected with all the other elements of the fruit of the Spirit: love, joy, peace, patience, kindness, faithfulness, gentleness, and self-control. From a different angle, goodness is connected with love and wisdom which are the basic common elements of religions as Bede Griffiths observed. Conscience nurtures good choices which manifest in love and wisdom.

Psychiatrist and philosopher Roger Walsh emphasizes ethical living as an essential part of spirituality. He observes that when we give somebody our love, that same love flowers in us first. He says: "This psychological and spiritual principle–what we intend for others we create for ourselves—is one of the most powerful and important, yet, sadly, also one of the least understood and appreciated, of all spiritual principles." Once it is understood, it transforms the basis of all relationships. The great secret of ethics is as the Buddha pointed out: "Whatever you do, you do to yourself."[10] Ethical living is living by goodness, making choices using conscience.

I close this chapter with the uplifting words of St. Paul in tune with conscience: "Finally, beloved, whatever is true, whatever is honorable, whatever is just, whatever is pure, whatever is pleasing, whatever is commendable, if there is any excellence and if there is anything worthy of praise, think about these things." (Phil 4:8)

---

9. Moody, *Light Beyond*, 39.
10. Walsh, *Essential*, 121.

Chapter Ten

Faithfulness

"Hold faithfulness and sincerity as first principles." — Confucius[1]

"The foundation stones for a balanced success are honesty, character, integrity, faith, love, and loyalty." — Zig Ziglar[2]

FAITHFULNESS OR FIDELITY IS a crucial element in relationships. Loyalty and dependability are connected with faithfulness. While the word "infidelity" is often used in reference to cheating in marriage, infidelity can be in any relationship. Having dealt with a lot of cases of marital infidelity, I find a story in the Greek poet Homer's *Odyssey* about the affair between goddess Venus and god Mars insightful and humorous. Sensuous Venus was fond of sex and society. Her husband Vulcan, god of night and blacksmiths, was sweet-tempered and powerful but ugly, old and lame. Vulcan's younger brother Mars, the god of war, was handsome, virile and aggressive, even brutal. Venus and Mars became passionate lovers. The god Apollo noticed it and told Vulcan about it. Vulcan wanted to take revenge on Venus and Mars. He produced a snare made of bronze chains so light even the gods could not see it and put it around his bed and told Venus he was leaving for Limnos. When Venus and Mars made love, they were caught in the net and Vulcan called Venus' father Jove who came with the other gods to see the sight. The goddesses did not join them out

---

1. Confucius, *Analects*, 1:8, ii.
2. Ziglar, *See You*, 83.

of shame. The gods roared with laughter. Vulcan demanded the dowry back from Jove. Neptune promised to pay the amount if Mars didn't. So, Vulcan released the lovers, and they left in separate directions.[3]

While affairs have been subjects of gossip, ridicule, mockery, laughter, and tears, they play a role in divorce. Twenty to forty percent of divorces are caused by an affair according to American Psychological Association research. 40 percent of adults with a history of cheating are separated or divorced compared to 17 percent who never cheated. Male cheaters fare better than female cheaters. Among cheaters, 61 percent of men and 44 percent of women are still married.[4]

Infidelity is a major cause of distress for the victim which could lead to depression, suicide attempts, substance abuse, and the like. It is very important to seek help in these situations. Cheating is clearly against conscience, but cheaters use various defenses to block their guilt. Many people's superegos accept or, in some cases, even encourage affairs. I have come across a few men who were proud of having had a fling with a beautiful woman and a few women who had similar feelings about a fling with a powerful and attractive man.

DEPENDENCE, INDEPENDENCE, INTERDEPENDENCE AND DEPENDABILITY

Authoritarians tend to be independent themselves and encourage followers to depend on them in many ways. It is an unhealthy pattern. Dependability is a good feature in a person who can and does provide the support someone else needs. Realistic dependence, i.e., a person with real limitations like physical disability, depending on others is appropriate. Conscience promotes healthy relationships. Distorted superegos promote relationship problems like excessive dependence or independence.

RELIGION AND FAITHFULNESS

Theistic religions teach the perfect dependability of God. 1 Kgs 8:56 says: "Blessed be the Lord, who has given rest to his people Israel according to all that he promised, which he spoke through his servant Moses." God's nature is unchanging. "Jesus Christ is the same yesterday and today and

---

3. Homer, *Odyssey*, 191–210.
4. Buscho, "Is Your Marriage," para. 4.

forever." (Heb 13:8) In his faithfulness, God protects us from evil. (2 Thess 3:3) God is just and fair. In Jer 17, God proclaims: "I the Lord test the mind and search the heart, to give to all according to their ways, according to the fruit of their doings."

A parable of the talents in Matt 25 is instructive. A man entrusted his property to his slaves as he was going on a journey. According to their abilities, he gave five talents to one, two talents to another and one talent to the third. Then he left. The slave who got the five talents traded with it and got five more talents. Similarly, the one who received two talents utilized it and got two more talents. But the man who got just one talent dug a hole in the ground and buried the talent in it. A long time later, the master returned, and he asked the slaves to settle the account. Each slave told the master what he had done with the talent. The master praised the first two who had doubled what was given to them and entrusted more things with them as if they were trustworthy. The one who had hidden the talent in the ground explained to the master that he did it out of fear of the master. The master called him wicked and lazy and told him he could have invested the money with a banker and got the talent with an interest. So, the one talent was taken away from him and he was punished. From the angle of conscience versus superego, the two slaves who utilized the talents they received to grow were guided by conscience, but the other man was probably guided by a very defensive superego.

The story of Mu Lian, one of the ten great disciples of Buddha, is literally out of this world. He was born into a rich family. His family happily connected with Buddhist monks and did charitable works. After his father died, Mu Lian left home to go to a temple to become a Buddhist monk. Under the influence of his younger brother, his mother started killing animals and eating meat. Soon she died. Thinking that she must be in heaven, Mu Lian searched for her in the Western Paradise, but Buddha informed him that the lady was detained in hell and was standing trial at the time. Buddha gave him a magic stick. Then he traveled to hell and passed through many obstacles and challenges from ghosts carrying his mother on his shoulders. Finally, they returned to the world and the mother corrected her wrongdoings. And Mu Lian was rewarded as one of the greatest disciples of Buddha based on his strong devotion to his mother.[5]

---

5. Wikipedia, "Mulian," paras. 1–3.

The Hindu epic *Mahabharata* has a story of a squirrel helping along with thousands of monkeys to build a bridge from India to Sri Lanka. The reason for building the bridge was for Lord Rama's group to save Sita, wife of Rama, from Ravana's control. Ravana had abducted Sita and taken her to his place in Sri Lanka. The monkeys were moving big stones in building the bridge. A brown squirrel carried pebbles in his mouth to help with the project. The monkeys laughed at the squirrel. One monkey even pulled the squirrel by the tail and threw him away. The squirrel crying out the name of Lord Rama landed in Rama's hand. Rama took the situation as a teaching moment. He praised the monkeys and the squirrel for their sincere hard work. He taught the monkeys to respect the efforts of the weak and small. He also pointed out how useful the pebbles were to fill the gaps between the big stones implying the specialness of the squirrel's work. The bullying monkey types are not using their consciences.[6]

Rabia of Basra (717–801 CE), the female Muslim mystic and saint, lived in Basra, Iraq. Rabia means "Fourth" as she was the fourth daughter of her family. Her family was very poor. After her father's death, she went off into the desert and lived a semi-reclusive life. She was known for her complete devotion to God–pure unconditional love of God. She lived a life of humility, love and devotion to God. Many people sought her spiritual guidance. She loved God for who God is, not from fear of hell or hope of heaven. She promoted the love of God in others. Rabia has been a great inspiration for Sufis and others connected with this mystical group which promotes peace, love, and healthy spirituality guided by conscience.

Responsibility and commitment are the other factors in faithfulness. Irvin Yalom observes: "The word "responsibility" itself denotes that capacity: "response" + "ability" - that is, the ability to respond."[7] This involves duty and using one's ability to respond in a humane or caring way, going beyond one's job description. In the parable of the Good Samaritan, we imagine the Rabbi and the Rabbi's Assistant who went by without attending to the victim of abuse lying on the roadside, were not avoiding their duty. Helping the victim was not part of their job description. Clearly, it was not part of the Samaritan's job either, but he responded beyond the call of duty. He did it out of his goodness and love.

---

6. Krishnamacharya, *Mahabharata*, 1–19.
7. Yalom, *Existential*, 286.

In the spiritual sense, we have the responsibility to utilize our special gifts or potential. Existential guilt is regret about wasted potential. So, there are three kinds of guilt: real guilt, neurotic guilt, and existential guilt. Real guilt is about real wrongdoing. One can deal with real or realistic guilt by repairing damage, accepting reasonable punishment and preventing repetition. Neurotic guilt is from unrealistic punitive judgment by a harsh superego, and the solution is for the person to recognize the underlying problem and balance the superego using conscience. For example, feeling excessive guilt about a fleeting bad thought. Existential guilt can be dealt with what we call "applying the spirit of the serenity prayer:" doing the best they can with their potential and accepting their realistic limits and calming unhealthy feelings.

Faithfulness involves commitment. Commitment to a pledge, agreement or obligation involves sincere effort to meet the expectation. I use the phrase "half faithful" to people who perform only half of their expectations in their roles at work or personal relationship. It applies to spouses who are not cheating but not meeting the natural sexual expectations of a marital relationship without good reasons. Overall, we can see how important the virtue of faithfulness is. It is a sign of psychological and spiritual maturity.

Chapter Eleven

Gentleness

"Our greatest strength lies in the gentleness and tenderness of your heart." — Rumi[1]

"I have three precious things which I hold fast and prize. The first is gentleness; the second frugality; the third is humility; which keeps me from putting myself before others. Be gentle and you can be bold; be frugal and you can be liberal; avoid putting yourself before others and you can become a leader among men." — Lao Tzu[2]

GENTLENESS IS A GREAT human quality which makes relationships easy and strong. It is the opposite of harshness and hardness. Interestingly, as he offered to be a source of rest for the weary and carrying heavy burdens, Jesus reassured them by saying he is "gentle and humble in heart." (Matt 11:28–29). Wouldn't we hesitate to approach a harsh and arrogant person for help when we are stressed out with burdens? The psychological connection between gentleness and humility is very insightful. Also, gentleness and humility are connected with conscience.

St. Paul says in Gal 6: "My friends, if anyone is detected in a transgression, you who have received the Spirit should restore such a one in a spirit of gentleness." And in Phil 4:5, he says: "Let your gentleness be known to everyone."

1. Rumi, *Essential*, 102.
2. Lao Tzu, *Sayings*, 33–36.

"As God's chosen ones, holy and beloved, clothe yourselves with compassion, kindness, humility, meekness, and patience." (Col 3:12) Meekness is gentleness.

"But the wisdom from above is first pure, then peaceable, gentle, willing to yield, full of mercy and good fruits, without a trace of partiality or hypocrisy." (Jas 4:17)

Prov 15:1 says: "A soft answer turns away wrath, but a harsh word stirs up anger."

Prov 25:15 says: "With patience a ruler may be persuaded, and a soft tongue can break bones."

The sages of the Axial Age were gentle, and they spread peace, compassion, goodness and gentleness. Many of them lived in the background of violence, anarchy and the mentality of "might is right."

Moses was a gentle leader. "Moses was very humble, more so than anyone else on the face of the earth." (Num 12:3) A man of many heroic actions, he was humble and gentle.

Huston Smith wrote about Prophet Muhammad: "Pure-hearted and beloved in his circles, he was, it is said, of sweet and gentle disposition."[3] Along this point, Karen Armstrong states: "Some Muslim thinkers regard the Jihad against Mecca as the climax of Muhammad's career and fail to note that he eventually abjured warfare and adopted a nonviolent policy."[4]

In Shakespeare's tragedy *Julius Caesar,* Mark Antony pays a great tribute to his defeated enemy Brutus:

His life was gentle; and the elements

> So mixed in him that Nature might stand up
> And say to all the world, *This was a man!* (Act V Scene V)[5]

Henry Wadsworth Longfellow (1807–1882) in his poem, *The Village Blacksmith,* describes a village blacksmith, a strong, well-built man who becomes tearful remembering his departed mother as he hears his daughter singing at the church.

> The smith, a mighty man is he
> With large and sinewy hands;
> And the muscles of the brawny arm
> Are strong as iron hands.

3. Smith, *World's,* 224.
4. Armstrong, *Muhammad,* 200.
5. Shakespeare, *Julius Caesar,* Act 5, Scene 5.

> He goes on Sunday to the church,
> And sits among his boys;
> He hears the parson pray and preach,
> He hears his daughter's voice
> Singing in the village choir,
> And it makes his heart rejoice.
> It sounds to him like his mother's voice
> Singing in Paradise!
> He needs must think of her once more,
> How in the grave she lies;
> And with his hard, rough hands he wipes
> A tear out of his eyes.[6]

As opposed to the idea in many cultures that strong men don't cry, Victor Hugo observed: "A dry eye goes with a dead soul."[7] Hugo was describing the hateful condition of Jean Valjean when he left prison after nineteen years. As noted in chapter nine, his crying after vainly trying to return the coin he stole from a poor boy, was a significant part of Jean Valjean's healing. Many people believe in being aggressive, very angry, insulting, name-calling and so on which are against conscience. Some politicians of this type seem to get a lot of support in the election campaigns.

Many people confuse gentleness as not being manly. Years ago, in my psychiatric practice I had some parents worried about their sons watching the gentle Mr. Roger's show on PBS for fear that the boys might become gay. I was able to educate them and clear their fear. One can be gentle and firm, or assertive. Aristotle connected gentleness with moderation in anger. He considered an excess of anger as well as the lack of anger in response to hurt as extremes or vices.

People have to be very careful about leaders who try to thrive by stimulating unreasonable anger or fear. Such unreasonable feelings could influence us through our superegos and distract our consciences. Before the Axial Age, aggressiveness prevailed. But the sages of the Axial Age promoted peace and nonviolence. Do we want to regress to the pre-Axial mentality? Firebrands and flamethrowers are guided by superegos.

Aristotle used gentleness as the virtue between being too quick to anger and being too detached and not getting angry in a situation where an angry reaction is appropriate. In *Nicomachean Ethics Book four*, chapter five, Aristotle says: "He then who is angry on the right occasions and

---

6. Longfellow, "Village," stanzas 1–3.
7. Hugo, *Les Misérables*, 93.

with the right persons, and also in the right manner, and at the right season, and for the right reason, and for the right length of time, is praised; we will call him gentle, therefore, since gentleness is used as a term of praise."[8] Such behavior shows an underlying conscience and also shows healthy self-control, the topic of our next chapter.

---

8. Aristotle, *Nicomachean*, 1120b1–5.

Chapter Twelve

Self-Control

"You have power over your mind-not outside events. Realize this, and you will find strength." — Marcus Aurelius[1]

"Educate your children to self-control, to the habit of holding the passion and prejudice and evil tendencies subject to an upright and reasoning will, and you have done much to abolish misery from their future, and crimes from society . . . " — Benjamin Franklin[2]

Prov 25:28 says: "Like a city whose walls are broken down is a man without self-control."

Self-control is our ability to manage our emotions, impulses and behavior to achieve long term goals. This is one of our superior qualities over animals. Religion and culture and our own superegos and consciences have commands and prohibitions or do's and don'ts. Self-control is important for us to act by these do's and don'ts. Without self-control one would fail more or less to produce the other eight virtues.

St. Paul expressed his conflict between his flesh and his spirit: "I do not understand my own actions. For I do not do what I want but I do the very thing I hate." (Rom 7:15) For I delight in the law of God in my inmost self, but I see in my members another law at war with the law of my mind, making me captive to the law of sin that dwells in my

---

1. Aurelius, *Meditations*, 29.
2. Franklin, *Autobiography*, 74.

members. (Rom 7:22-23) Given Paul's list of works of the flesh which include drunkenness, sexual immorality, rage, envy, jealousy and strife, Paul's conflict would probably have involved conflict between his ideals and various temptations.

In Cor 8:24–27, Paul says: "Do you not know that in a race the runners all compete but only one receives the prize? Run in such a way that you may win. Athletes exercise self-control in all things; they do it to receive a perishable wreath; but we an imperishable one. So, I do not run aimlessly, nor do I box as though beating the air; but I punish my body and enslave it, so that after proclaiming to others, I myself should be disqualified." The sayings, "keep the eyes on the prize" and "practice makes perfect" are popular because they help. In chapter one, I gave several examples of people who overcame addiction or extremism by controlling their behavior and transforming themselves using the guidance of conscience.

SPECIAL IMPORTANCE OF SELF-CONTROL

Aristotle emphasized self-control. He explained that when you go through with a choice you've made after proper deliberation, not distracted by temptation you are showing self-control. If you fall for the temptation, you don't have self-control. The other eight virtues in the "fruit of the spirit" depend on self-control to become effective, making self-control so special. Self-control often involves delaying gratification because immediate satisfaction of a need or a desire is unhealthy or inappropriate. Many obese people have difficulty in delaying or denying the desire to eat something unhealthy for them. As we gain control over one kind of wrong choice, we feel more confidence in controlling other choices.

Thucydides said: "Self-control is the chief element in self-respect, and self-respect is the chief element in courage."[3] As we make good choices, judge with our consciences and act with self-control, our self-esteem goes up. So also, our courage goes up in this situation because courage invokes the good feeling about making good choices.

About self-control, the Dalai Lama said: "practically speaking, the best control is self-control. Through internal change, crime can be stopped and peace brought to society." Self-examination is most important, and thus the Buddhist theory of self-responsibility is useful

---

3. Thucydides, *History*, para. 19.

as it entails self-examination and self-control in consideration of both one's own and others' interests.[4] We often hear about willpower in this connection.

Regarding the role of willpower, the Dalai Lama says: "Without willpower and determination, even something you might have achieved easily cannot be achieved. If you have willpower and reasonable courage–not blind courage–but courage without pride–even things which seemed impossible at a certain stage turn into being possible because of continuing effort inspired by that courage. Thus, determination is very important."[5]

Along with determination, some other factors such as wish, hope, imagination, and reinforcements or rewards play their parts in pursuing a goal. The more appealing the outcome, the more attractive the goals, the more hopeful the result and the more reinforcements we receive for a choice, the better chance for the success of the choice.

The 12-step programs for addiction succeed by depending on a higher power, utilizing the support of the recovery group and the individual help from a sponsor. In my psychiatric practice, many patients with addiction who had problems choosing a higher power successfully followed my recommendation to choose conscience as their higher power.

Various religions and ethical teachings give great importance to self-control. Thirukkural, a great ethical work, written by the Indian sage Thiruvalluvar probably in the first century CE is full of praise for self-control. It claims that self-control would place a person among gods, and lack of self-control would cause a miserable life. Also, it claims that self-control guided by wisdom would result in everlasting fame. I think the sages of the Axial Age prove this point.

In his book *Emotional Intelligence,* Psychologist Daniel Goleman emphasizes the importance of emotional intelligence which can matter more than IQ. Emotional Intelligence is the capacity to manage one's own emotions and interact well with others by being aware of others' feelings.[6] I have said before that applying the golden rule of doing to others as we want them to do to us is an essential part of using conscience. We can see the importance of using our feelings and being aware of the feelings of others we are dealing with in using conscience. While conscience

4. Dalai Lama, *Kindness,* 27.
5. Dalai Lama, *Kindness,* 158.
6. Goleman, *Emotional,* 8.

has the flexibility to understand another's different outlook, superegos may be too rigid to understand well a different outlook than one's own.

An interesting person I treated had several issues related to control. This lady in her forties was a nervous person. She was trying to follow the dietary restriction her primary care physician had recommended for weight control, especially to stop snacking on ice cream or potato chips, which were her comfort foods. The doctor had recommended reducing the carbohydrates and increasing the vegetables in her diet. She took her doctor's recommendations seriously and started thinking a lot about these controls she should live with. Obsessing about these controls made her more tense. She had some hangup about control because her father was a "control freak." With these issues going on, she became more tense and her struggle to avoid her comfort food became more intense and she failed many times.

I recommended that she should not think about dietary control often; think of it only when she shopped for food, when she cooked and when she served her food and ate. Also, she was told she could think of dietary control as beautiful behavior and beauty lies in harmonious blending. She was encouraged to practice meditation, but she was resistant because she thought of it as a Hindu practice. I educated her about meditation and told her about the Catholic monk Fr. John Main in Canada who used a Christian "mantra" or sacred word "maranatha" to repeat in the mind for meditation. Maranatha is a word in the Aramaic language Jesus spoke, and it means "Lord, come in my heart." Meeting in weekly sessions, it took her a few months to become stable.

Spiritual exercises like prayer, meditation, yoga, fasting and reading sacred books and singing sacred songs help to have self-control. Conscience promotes self-control. Some people's superegos push them too far in their need for control and cause them to be stubborn, которая is a problem. Stubbornness is one of the features of perfectionistic or compulsive personality. Pope Francis, a champion of healthy conscience, in his book *Let Us Dream*, described some people with "isolated conscience" who are very rigid and critical of the Church, bishops, and the Pope.[7] Such people tend to think in either good or bad terms, and they hardly have mercy towards those they are critical of. I suspect these may be perfectionists. Aristotle had noted that the stubborn person favors the pleasure of self-righteousness over being actually virtuous. Self-righteousness

---

7. Pope Francis and Austen Ivereigh, *Let Us Dream*, 69.

is connected to superego. With this chapter, we come to the end of the chapters, and next we move on to the conclusion.

Conclusion

"The safest course is to do nothing against one's conscience. With this secret, we can enjoy life and have no fear from death." — Voltaire[1]

"No external conditions can guarantee our life, which is attended with inevitable sufferings and infallibly terminated by death, and which consequently can have no significance except in the constant accomplishment of what is demanded by the Power which has placed us in life with a sole certain guide–the rational conscience."

— Leo Tolstoy (The Kingdom of God is within you)[2].

"Humanity's intellectual nature finds at last its perfection, as it needs to, in wisdom, which gently draws the human mind to look for and to love what is true and good."

— Austin Flannery, O.P. (From Vatican Council II)[3]

MARTIN LUTHER KING JR. wrote at the end of *Why We Can't Wait*: "Man was born into barbarism when killing his fellow man was a normal condition of existence. He became endowed with a conscience. And he has reached now the day when violence toward another human being must become abhorrent as if eating another's flesh. Nonviolence, the answer to the Negro's need, may become the answer to the most desperate need of all humanity."[4]

1. Voltaire, *Letters*, 1.
2. Tolstoy, *Kingdom*, 368.
3. Flannery, "Gaudium," 177.
4. King, *Why*, 191.

Regarding King's statement about "man became endowed with a conscience," I believe a significant part of it occurred during the Axial Age. We have seen in chapter two how spirituality, conscience, and many religions—Confucianism, Daoism, and Buddhism—developed during the Axial Age. Also, Hinduism and Judaism which existed before the Axial Age transformed during the Axial Age, emphasizing personal transformation rather than rituals. It is a shame that the Axial Age is rather unknown. Reflecting on the importance of the Axial Age, Bede Griffiths wrote: "It is impossible to exaggerate the importance of this moment of human history. It is the point at which man reaches the knowledge of himself…"[5] In an article, *The Axial Age of Human History: A Base for the Unity of Mankind* published in 1948, Jaspers wrote: "The age of myth–the age of the static and self-evident–came to an end, and there began the battle of rationality and practical experience against myth (*logos versus mythos*): the battle for the transcendence of the one God against the demons who did not exist; the battle of an aroused ethical sense against the false gods. Religion was informed with ethics, and thus the idea of divinity was enhanced.... The mythical world slowly receded, but it remained in the beliefs of the masses, the background of all life (and therefore it could triumph again in later periods over wide areas)."[6]

I recommend that the reader read the above quote again and reflect on the profound history of human spiritualization beautifully expressed. In the Introduction, we dealt with stages of human cultural evolution from mythical to theoretic, from myth to reason. The insight that religions were rendered ethical is crucial. Being ethical is the common ground of the religions in the Axial Age. Thus, the Axial Age spirituality largely overcame the two frequent religious problems Mark Twain humorously expresses: "He [Man] is the only animal who has the True Religion—several of them. He is the only animal that loves his neighbor as himself and cuts his throat if his theology is not straight."[7] Unity in diversity is part of nature and life. Variety with ethics promotes harmony, not hostility. Ethics is consistent with conscience. During the Axial Age, the religions were in separate regions of the world, but they had strong common ground of transcending the mythical, being rational and strongly ethical. In another situation, I have given the example of Kerala, India where several religions have coexisted peacefully for two thousand years. Millions of

5. Griffiths, *Marriage*, 60.
6. Jaspers, *"Is Science,"* paras. 1–39.
7. Twain, *Man's Place*, 125.

Chinese practiced Confucianism, Taoism and Buddhism for centuries before the Communist rule. Conscience and the fruit of the Spirit with its nine elements, or the nine virtues, are intimately linked. As we have seen in the preceding chapters, strengthening conscience enhances the virtues and enhancing the virtues strengthens conscience.

Before the Axial Age, the function of religion was cosmic maintenance, that is, the human race supporting the gods with ceremonies and offerings such as food ("Feeding the gods" said someone) and sacrifices. The proper function of the universe like the sun rising in the morning depended on such cosmic maintenance. In the Axial Age, the function of religion changed to the spiritual transformation of individuals and communities. Conscience plays a crucial role in the transformation. With these insights we can have a good perspective on religion, spirituality, and conscience. Horrible amounts of conflicts and suffering have occurred in connection with a lot of people who have religious affiliation or identity without proper spirituality and conscience. As I write this in March 2025, I am reminded of the tragic violence going on in the Palestinian Israeli conflict since October 7, 2023, where a lot of people seem to have religion without conscience. Also, the attack on Ukraine by Russian President Vladimir Putin since 2022 and the support of him by the Russian Orthodox Church leader Patriarch Kirill seems to show religion without conscience. The spiritual defect of such situations of religion without conscience indicate the intense need for the utilization of conscience.

Women's rights, civil rights, and various minority rights have been supporting conscience and reducing the unreasonable and unfair power of superego. Despite that, significant unfair discrimination continues and a lot of biases of various kinds still exist.

Various forms and shades of lies are promoted by many not only free of shame or guilt but even pushed with pride. That kind of damage to respect for truth seriously undermines conscience. It is said that truth is the first casualty of war. Even in various unfair competitions, especially in intense political fights, lies have become a frequently used weapon. The saying that negative advertisements succeed has been proven correct many times in recent years. But conscience goes beyond success.

Societies or human communities are human organizations with different influences and guidelines from its members. Leaders of groups tend to have disproportionate say in the rules, regulations and the power structure of the group. Group members tend to internalize the group's rules or value system, and it becomes their superegos. So, we can understand how an unfair value system could exist in societies if people don't use their consciences, examine the systems and work to change unfair systems rather than adjust to them. That is what the great sages and people like Gandhi and King did. In the case of Las Casas in chapter three, a passage he was reading stimulated his conscience against his own superego supporting slavery and transformed himself against slavery and helped others to change.

Russell Moore, editor-in-chief of *Christianity Today*, in his book *Losing Our Religion*, has addressed how Christianity in America, especially Evangelical Christianity, has lost credibility, authority, identity, integrity, and stability. He is critical of the decline in the importance of character as part of the politicization of Christianity in recent years against conscience. Moore wrote against the spreading of lies going on. He wrote about the scandal of Jerry Falwell Jr. who lost his position as the Chancellor of Liberty University, the largest evangelical university, when the information came out that many times, he had watched a pool boy having sex with his wife. Falwell's defense was that he was a lawyer and businessman, not a preacher. About this Moore wrote: "He said that he was a lawyer, not a preacher—as though the commands to integrity, obedience, repentance, and mercy were ordination vows instead of the call of Jesus on every one of his disciples, and even before that written by God on the consciences of every human being."[8] I hope such constructive criticism and push to use conscience by Moore would stimulate the consciences of a lot of Christians who need such change.

Among various political systems, democracy is the best because it gives members of the country the most freedom to use conscience. But when political parties in the system work against conscience, it diminishes the level of conscience in the system and in the country. On September 13, 2024, Pope Francis encouraged US Catholics to use their consciences and pick the lesser of two evils against life, one that kicks out immigrants and one who supports abortion. The Pope was rejecting the single-issue voting (voting based just on antiabortion). Media sources are very important for providing truthful and useful information, but to the extent they deviate from conscience in their work, they become harmful to people and the democratic process in society. Beware of any media

---

8. Moore, *Losing*, 115.

outlet claiming to be pro-Christian but goes against conscience in their activities.

In our scientific age, the examples of Teilhard de Chardin, Erwin Schrödinger, and others who have combined great depth in scientific and spiritual fields are especially inspiring. I am also reminded of the studies about Near-Death Experiences in many cases when a being of light reviews the person's life and enquires whether the person has gained love and knowledge. And the knowledge seems to be of wisdom. Love and wisdom are closely connected with living by conscience.

To reiterate, the difference between the judgment of conscience compared to that of the superego and the PIG are very important for our understanding. It cannot be said enough, Conscience is our best guide. Conscience guides the individual to choose what is good (useful, not harmful), using reason, the Golden Rule, moderation, and respect for truth. Learning about the Axial Age clarifies and strengthens our perspective on spirituality, religion, and conscience. Religion with conscience is a social and spiritual organization that is a positive force but religion without conscience is a spiritual defect more or less problematic. The human race is at a crucial stage with intense struggle between destructive and creative forces: climate crises and efforts to mitigate it, nuclear weapons and the efforts to control them, artificial intelligence and its potential to be used creatively and prevent it from being destructive. The word conscience is used thirty times in the New Testament and the apostles Paul and Peter gave great importance to conscience. Given the level of psychological, spiritual and historical information available now, people of all religions, and Christians in particular, have a unique opportunity and responsibility to understand and promote the use of conscience. Jesus reinforced the spirit of the Axial Age with his teaching and example. He even took a step further in teaching us to love our enemies. With conscience as our master guide and social values in tune with conscience, we can really enjoy the fruit of the Spirit and avoid the destructive results of handling our needs without conscience.

Notes

PERSONALITY DISORDERS

I will give some features of various personality disorders here based on my training and experience. If the reader wants to know more about the topic, I recommend checking it in the Mayo Clinic description on the Internet (https://www.mayoclinic.org/diseases-conditions) or a psychiatric textbook or discussing it with a professionally trained person. The Textbook I have used is *Diagnostic and Statistical Manual of Mental Disorders Fifth Edition* published by American Psychiatric Press.[1]

Borderline personality disorders:

Borderline personality disorders tend to overreact to real or perceived rejection and show excessive anger and may do self-harm like cutting on oneself.

Paranoid personality disorder:

Paranoid personality disorder tends to be suspicious of others, read hidden motives in others, hypersensitive to criticism, holds grudges, prone to anger and retaliation, cold and controlling in relationships.

Histrionic or Hysterical personality disorders:

---

1. American Psychiatric Association, *Diagnostic*, 645–84.

Histrionic or Hysterical personality disorders tend to be attention-seeking, manipulative, very emotional, and seductive.

Dependent personality disorders:

Dependent personality disorders are characterized by excessive dependence on others.

Perfectionistic or Compulsive personality disorders (OCPD):

Perfectionistic or Compulsive personality disorders tend to be rigid, judgmental, and have unrealistic expectations of self and others.

In general, people with personality disorders tend to blame others for problems resulting from their disorder. Perfectionists tend to blame themselves excessively too, but they might hide it from others.

The "self-righteous prig" C.S. Lewis talked about in the beginning of chapter one would be deficient in his self-evaluation and excessive in his judgment of others and sounds like a perfectionist.

Schizoid personality disorders:

Schizoid personality disorders tend to isolate themselves and show not much desire to adjust well in society.

Schizotypal personality disorders:

Schizotypal personality disorders show odd or peculiar appearance, thinking, and behavior and tend to isolate.

Narcissistic personality disorder:

Narcissistic personality disorder is characterized by grandiose esteem of themselves and devaluation of others, especially others who they consider as competition, and are arrogant and envious.

Antisocial personality disorder:

Antisocial personality disorders tend to commit crimes and show no remorse; many of them may have criminal superegos which approve of criminal behavior. They tend to be impulsive, irresponsible, and undependable because of lying, manipulation, and lack of guilt and shame.

Avoidant personality disorders:

Avoidant personality disorders tend to avoid dealing with even somewhat difficult choices, tend to be excessively shy, introverted and too sensitive to rejection.

NOTE: There are people with mixed personality disorders with features of more than one type noted above and some with nonspecific personality disorders who do not fit in any of the above types.

EWERT H. COUSINS' IDEA OF A SECOND AXIAL PERIOD

Cousins says we can discern a transformation of consciousness into a global consciousness in the 21st century which he calls the Second Axial Period. He includes a convergence of different cultures as a part of this. By the meeting of different religions and cultures, the global consciousness gets complexified. In this period, religions have two tasks: join the dialogue of religions and direct their energies to solve the common human problems.

Cousins emphasizes the views of Pierre Teilhard de Chardin, as we saw earlier, who integrated spirituality and science. Cousins presents the teachings of Raimundo Panikkar as the systematic theology of the future in his book *Christ of the 21st Century*.[2] I have discussed some things about Panikkar (Chapter Six, *Parliament of the World's Religions* section). He had doctorates in chemistry, theology and philosophy. I have attended several of his enlightening talks. In one of his talks, somebody asked what one should do if a religious leader pursues a wrong agenda and he answered: "Practice holy disobedience."

It was no secret during the Parliament of the World's Religions in Barcelona in 2004 that Panikkar had been married for several years and was functioning fully as a Roman Catholic priest. His name, Panikkar, is a Hindu name from Kerala, India which is my home state. A Catholic priest from Kerala I met in Barcelona told me he wondered how Panikkar was married and functioned as a Catholic priest. I have great respect and admiration for Chardin and Panikkar.

My view is that if we are to name a Second Axial Period, the 20th century deserves the qualification for a great many reasons including the following: the Gandhian revolution, the formation of the U.N., the second Parliament of the World's Religions when the Global Ethic was declared, quantum theory and its implication about consciousness, the spread of yoga and meditation, the Second Vatican Council, the teachings of Thomas Merton, Dalai Lama, Deepak Chopra, the Near Death Experience studies, Jaspers' view of the Axial Age, Freud's and Jung's psychologies, and many religious mystics.

2. Cousins, *Christ*, 73–104.

About the Author

N. S. Xavier, M.D., is a psychiatrist who integrated spirituality in his practice in Birmingham for forty-one years. Dr. Xavier has been teaching about Conscience and Eastern Religions in the Spirituality and Medicine course at UAB for seventeen years. His book, *Fulfillment Using Real Conscience,* has received good reviews in *Psychiatric Times, Christian Ethics Today,* endorsements from Dr. Deepak Chopra, Nobel Peace winner President Oscar Arias, Fr. Richard Rohr, Bishop John Shelby Spong, and blessings from Pope Francis. He is also the author of *The Two Faces of Religion,* an exploration of the healthy and sick sides of religion. It received endorsements by Professor Wayne Oates, Jesse Milby, Seshagiri Rao, and Nobel Laureate Elie Wiesel. His documentary, *"The World's Most Enlightening Region"* is about the unique history of two-thousand years of harmony among Hindus, Jews, Christians, and Muslims from the seventh century. It also addresses the extremism within each of these religions which was overcome by using conscience. The documentary was shown at The Parliament of the World's Religions, has aired twice on Alabama Public Television, and is available on YouTube. Notably, the documentary has been used in a Peace Studies course at the Loyola Institute of Peace and International Affairs, Kochi, India. Rev. Kevin Higgs, Rev. Ray Wade, and Xavier gave a presentation on Christian Nonviolence at the Parliament of the World's Religions in Chicago on August 14, 2023.

A psychiatrist insightful of conscience and knowledgeable about World Religions, particularly Christianity, Dr. Xavier seeks to provide a pragmatic perspective on how to use the guidance of conscience to make good choices and produce what St. Paul called the Fruit of the Spirit: love, joy, peace, patience, kindness, goodness, faithfulness, gentleness, and self-control. Such benefits are wonderful for individuals, families, communities, and the world. This book also addresses why people make bad choices and how to avoid those choices and their detrimental consequences. This has become crucial in a world full of conflicts with potential for catastrophe, even to the point of human extinction.

Bibliography

Alberta, Tim. *The Kingdom, The Power, and The Glory.* New York: HarperCollins, 2023.
Ajoy, April. *Star-Spangled Jesus.* New York: Worthy, 2024.
American Psychiatric Association. *Diagnostic and Statistical Manual of Mental Disorders.* 5th ed. Washington, DC: American Psychiatric Publishing, 2013.
Anālayo, Bhikkhu. "The Buddha and His Son." Insight Meditation Society. Accessed May 31, 2025. https://www.dharma.org/the-buddha-and-his-son.
Aristotle. *Nicomachean Ethics Book Four.* Translated by W.D. Ross. New York: Oxford University Press, 1924.
———. *Poetics.* Translated by Gerald F. Elses. Ann Arbor: University of Michigan Press, 1967.
———. *Rhetoric Book II.* Translated by W. Rhys Roberts. New York: Dover, 2004.
Armstrong, Karen. *The Great Transformation.* New York: Alfred A. Knopf, 2006.
———. *Muhammad.* New York: HarperOne, 2006.
———. *Twelve Steps to a Compassionate Life.* New York: Anchor, 2011.
Atwoli, Lukoye, et al. "Call for Emergency Action to Limit Global Temperature Increases, Restore Biodiversity, and Protect Health." *MBio, an Open Access Journal published by the American Society for Microbiology* 12.5 (2021). https://pmc.ncbi.nlm.nih.gov/articles/PMC8546844.
Augustine. *Confessions.* Edited and translated by Philip Burton with an introduction by Robin Lane Fox. New York: Alfred A. Knopf, 2001.
———. *The Confessions of St. Augustine.* Edited and translated by Rex Warner. New York: The New American Library, 1963.
Aurelius, Marcus. *Meditations.* Edited and Translated by Martin Hammond. New York: Penguin, 2006.
Balmer, Randall. "Still Wrestling With the Devil." *Christianity Today.* March 2, 1998. https://www.christianitytoday.com/1998/03/still-wrestling-with-devil.
Barr, Stephen M. "St. Augustine and the Beginning of Time." Society of Catholic Scientists. January 30, 2020. https://catholicscientists.org/articles/st-augustine-beginning-of-time.
Barrett, David B., et al. *World Christian Encyclopedia.* Oxford: Oxford University Press, 2001.
Beck, Glenn. *Addicted to Outrage.* New York: Threshold Editions/Mercury Radio Arts, 2018.
Bellah, Robert N. *Religion in Human Evolution.* Cambridge, MA: Harvard University, MD Press, 2017.

Bellah, Robert N., and Hans Joas. *The Axial Age and Its Consequences.* Cambridge, MA: Belknap Press of Harvard University Press, 2012.
Bellarmine University. "About Eureka!" https://www.bellarmine.edu/learningcommunity/eureka/about.
Berger, James M., and J. D. Crowley. *Conscience.* Wheaton, IL: Crossway, 2016.
Berger, James M. *Extremism.* Cambridge, MA: MIT Press, 2018.
Bharakda, Arif. "The Greatness of the Prophet Muhammed: The Story of the Lady Who Threw Garbage." September 3, 2024. https://themuslimvibe.com/faith-islam/the-greatness-of-the-prophet-muhammed-the-story-of-the-lady-who-threw-garbage.
Borg, Marcus J. *The Heart of Christianity.* New York: HarperCollins, 2003.
Boudinhon, Auguste. "Excommunication." *New Advent Catholic Encyclopedia* (website). New York: Robert Appleton Company, 1909. https://www.newadvent.org/cathen/05678a.htm.
Buber, Martin. *Good and Evil.* Translated by Ronald Gregor Smith and Michael Bullock. New York: Scribner's Sons, 1952.
Buscho, Ann Gold. "Is Your Marriage Doomed After an Affair?" *Psychology Today,* February 1, 2022.
Campolo, Tony. *Following Jesus Without Embarrassing God.* Nashville: Nelson, 1997.
Camus, Albert. "Peace, The Only Combat: Between Hell and Reason." *Combat Magazine,* August 8, 1945.
Cason, Mike. "Gov. Kay Ivey Signs Bill Allowing Yoga in Alabama Public Schools." May 20, 2021. https://www.al.com/news/2021/05/gov-kay-ivey-signs-bill-allowing-yoga-in-alabama-public-schools.html.
CBS News. "Alabama Fan Receives Three Years for Auburn Tree Poisoning." March 22, 2013. https://www.cbsnews.com/news/alabama-fan-receives-3-years-for-auburn-tree-poisoning.
Center for Strategic and International Studies, Brief by Seth G. Jones and Catrina Doxsee, Published June 17, 2020. https://www.csis.org/analysis/escalating-terrorism-problem-united-states.
Centers for Disease Control and Prevention. "Rates of COVID-19 Cases or Deaths by Age Group and Vaccination Status." Accessed February 25, 2025. https://data.cdc.gov/Public-Health-Surveillance/Rates-of-COVID-19-Cases-or-Deaths-by-Age-Group-and/3rge-nu2a.
Chardin, Pierre Teilhard. *Phenomenon of Man.* Translated by Bernard Wall. New York: HarperCollins, 1965.
———. As quoted in *The Joy of Kindness,* by Robert J. Furey. New York: Crossroad, 1993.
Chenoweth, Erica. "The Future of Nonviolent Resistance." *Journal of Democracy* 31.3 (2020) 69–84.
Chenoweth, Erica, and Maria Stephan. *Why Civil Resistance Works.* New York: Columbia University Press, 2012.
Chopra, Deepak. Foreword to *Radical Kindness: The Life-Changing Power of Giving and Receiving,* by Angela C. Santomero. New York: HarperCollins, 2019.
Claiborne, Shane. *Rethinking Life.* Edited by Amy Pagliarella. Grand Rapids: Zondervan, 2023.

CNBC. "How Photographs Saved the Israel-Egypt Peace Talks." October 2, 2024. https://www.cnbc.com/2014/10/02/how-photographs-saved-the-israel-egypt-peace-talks.html.
Collins, Francis S. *The Road to Wisdom*. New York: Hachette, 2024.
Confucius. *The Analects of Confucius: A Philosophical Translation*. Translated by Roger T. Ames and Henry Rosemont, Jr. New York: Ballantine, 1999.
Cousins, Ewert. *Christ of the Twenty-First Century*. Rockport, MA: Element, 1992.
Covey, Stephen R. "The Way to a Valueless Society." *World Without Violence*. Edited by Arun Gandhi. Memphis, TN: M. K. Gandhi Institute for Nonviolence, 1999.
Cox, Daniel A. "After the Ballots Are Counted: Conspiracies, Political Violence, and American Exceptionalism." American Enterprise Institute, February 11, 2021. https://www.aei.org/research-products/report/after-the-ballots-are-counted-conspiracies-political-violence-and-american-exceptionalism.
Dalai Lama, The Fourteenth. *Kindness, Clarity, and Insight*. Translated and edited by Jeffrey Hopkins, coedited by Elizabeth Napper. Ithaca, NY: Snow Lion, 1984.
Dalai Lama and Desmond Tutu. *The Book of Joy: Lasting Happiness in a Changing World*. Edited by Douglas Abrams. New York: Avery, 2016.
Dawkins, Richard. *The God Delusion*. Boston: Houghton Mifflin Harcourt, 2006.
Dean, John W. *Conservatives Without Conscience*. New York: Viking, 2006.
Djupe, Paul A., and Ryan P. Burge. "A Conspiracy at the Heart of It: Religion and Q." November 6, 2020. https://religioninpublic.blog/2020/11/06/a-conspiracy-at-the-heart-of-it-religion-and-q.
Dobson, Ed, et al. *The Fundamentalist Phenomenon: The Resurgence of Conservative Christianity*. Grand Rapids: Baker, 1986.
Donald, Merlin. *Origins of the Modern Mind*. Cambridge, MA: Harvard University Press, 1993.
Dong, Yuhong. "From Blindness to 360-Degree Vision–What 4,000 Near-Death Cases Bring to Light." *Epoch Times*, October 19, 2024. https://www.theepochtimes.com/health/from-blindness-to-360-degree-vision-what-4000-near-death-cases-bring-to-light-5731725.
Dostoyevsky, Fyodor. *The Brothers Karamazov*. Translated by Andrew R. MacAndrew. New York: Bantam, 1970.
Easwaran, Eknath, ed. *The Upanishads*. Translated by Eknath Easwaran. Tomales, CA: Nilgiri, 2007.
———. *The Dhammapada (Buddha)*. Translated by Eknath Easwaran. Blue Mountain Center of Meditation. New York: Penguin, 1986.
Eckhart, Meister. *Selected Writings*. Translated by Thomas V. LeBeau. Chicago: Modern Language Association, 2014.
Einstein, Albert. "The Einstein Theory of Living." *New York Times*, March 12, 1944, 16.
———. *The World as I See It*. New York: Citadel, 2000.
———. *The World as I See It*. Abridged ed. Chicago: Philosophical Library, 1949.
Emerson, Ralph Waldo. *Nature*. Boston: James Munroe, 1836.
———. *Self-Reliance, and Other Essays*. New York: Dover, 1993.
Flannery, Austin, O. P., ed. *Vatican Council II: The Conciliar and Post Conciliar Documents*. "Gaudium et Spes, Pastoral Constitution on the Church in the Modern World." Collegeville, MN: Liturgical Press, 1980.
Fox, Matthew. *Original Blessing*. Santa Fe: Bear, 1983.

Franklin, Benjamin. *The Autobiography of Benjamin Franklin*. Edited by Frank Woodworth Pine. New York: Touchstone, 2004.

Fredericks, James L. "At the Limits: Raimundo Panikkar's Long Theological Journey." *Commonwealth Magazine*, November 15, 2010. https://www.commonwealmagazine.org/limits.

French, David. "Christian Political Ethics Are Upside Down." *The Dispatch*. Accessed August 21, 2022. https://thedispatch.com/newsletter/frenchpress/christian-political-ethics-are-upside.

Freud, Sigmund. *New Introductory Lecture on Psychoanalysis*. Translated and edited by James Strachey. New York: Norton, 1965.

Fromm, Erich. *To Have or To Be*. Edited by Ruth Nanda Anshen. New York: Bantam, 1981.

———. *The Art of Loving*. New York: Harper & Bros., 1956.

Fry, Douglas P. *Beyond War*. New York: Oxford University Press, 2007.

Furey, Robert J. *The Joy of Kindness*. New York: Crossroad, 1993.

Gandhi, M. K., *An Autobiography* or *The Story of My Experiments with Truth*. Translated by Mahadev Desai. General Editor Shriman Narayan. New York: Penguin, 1982.

———. *Young India*. New York: Huebsch, 1923.

Garraty, John A., and Peter Gay, eds. *The Columbia History of the World*. New York: Harper & Row, 1974.

Goleman, Daniel. *Emotional Intelligence*. 10th ed. New York: Bantam, 2007.

Griffiths, Bede. *The Marriage of East and West*. Springfield, IL: Templegate, 1982.

———. *Universal Wisdom*. London: Fount/HarperCollins, 1994.

Griswold, Eliza. *Circle of Hope: A Reckoning with Love, Power and Justice in an American Church*. New York: Farrar, Straus and Giroux, 2024.

Guidepost Solutions. "Southern Baptist Convention Executive Committee Sexual Abuse Task Force Independent Investigation Report." May 22, 2022. https://guidepostsolutions.com/sbc-ec-investigation/, https://www.documentcloud.org/documents/22031737-final-guidepost-solutions-independent-investigation-report.

Equal Justice Initiative. "The Legacy Sites." Accessed May 22, 2025. https://legacysites.eji.org/about.

Hamer, Dean. As quoted in *Adi Shankaracharya* by Pavan K. Varma. Chennai: Tranquebar, 2018.

Hayhoe, Katharine. Samford University Howard College of Arts and Sciences Annual J. Roderick Davis Lecture in Partnership with Cumberland School of Law and the Office of the Provost, Birmingham, AL. February 13, 2024. Video, 1:20:10. https://vimeo.com/914920763.

Hoffer, Eric. *The True Believer*. New York: Harper & Row, 1966.

Holland, Tom. *Dominion*. New York: Basic, 2019.

Humphreys, Fisher, and Philip Wise. *Fundamentalism*. Macon, GA: Smyth & Helwys, 2004.

Huxley, Aldous. *The Perennial Philosophy*. New York: Harper & Row, 1945.

Hoffer, Eric. *The True Believer*. New York: Harper & Row, 1966.

Homer. *The Odyssey*. Translated by Robert Fagles. New York: Penguin, 1999.

Huecker M. R., et al. *Domestic Violence*. Treasure Island, FL: StatPearls, 2023. https://www.ncbi.nlm.nih.gov/books/NBK499891.

Hugo, Victor. *Les Misérables*. Translated by Lee Fahnestock and Norman MacAfee. Original translation by Charles E. Wilbour. New York: Penguin, 1987.
James, William. *The Varieties of Religious Experiences*. Edited by Martin E. Marty. New York: New American Library, 1958.
Jaspers, Karl. "Is Science Evil? Answering the Attack on Modern Knowledge and Technology." *Commentary Magazine*, March 1950. Accessed May 24, 2024. https://www.commentary.org/articles/karl-jaspers/is-science-evilanswering-the-attack-on-modern-knowledge-and-technology.
———. *The Origin and Goal of History*. Translated by Michael Bullock. New York: Routledge Classics, 2021.
Jefferson, Thomas. "From Thomas Jefferson to Benjamin Rush, 21 April 1803." Founders Online. https://founders.archives.gov/documents/Jefferson/01-40-02-0178-0001.
Jia, Katherine M., et al. "Estimated Preventable COVID-19-Associated Deaths Due to Non-Vaccination in the United States." *European Journal of Epidemiology* 38.11 (2023) 1125–28. doi:10.1007/s10654-023-01006-3. https://pmc.ncbi.nlm.nih.gov/articles/PMC10123459.
Johnson, Daryl. *Hate Land*. Lanham, MD: Prometheus, 2019.
Johnston, William. *Arise, My Love: Mysticism for a New Era*. New York: Orbis, 2000.
Jones, E. Stanley. *Gandhi: Portrait of a Friend*. Nashville: Abingdon Classics, 1973.
Keats, John. "A Thing of Beauty is a Joy Forever." *Endymion,* Book I, line 1 (1818). https://www.gutenberg.org/files/24280/24280-h/24280-h.htm.
———. "Ode on a Grecian Urn." Lines 49–50 (1819). https://www.poetryfoundation.org/poems/44477/ode-on-a-grecian-urn.
Khan, Hazrat Inayat. *Mastery Through Accomplishment*. Translated and edited by Donald A. Graham. New Lebanon, NY: Sufi Order Publication, 1978.
Khayyam, Omar. *Rubaiyat*. Translated by Edward FitzGerald. New York: Penguin, 2000.
King, Martin Luther Jr. "Letter from Birmingham Jail." In *Why We Can't Wait*. New York: Signet, 1963.
———. *Strength to Love*. Edited by Melvin Arnold and Charles L. Wallis. New York: Harper & Row, 1963.
———. *Testament of Hope*. Edited by James M. Washington. San Francisco: Harper, 1986.
———. *Why We Can't Wait*. Edited by Stanley Levison and Clarence Jones. New York: Signet, 2000.
Kornfield, Jack. *Buddha's Little Instruction Book*. New York: Bantam, 1994.
Krishnamacharya, N.V.R. "Episode 91 on Prekshaa." *The Mahabharata*. Translated by N.V.R. Krishnamacharya. Tirupati, India: Tirumala Tirupati Devasthanams, 1983.
———. "The Squirrel and Hanuman: Lessons from the Ramayana." *The Mahabharata*. Translated by N.V.R. Krishnamacharya. February 2, 2015. https://www.bhagavatam-katha.com/ramayana-story-little-squirrel-who-helped-lord-rama.
Kushner, Harold S. *When All You've Ever Wanted Isn't Enough*. New York: Summit, 1986.
Lao Tzu. *Tao Te Ching*. Translated by Arthur Waley. Wordsworth Classics of World Literature. Ware, England: Wordsworth Editions, 1996.
———. *The Sayings of Lao Tzŭ*. Translated by Lionel Giles. London: The Orient Express, 1904.
Lea, H.C. *A History of the Inquisition of Spain*. Vol. 3, Book 8. London: Macmillan, 1922.

Lee, Harper. *To Kill a Mockingbird*. Edited by Tay Hohoff. New York: Warner, 1960.

Lewis, C.S. *Mere Christianity*. New York: Macmillan, 1952.

Longfellow, Henry Wadsworth. "The Village Blacksmith." In *Complete Poetical Works*. Edited by H. W. Longfellow. Boston: Houghton Mifflin, 1886.

MacGregor, Geddes. *Reincarnation in Christianity*. Wheaton, IL: Quest, 1990.

Macmillan, Margaret. *War: How Conflict Shaped Us*. New York: Random House, 2020.

Malone, David. "Fundamentals." Wheaton College, Buswell Library Special Collections. May 29, 2009. https://recollections.wheaton.edu/2009/05/fundamentals.

Marist Institute for Public Opinion. "A Nation Divided? Nearly Half of Americans Think U.S. Could See Another Civil War." May 21, 2024. https://maristpoll.marist.edu/polls/a-nation-divided.

Maslow, Abraham H. *Religions, Values, and Peak-Experiences*. New York: Penguin, 1975.

Mason, George A. "Applying Christian Wisdom." *Christian Ethics Today*, Issue 127. Accessed March 23, 2023. https://www.christianethicstoday.com/wp/applying-christian-wisdom.

May, Gerald G. *Addiction and Grace*. San Francisco: Harper & Row, 1991.

May, Rollo. *Freedom and Destiny*. New York: Norton, 1981.

McAleer, Tony. *The Cure for Hate: A Former White Supremacist's Journey from Violent Extremism to Radical Compassion*. Vancouver: Arsenal Pulp, 2019.

McKinney, Janie Forsyth. "As a Twelve-year-old, I Defied the KKK to Comfort Freedom Riders Injured in a Firebombing." *Los Angeles Times*. May 9, 2021. https://www.latimes.com/opinion/story/2021-05-09/op-ed-freedom-riders-60th-anniversary.

Merton, Thomas. *The Asian Journal of Thomas Merton, Edited from Merton's Notebook*. Edited by Naomi Burton Stone et al. New York: New Directions, 1975.

———. *Contemplation in a World of Action*. Edited by William H. Shannon. New York: Image, 1973.

———. Foreword to *The Mysticism of The Cloud of Unknowing*, by William Johnston. New York: Desclee, 1967.

———. *Love and Living*. Edited by Naomi Burton Stone and Brother Patrick Hart. New York: Bantam, 1980.

———. *The Way of Chuang Tzu*. New York: New Directions, 1969.

Moody, Raymond A., Jr. *The Light Beyond*. Edited by Lillian Watson. New York: Bantam, 1988.

———. *Life After Life*. Foreword by Eben Alexander. New York: Harper Collins, 2015.

Moore, Russell. *Losing Our Religion: An Altar Call for Evangelical America*. New York: Sentinel, 2023.

Moore, Walter. *Schrödinger: Life and Thought*. Cambridge: Cambridge University Press, 1989.

Mother Teresa of Calcutta. "Mother Teresa on Religion." Missionaries of Charity. https://missionariesofcharity.org/mother-teresa-on-religion-read-more.html.

Murthy, Vivek H. *Together: The Healing Power of Human Connection in a Sometimes Lonely World*. New York: Harper Collins, 2020.

Muesse, Mark W. *The Age of the Sages: The Axial Age in Asia and the Near East*. Minneapolis: Fortress, 2013.

Naselli, Andrew David, and J. D. Crowley. *Conscience: What It Is, How to Train It, and Loving Those Who Differ*. Wheaton, IL: Crossway, 2016.

Niebuhr, Reinhold. *Moral Man and Immoral Society*. Louisville: Westminster John Knox, 2021.

———. "The Serenity Prayer." In *The Essential Reinhold Niebuhr: Selected Essays and Addresses*, edited by Robert McAfee Brown. New York: Harper & Row, 1951.

Nietzsche, Friedrich. *Beyond Good and Evil*. Translated by Helen Zimmern. New York: Dover, 1998.

NPR. "NPR Exclusive: U.S. Overdose Deaths Plummet, Saving Thousands of Lives." September 18, 2024. https://www.npr.org/2024/09/18/nx-s1-5107417/overdose-fatal-fentanyl-death-opioid.

Nussbaum, Martha C. "Roger Williams and John Cotton." In *Liberty of Conscience*. New York: Basic, 2008.

Parnia, S., et al. "New Evidence Indicates Patients Recall Death Experiences After Cardiac Arrest." *Elsevier's Science Daily*, September 14, 2023. https://www.sciencedaily.com/releases/2023/09/230914175140.htm

Pasternak, Boris Leonidovich. *Doctor Zhivago*. Translated by Manya Harari and Michael Hayward. New York: Pantheon, 1958.

Peck, M. Scott. *The Road Less Traveled: A New Psychology of Love, Traditional Values, and Spiritual Growth*. New York: Simon & Schuster, 1978.

Pew Research Center. "About Three-in-Ten U.S. Adults Are Now Religiously Unaffiliated." December 14, 2021. https://www.pewresearch.org/religion/2021/12/14/about-three-in-ten-u-s-adults-are-now-religiously-unaffiliated.

———. "Attitudes Toward Spirituality and Religion." May 29, 2018. https://www.pewresearch.org/religion/2018/05/29/attitudes-toward-spirituality-and-religion.

———. "Forty-Five Percent of Americans Say U.S. Should Be a 'Christian' Nation." October 27, 2022. "https://www.pewresearch.org/religion/2022/10/27/45-of-americans-say-u-s-should-be-a-christian-nation.

———. "How Religion Intersects with Americans' Views on the Environment." November 17, 2022. https://www.pewresearch.org/religion/2022/11/17/how-religion-intersects-with-americans-views-on-the-environment.

———. "Religion in India: Tolerance and Segregation." June 29, 2021. https://www.pewresearch.org/religion/2021/06/29/religion-in-india-tolerance-and-segregation.

———. "Religious 'Nones' in America: Who They Are and What They Believe." January 24, 2024. https://www.pewresearch.org/religion/2024/01/24/religious-nones-in-america-who-they-are-and-what-they-believe.

———. "Republicans More Likely than Democrats to Believe in Heaven, Say Only Their Faith Leads There." November 23, 2021. https://www.pewresearch.org/short-reads/2021/11/23/republicans-more-likely-than-democrats-to-believe-in-heaven-say-only-their-faith-leads-there.

———. "Spirituality Among Americans." December 7, 2023. https://www.pewresearch.org/religion/2023/12/07/spirituality-among-americans.

———. "Two-thirds of U.S. Catholics Unaware of Pope's New Restrictions on Traditional Latin Mass." October 7, 2021. https://www.pewresearch.org/short-reads/2021/10/07/two-thirds-of-u-s-catholics-unaware-of-popes-new-restrictions-on-traditional-latin-mass.

Picciolini, Christian. *Breaking Hate*. New York: Hachette, 2020.

Pinker, Steven. *Enlightenment Now: The Case for Reason, Science, Humanism, and Progress*. New York: Allen Lane, Penguin Random House, 2018.

Plato. *Apology.* Retrieved from Perseus Digital Library https://data.perseus.org/citations/urn:cts:greekLit:tlg0059.tlg002.perseus-grc1:17a.

———. *Phaedo.* Oxford: Clarendon, 1911.

———. *The Republic. Book IV.* Translated by Allan Bloom. New York: Basic, 1993.

Pope Francis. *Laudato Si'. On Care for Our Common Home. Encyclical Letter.* Vatican City: Vatican Press, 2015.

Pope Francis, and Austen Ivereigh. *Let Us Dream: The Path to a Better Future.* New York: Simon & Schuster, 2020.

———. The Holy See. "Pope Francis' Dialogue with the Students of the Albertelli Lyceo in Rome." December 20, 2019. https://www.vatican.va/content/francesco/pt/speeches/2019/december/documents/papa-francesco_20191220_visita-liceo-albertelli.html.

Rabbi Hillel. "Jewish Holy Scriptures: Ethics of the Fathers (Pirkei Avot)."Jewish Virtual Libaray. https://www.jewishvirtuallibrary.org/ethics-of-the-fathers-pirkei-avot.

Radhakrishnan, S. *Eastern Religions and Western Thought.* Delhi: Oxford, 1990.

———. *Indian Religions.* Delhi: Orient, 1983.

Rajaram, M., ed. *Thirukkural.* Translated by M. Rajaram. New Delhi: Rupa, 2009.

Ramachandran, G. "The Essence of Gandhi." https://www.mkgandhi.org/g_relevance/Epilogue.php

Ricks, Thomas E. *Waging a Good War: A Military History of the Civil Rights Movement, 1954–1968.* New York: Picador, 2023.

Riggleman, Denver. *Bigfoot...It's Complicated.* United States: Outskirts, 2020.

Robinson, David W. *Conscience and Jung's Moral Vision: From Id to Thou.* New York: Paulist, 2005.

Rohr, Richard. *Immortal Diamond.* San Francisco: Jossey-Bass, 2013.

Romero, Robert Chao, and Marcos Canales. *Las Casas on Faithful Witness.* Sacred Roots Spiritual Classics. Wichita, KS: TUMI; Upland, IN: Samuel Morris, 2022. https://pillars.taylor.edu/spiritualclassics/5.

Rubenstein, Richard E. *When Jesus Became God: The Epic Fight over Christ's Divinity in the Last Days of Rome.* New York: Harcourt, 1999.

Rubin, Theodore Isaac. *Compassion and Self-hate.* New York: Ballantine, 1975.

Rudd, Kevin. *The Avoidable War.* New York: Public Affairs, 2023.

Rumi. *The Essential Rumi.* Translated by A. J. Arshaghyan. New York: HarperOne, 2003.

Santomero, Angela C. *Radical Kindness: The Life-Changing Power of Giving and Receiving.* New York: Harper Collins, 2019.

Sasse, Ben. *Them: Why We Hate Each Other—and How to Heal.* Edited by Tim Bartlett. New York: St. Martin's, 2018.

Schopenhauer, Arthur. *Essays and Aphorisms.* Translated by R. J. Hollingdale. London: Penguin, 2014.

Scott, Randall K. *Like a Shadow That Never Departs.* Self-published, iUniverse, 2021.

Shapiro, Ben. *The Authoritarian Moment.* New York: Harper Collins, 2021.

Shapiro, Rami M. *Perennial Wisdom for the Spiritually Independent.* United States: Skylight Paths, 2013.

Shakespeare, William. *Hamlet.* Edited by Harold Bloom. New York: Chelsea House, 2004.

———. *Julius Caesar.* Edited by Roma Gill. Oxford: Oxford University Press, 2001.

———. *The Tragedy of King Richard III.* Edited by Roma Gill. Oxford: Oxford University Press, 2001.

———. *The Tragedy of King Richard III*. Edited by Roma Gill. Oxford: Oxford University Press, 2001.
Shankara, Adi. *Crest – Jewel of Discrimination*. Translated by Swami Prabhavananda and Christopher Isherwood. Hollywood: Vedanta, 1970.
Shimron, Yonat. "Study: Most Americans Are Spiritual, but a Growing Number Say They Are Not Religious." *Religion News Service*, December 7, 2023. https://religionnews.com/2023/12/07/study-most-americans-are-spiritual-but-a-growing-number-say-they-are-not-religious.
Smedes, Lewis B. *Forgive and Forget*. New York: Harper & Row, 1984.
Smith, Huston. *The World's Religions*. New York: HarperCollins, 1991.
Smith, Kenneth L., and Ira G. Zepp Jr. *Search for the Beloved Community: The Thinking of Martin Luther King Jr*. Edited by Kenneth L. Smith and Ira G. Zepp Jr. King of Prussia: Judson, 1986.
Smithsonian Institute. "What Does it Mean to be Human?" Last updated January 3, 2024. https://humanorigins.si.edu/evidence/human-fossils/species/homo-sapiens.
Sophocles. *Antigone*. Translated by Sir George Young. Edited by Stanley Appelbaum. New York: Dover, 1993.
Sorabji, Richard. *Moral Conscience Through the Ages*. Chicago: University of Chicago Press, 2014.
Spong, John Shelby. *Unbelievable: Why Neither Ancient Creeds Nor the Reformation Can Produce a Living Faith Today*. Edited by Christine Mary Spong. New York: Harper Collins, 2018.
Stanley, Andy. *Not in It to Win It: Why Choosing Sides Sidelines the Church*. Grand Rapids: Zondervan, 2022.
Stevenson, Bryan. *Just Mercy: A Story of Justice and Redemption*. New York: Spiegel & Grau, 2015.
Stockholm International Peace Research Institute. "World Military Expenditure Reaches New Record High as European Spending Surges." April 24, 2023. https://www.sipri.org/media/press-release/2023/world-military-expenditure-reaches-new-record-high-european-spending-surges.
Sullivan, Francis A. *Salvation Outside the Church?* New York: Paulist, 1992.
Taylor, Barbara Brown. *Holy Envy*. New York: HarperCollins, 2018.
The Economist. "The Beating of Argentina's Former First Lady Fits a Shameful Pattern." October 12–18, 2024. https://www.economist.com/the-americas/2024/10/10/the-beating-of-argentinas-former-first-lady-fits-a-shameful-pattern.
———. "Xi Jinping Is Trying to Fuse the Ideologies of Marx and Confucius." November 4, 2023. https://www.economist.com/china/2023/11/02/xi-jinping-is-trying-to-fuse-the-ideologies-of-marx-and-confucius.
———. "Women in the Middle East Are Leading a Revolt Against Prudish Men." January 5, 2023. https://www.economist.com/middle-east-and-africa/2023/01/05/women-in-the-middle-east-are-leading-a-revolt-against-prudish-men.
The Guardian. "I Yelled Out That I Have Kids: Police Officer Describes Attack by Capitol Rioters." January 16, 2021. https://www.theguardian.com/us-news/video/2021/jan/16/i-yelled-out-that-i-have-kids-police-officer-describes-attack-by-capitol-rioters-video.
Thucydides. *History of the Peloponnesian War*. Translated by Richard Crawley. New York: Dent, 1910.

Tillich, Paul. *The Eternal Now*. New York: Scribner's Sons, 1964.
Tolstoy, Leo. *The Kingdom of God Is Within You*. Translated by Constance Garnett. Lincoln: University of Nebraska Press, 1984.
Treece, Henry. *The Crusades*. New York: Barnes and Noble, 1994.
Twain, Mark. *Letters from the Earth*. Edited by Bernard DeVoto. New York: Harper & Row, 1962.
———. *Man's Place in the Animal World*. Edited by Shelley Fisher Fishkin. Berkeley: University of California Press, 2010.
———. *The Adventures of Huckleberry Finn*. London: William Collins, 2010.
Varma, Pavan K. *Adi Shankaracharya*. Translated by Dhiraj Kumar. Chennai: Tranquebar, 2018.
Vātsyāyana, Mallanaga. *The Complete Kāma Sūtra: The First Unabridged Modern Translation of the Classic Indian Text by Vāyana*. Translated by Daniélou Alain. Rochester, VT: Park Street, 1994.
Voltaire. "Letters on Various Subjects: 1762." *Letters on England*. Translated by Leonard Tancock. New York: Penguin, 1980.
Wade, Wyn Craig. *The Fiery Cross: The Ku Klux Klan in America*. New York: Simon and Schuster, 1987.
Wallis, Jim. *The False White Gospel: Rejecting Christian Nationalism, Reclaiming True Faith, and Refounding Democracy*. New York: St. Martins Essentials, 2024.
Walsh, Roger. *Essential Spirituality*. New York: Wiley & Sons, 1999.
Washington, George. "George Washington's Farewell Address." The Avalon Project, Lillian Goldman Law Library, September 17, 1796. Accessed May 24, 2025. https://avalon.law.yale.edu/18th_century/washing.asp.
Wells, H. G. *The Outline of History*. Edited by Raymond Postgate. New York: Doubleday, 1961.
Wesley, John. *Sermons on Several Occasions: A New Edition (1771)*. Quoting Sermon 50, "The Use of Money." Grand Rapids: Christian Classics Ethereal Library. Accessed May 31, 2025. https://ccel.org/ccel/w/wesley/sermons/cache/sermons.pdf.
Whitehead, Alfred North. *Process and Reality*. Edited by David Ray Griffin and Donald W. Sherburne. New York: Free Press, 1979.
Wikipedia. "Arthur Schopenhauer." Last edited on 30 May 2025. https://en.wikipedia.org/wiki/Arthur_Schopenhauer.
———. "Assassination of Anwar Sadat." Last edited on 19 May 2025. https://en.wikipedia.org/wiki/Assassination_of_Anwar_Sadat.
———. "Assassination of Mahatma Gandhi." Last edited on 28 May 2025. https://en.wikipedia.org/wiki/Assassination_of_Mahatma_Gandhi.
———. "Assassination of Yitzhak Rabin." Last edited on 24 May 2025. https://en.wikipedia.org/wiki/Assassination_of_Yitzhak_Rabin.
———. "Cochin Jews." Last edited on 8 May 2025. https://en.wikipedia.org/wiki/Cochin_Jews.
———. "Erwin Schrödinger." Last edited on 27 May 2025. https://en.wikipedia.org/wiki/Erwin_Schrödinger.
———. "George Floyd Protests." Last edited on 1 June 2025. https://en.wikipedia.org/wiki/George_Floyd_protests.
———. "Golden Rule." Last edited 30 May 2025. https://en.wikipedia.org/wiki/Golden_Rule.

———. "Inquisition." Last edited on 30 May 2025. https://en.wikipedia.org/wiki/Inquisition.

———. "Mughal War of Succession (1658–1659)." Last edited on 31 May 2025. https://en.wikipedia.org/wiki/Mughal_war_of_succession_(1658–1659).

———. "Mulian Rescues His Mother." Last edited on 5 May 2025. https://en.wikipedia.org/wiki/Mulian_Rescues_His_Mother.

———. "Origen." Last edited on 4 June 2025. https://en.wikipedia.org/wiki/Origen.

———. "Peace of Westphalia." Last edited on 25 May 2025. https://en.wikipedia.org/wiki/Peace_of_Westphalia.

———. "QAnon." Last edited on 31 May 2025. https://en.wikipedia.org/wiki/QAnon.

———. "Succession of the Roman Empire." Last edited on 5 June 2025. https://en.wikipedia.org/wiki/Succession_of_the_Roman_Empire.

———. "The War Prayer." Last edited on 31 March 2025. https://en.wikipedia.org/wiki/The_War_Prayer.

Wilbur, Ken, editor. *Quantum Questions: Mystical Writings of the World's Great Physicists*. Boulder, CO: Shambhala, 1984.

———. *Quantum Questions: Mystical Writings of the World's Great Physicists*. Boulder, CO: Shambala, 1984.

———. "The Mystic Vision" by Erwin Schrödinger. In *Quantum Questions: Mystical Writings of the World's Great Physicists*. Boulder, CO: Shambala, 1984.

Wilkinson & Finkbeiner. "Divorce Statistics: Over 115 Studies, Facts and Rates for 2022." July 26, 2022. https://www.wf-lawyers.com/divorce-s...ics-and-facts.

Worland, Justin. "The Conscience: Greta Thunberg, 2019 Person of the Year." *Time Magazine* 194, December 23, 2019. 27–28, 50–65.

Yahya, Harun. *The Importance of Conscience in the Quran*. Okmeydani-Istanbul/Turkey: Global, 2018.

Yajnavalkya. *Brihadaranyaka Upanishad: The Upanishads*. Translated by Max Müller. New York: Dover, 1962.

Yalom, Irvin D. *Existential Psychotherapy*. New York: Basic, 1980.

Zhekov, Yordan. *Conscience in Recovery from Drug Addiction*. Independently published, 2019.

———. *Conscience Therapy: Unveiling the Power of Spirituality in Conscientious Transformation*. Independently published, 2022.

Ziglar, Zig. *See You at the Top*. New Orleans: Pelican, 1975.

Index

12-step, 28, 43, 44, 45, 149, 226
9/11, 50

AA, 43, 44, 45, 132
Aboriginals, 190
Abortion, 50, 135, 232
ackee, 201
Acropolis, 75
Activism, 11, 52, 64, 187
Acupuncture, 69
Addiction, 2, 10, 15, 24, 28, 44–45, 53, 149, 156, 161, 167–168, 204, 208, 225–26
Advaita, 59, 177
Aeschylus, 7
Affairs, 85, 129, 178, 216
Agnostic, 32
Ajoy, April, 134
Akbar the Great, 63
Alabama Public Television, 239
Alabama, 38–39, 61, 128, 152, 239, 242
Alberta, Tim, 133
Alcoholics Anonymous, 132
Alexander, Eben, 92, 246
Ali, Hyder, 180
All in One, 78
Allah, 90, 107, 165
Allied Powers, 198
Altemeyer, Bob, 40
Ambrose, 108
American Abolitionists, 188
American Enterprise Institute, 127, 243

American Evangelicals in an Age of Extremism, 133
American Psychiatric Press, 235
American Psychological Association, 216
American Revolution, 122
Amma, 178. *See also* Sri Mata Amritanandamayi
Amos, 7, 84
Anabaptist, 120
Ananda, 55, 82, 172, 211
Ananias, 58
Anarchists, 50
Anathema, 107
Animal Liberation Front, 50
Animal Self, 24
Anti-tribe, 52
Antifa, 50
Antigone, 203, 204, 249
Antisocial personality, 237
Anxiety, 28, 30, 34, 41, 43, 51, 158, 171, 191, 193, 204, 207, 210
Apollo, 73, 215
Apostle John, 97
Arabic, 46, 112, 114, 182
Archimedes, 167
Arianism, 106
Arias, Oscar, 239
Aristotle, 5, 7, 66, 72–74, 114, 119, 148, 157, 222–23, 225, 227, 241
Arius, 102–106
Arjuna, 183
Armstrong, Karen, 9, 64, 70, 75, 88, 221
Arnold Toynbee, 122

Ashoka, 82, 122
    greatest of kings according to H. G. Wells, 8
    and Axial Age, 173–74
Assassin, 46
Assemblies of God, 156
Association for Humanistic Psychology, 32
Assyrian, 83, 85
Athanasius, 103, 104, 106
Atheism, 31
Atman, 59, 76–79, 82, 177
Auburn, 38, 242
Augustine, 57, 107–109, 111, 241
Aurangzeb, 63
Australia, 190
Authoritarian(ism), 39–40, 62, 248
Averroes, 114
Avoidant personality, 237
AWAreness during REsuscitation (AWARE), 91
Axial Age, 8, 54, 72, 75, 77, 82, 90, 132, 139, 191, 196, 226, 238, 242
    as defined by Karl Jaspers in 1949, 6
    Sages and philosophers of the Axial Age, 7
    development of conscience in, 10
    Karl Jaspers' The Origin and Goal of History, 64–65
    Great transformation in, 88–89
    sages stimulated people's consciences to promote goodness, 210-11
    Gentleness of the sages, 221–22
    Religions coexisting peacefully, 230–31
    Jesus reinforced Axial Age spirit, 233
Axis Period, 64

baboons, 189
Babylon(ians), 86–87, 179
Baha'i, 60
Baptism, 98
Barr, Stephen M., 111
Bartolomé de las Casas, 119
Basra, Iraq, 218
Beatitudes, 98

Bedouin, 9
Begin, Menachem 199
Bellah, Robert N., 7, 175
Berger, J.M., 46
Beyond War, 189, 244
Bible Belt, 128
Bigfoot, 34, 248
Bindusara, 175
birth control, 110
Black, Derek, 48
Black, Hugo, 151
Bodhi Tree, 80
Bond, Julian, 126
Bonobos, 188–189
Book of Revelation, 97
Book of Sirach, 119
borderline personality, 15, 235
Borg, Marcus J, .93
born again, 92, 93
Brahman, 76, 78–79, 82, 177
Breaking Hate, 47, 247
Brethren, 156
Brihadaranyaka Upanishad, 76, 80, 251
Brutus, 221
Buber, Martin 212
Buddha, 5, 7, 13–14, 23, 34, 43, 55, 80–82, 102, 202, 211–14, 217, 241, 243, 245
Buddhism, 14, 34, 44, 55, 60–61, 80–81, 102, 107, 109, 171, 173–175, 197, 211, 217, 225
    life after death and reincarnation, 67, 78
    and Ashoka, 82
    Merton on rebirth, (Contemplation in a World of Action), 93–94
    and mysticism, 168
    patience in Buddhism, 202
    development during Axial Age, 230–231
buffalo, 202

Camp David, 199
Campolo, Tony, 110, 190
Camus, Albert, 173
Capitol, 42, 127, 249

INDEX

Carter, James Earl, 139. *See also* Carter, Jimmy
Carter, Jimmy, 127, 199. *See also* Carter, James Earl
Cathar, 116
Catholic Church, 17, 109, 110, 116, 118, 120, 123, 129, 179
Catholic Counter Reformation, 120
Catholic, 27–29, 34, 43, 46, 79, 94, 116–18, 123, 129, 151, 162, 178–79, 196–97, 227, 232, 241–42
   differentiate conscience from superego and apply conscience, 17
   Pope Francis and climate crisis, 36
   history of Catholic and Protestant conflict, 41
   monk and famous writer Thomas Merton, 55–56
   Orthodox division, 106–107
   Augustine, 107–110
   Reformation, 120–21
   Pannikar, 238
celibacy, 60, 105, 112, 120, 179
Center for Strategic and International Studies, 49
Chanakya, 175
Chandragupta Maurya, 175
Chardin, Pierre Tielhard, 54, 138, 233, 238, 242
Chaura, Chauri, 187
Cheney, Dick, 134
Chenoweth, Erica, 186
Cheraman Dynasty, 176
Cheraman Mosque of Kodungallur, 181
Children's Crusade of 1212, 113
chimpanzees, 188, 189
China, 7, 61, 65–68, 184–186
Chopra, Deepak, 209, 239
Christian Broadcasting Network, 135
Christian Fundamentalism, 64, 123
Christian Nationalism, 135, 192, 250
Christian Nonviolence, 197, 198, 239
Christianity, 39, 60, 70, 86, 88, 93–97, 101–17, 120, 126, 132, 136, 138, 151, 158, 160, 163, 199, 239, 241–43, 246
   following conscience vs. contradicting conscience, 8
   St. Paul's conversion and ministry, 57–58
   Aristotle's influence, 74
   Inclusiveness, 93
   Nicene Creed, 106
   St. Augustine of Hippo, 107
   Crusades, 112–116
   historical significance of Conscience in Christianity, 129
   rejection within church, 147
   white Christian nationalism, 191–192
   loss of credibility, authority, identity, integrity, and stability, 232–233
Chuang Tzu, 70, 246
Circle of Hope, 135, 244
Civil rights movement, 16–17, 126, 131, 151, 187–88
Claiborne, Shane, 190–91, 242
clean energy, 35, 164
Clement of Alexandria, 101
climate crisis, 21, 27, 35–37, 138, 164, 169, 190, 198
CNN, 136
Cochin, 176, 179–80, 250
coconut, 146
Collins, Francis, 111, 129
Columbus, 118
commitment, 5, 33, 139, 161, 196–97, 218, 219
compassion, 5, 9, 23, 28, 33, 47, 56, 70, 82–86, 92, 100–102, 115, 152, 171–72, 178, 207–209, 221
   Active aspect of wisdom, 14
   Role of superego, 41–42
   And Axial Age, 64–65
   Jesus's command to love one another, 137
   strongest human therapeutic agent, 150
   Ashoka's promotion of compassion, 173–174
Confucianism, 60, 61, 67–69, 230–231

Confucius, 5, 7, 9, 65–68, 88, 215, 243, 249
Congressional Gold Medal, 126
Conscience Therapy, 15, 44, 251
conscience, 1–10, 11–18, 21–26, 30–39, 40–45, 47–59, 61–68, 70–79, 82–86, 88–90, 92–102, 104–112, 114–17, 119–24, 126–39, 142–46, 149–56, 158–60, 162–164, 166–76, 180–86, 188–89, 191–97, 199–200, 204, 207, 216–20, 222–27, 229–33, 239
- thirty times in the New Testament, 8
- spirituality without conscience as "Spiritual defect, 19
- shifting blame, 27–28
- Gandhi approach, 52–53
- Sepulveda conscience was stimulated, 119-120
- Southern Baptist Convention abuse report, 138
- Les *Misérables* Jean Valjean transformation by awakened conscience, 212-214

Connection with gentleness and humility, 220
Conservatives Without Conscience, 40
Constantine (the Great), 103–106, 191
contemplation, 93–94, 155, 246
contraception, 110, 111
Costa Rica, 195–96
Cotton, John, 34, 247
Council of Clermont, 112
Council of Nicaea, 104, 105
Council of Nicomedia, 106
Cousins, Ewert H., 89, 238
Covey, Stephen, 52
COVID-19, 1, 3, 15–16, 27, 133, 136, 145, 178, 190, 242, 245
Coyle, James Edwin, 151
Creed, 105–107
crotons, 200
Crow, Jim, 128
Crusades, 27, 112–14, 130, 250
Cuban Missile Crisis, 185

cults, 156
Cung, Nguyen Sinh, 125
Cyrus, 8, 87, 88

Daedalus, 73
Dalai Lama, 148, 171–72, 197, 209, 225–26, 238, 243
Daoism, 230
Darius, 175
Dawkins, Richard, 31
Dean, John W., 40
Deer Park, 81
Dees, Morris, 126
defiled conscience, 53
democracy, 139, 192, 232
Democrat, 38, 61
Democritus, 31
Denison University, 127
Department of Perceptual Studies, 77
Dependent personality, 236
depression, 5, 28, 30, 34, 51, 146, 149–50, 158, 194, 207, 216
Deus vult, 113
devil, 5, 6, 27, 38, 69, 87, 90, 202, 211, 241
dhamma, 81, 174
Dhammapada, 34, 81, 243
dharma, 81, 110, 174, 175, 241
diabolical self, 23, 24
Diagnostic and Statistical Manual of Mental Disorders, 235
Dionysus, 74, 103
Divinity of Jesus, 106
divorce, 147, 161–62, 216, 251
Djupe, Paul, 127
Dobson, Ed, 62
Doctor Zhivago, 166
Doctrine of the Mean, 5, 66
dog, 98, 104, 208
dogma, 110
Dominican, 117, 119
Donald, Merlin, 7, 75
Dong, Yuhong, 92
dopamine, 51, 160
Dostoyevsky, Fyodor, 33, 117–18, 243
Drug trafficking, 195
Duke, David, 48
Eagle Forum, 61

Earth Liberation Front, 50
Easwaran, Eknath, 76, 243
Eckhart, Meister, 166, 243
Edict of Milan, 103
Egan, Timothy, 125
ego, 10
Eightfold paths, 81
Einstein, Albert, 31, 168, 200, 206, 243
election, 35, 222
Emerson, Ralph Waldo, 173, 200
Emotional Intelligence, 226, 244
empathy, 11, 207
Emperor Frederick II of Germany, 114
Encyclical, 36, 248
endorphins, 51
Endymion, 166, 245
Equal Justice Initiative (EJI), 128, 244
Erinyes, 75
ethical conscience, 53
ethical, 2, 9, 25, 53, 60, 79, 85, 87, 102, 119, 164, 171, 214, 226, 230
ethics, 55, 88, 121, 214, 230, 244, 248
Eudaimonia, 74
Eumenides, 75
Eureka, 167
Euripides, 7
Eusebius, 102, 103, 104, 106
Evangelical, 36, 127, 232, 246
evil conscience, 53
excommunication, 107, 147, 242
existential guilt, 219
extremism, 23, 46, 106, 133, 242, 246
Ezekiel, 6, 7, 86, 180

Faith and Freedom Coalition, 133
faith, 1, 30–32, 44, 57–58, 60, 63, 96, 106, 111, 113–115, 124, 127, 134–37, 143, 171, 192, 197, 204, 215, 242, 247
   some people destroy faith by rejecting conscience, 8
   Shah Jahan and interfaith harmony, 63
   Parting of the sea for Moses, 113
   Martin Luther and Reformation, 120
   testing of your faith produces endurance, 201
faithfulness, 215, 219
Faiths United to Save Democracy, 192
Falwell, Jerry, 62, 232
fanaticism, 9, 62, 63, 94, 105, 179
Fanone, Mike, 42
Farid, Shayk, 181
fasting, 63, 205, 227
Festal Letter of 399, 103
Finkbeiner LLP law firm, 161
Flannery, Austin, O.P., 229
Floyd, George, 188, 250
Forgive and Forget, 195, 249
Forsyth, Janie, 152, 246. *See also* McKinney, Janie
Founding Fathers, 132
four noble truths, 81
Fox News, 136
Fox, George, 122
Fox, Matthew, 18, 109
Francis of Assisi, 31, 116, 191
Franciscan order, 115, 116
Franklin, Benjamin, 224
Freedom Monument Sculpture Park, 128
Freedom Riders, 152, 246
French, David, 16
Freud, Sigmund, 9, 10, 64
Fromm, Erich, 145, 171
Fruit of the Spirit, 2, 16–17, 100, 106, 138, 141, 163, 172–74, 205, 214, 231, 233
fruit, 27, 79, 82, 108, 146, 201–202, 211, 217, 225
Fry, Douglas, 189
Fulfillment Using Real Conscience, 30, 42, 149
fundamentalism, 52, 62, 124, 127

Galileo Galilei, 117
Galvani, Cardinal Pelagius, 191
Gandhi, 5, 11, 19, 52, 53, 62, 89, 122, 147, 154, 159, 169, 179, 182, 187–88, 195, 205, 210, 232, 243–45, 248, 250

(Gandhi continued)
    Gandhi and the "inner voice" referring to conscience, 3
    Gandhi used his conscience to stimulate the consciences of his followers, 130–131
    Martin Luther King Jr. and nonviolent Gandhian principles in Civil Rights Movement, 131, 151
Gandhi, Arun, 147
Gandhian, 11, 13, 52, 151, 180, 238
Gaza, 13
George Floyd peaceful protests, 188
Georgetown University's Bishop Desmond Tutu Chair in Faith and Justice, 192
global warming, 35, 36, 37, 154
gnostic, 116
Goa, 117, 178
God, 8–11, 19, 25–26, 29–31, 35–36, 44, 57, 60, 64–65, 67, 73–74, 82–86, 90–94, 96, 98, 101–103, 106–111, 113–14, 122, 127, 129, 136, 141, 143, 155–56, 163–64, 170, 172, 177, 183–84, 201, 206, 211–13, 216–18, 221, 224, 229–32
    ultimate reality and truth, 5–6
    religious but not spiritual, 55
    Ezekiel prophetic call, 70
    fear of God, 147
    made in the image and likeness of God, 190–191
Golden Mean, 5, 65, 66
Golden Rule, 4–10, 13, 21, 23, 26, 33, 39, 40, 65, 66, 88, 96, 134, 153, 156, 159, 171, 192, 196–97, 233, 250
Goleman, Daniel, 226
Gomer, 84
Good Samaritan, 99–100
Gotama, 80, 81
Graham, Billy, 17
Grand Inquisitor, 33, 116, 117
grandiose, 237
greed, 163
Gregory IX, 114

Griffiths, Bede, 79, 90, 92, 197, 214, 230
Griswold, Eliza, 135
Griswold, Frank, 135
guilt, 3–5, 10, 25–29, 39, 41, 43–44, 136, 149, 174, 193, 204, 213, 216, 219, 231, 237

H.G. Wells, 8, 107, 113, 115, 117, 175
Haidt, Jonathan, 155
Hamas, 13, 199
Hamer, Dean, 94
Hamlet, 130, 248
Hanukkah, 180
Harrusi III, 198
Hashishin, 46
Hayhoe, Katherine, 36
healthcare system, 37
Heisenberg, 78
Helena, 103, 105
Hemon, 203–204
Heschel, Abraham Joshua, 206
Hillel, 9, 152, 248
Himalayas, 80
Hindson, Ed, 62
Lord Ayyappa, 181
Hindu, 7, 41, 47, 54, 59, 61–63, 75, 82, 94, 110, 130, 172, 176–79, 181, 183, 197, 208, 218, 227, 238
Hinduism, 14, 59, 60–63, 78–79, 82, 107, 164, 199, 230
histrionic or hysterical personality, 235–236
Hitler, Adolf, 3
Hoffer, Eric, 58
Hollis, Tom, 129
Hollywood, 127
Holt-Lunstad, Julianne, 51
Holy Communion, 172
Holy Envy, 18, 94, 249
Holy Ghost, 107, 114
Holy Land, 112–14
Holy Roman Empire, 121, 132
Holy See, 118
Homer, 215–16, 244
Homo Sapiens, 9
homosexual, 110

hope, 36, 85, 117, 132, 139, 160, 169, 172, 191–92, 201, 203–204, 218, 226, 232
Hosea, 7, 84
Huckleberry Finn, 12–13, 250
Hugo, Victor, 88, 175, 212, 222
Huxley, Aldous, 89
hyper-fundamentalism, 62

Icarus, 73
identity, 41
Ignatius of Loyola, 117
immigrants, 47, 232
Immortal Diamond, 89, 248
incels, 50
Indian sages, 75
infidelity, 161, 215
inner parrot, 3–4, 6, 8–9, 21, 23, 97
inner voice, 1–4, 70–71
Inquisition, 116–18, 245, 251
IQ, 226
Isaiah, 7, 85, 88
Isha Upanishad, 78
ISIS, 17, 62
Islam, 17–18, 60–61, 63, 88, 90, 93–94, 114, 117, 176, 181, 199, 208
Israel, 7, 13, 83–86, 88, 139, 180–81, 199, 216, 243
Israeli Palestinian conflict, 13
Ivey, Governor Kay, 61

Jahan, Shah, 63
Jainism, 60
Jamaica, 201
James, William, 56, 159
January 6, 127
Jaspers, Karl, 6, 7, 64–65, 94, 230, 238, 245
Jataka Tales, 202
Jefferson, Thomas, 95
Jeremiah, 6, 7, 85, 86
Jericho, 207
Jerusalem, 85–86, 88, 99, 112–13, 179, 181
Jesuit, 79, 117, 121, 138
Jesus, 8, 29, 32–33, 57–58, 61, 66, 84, 92–96, 98–100, 102–108, 115, 117, 123–24, 130, 133–37, 141, 147, 151, 158, 163–64, 170, 173, 176, 180, 188, 190–92, 201, 206–207, 210–211, 216, 220, 227, 232–33, 241–42
woman caught in adultery, 4–5
Jesus's teaching of turning the other cheek stimulate the conscience, 11
casting out demons in Jesus's name, 38
communion bread and wine turning into the body and blood of Jesus (transubstantiation), 120
Jewish, 7, 46, 48–49, 57, 62, 86, 88, 90, 97, 99, 114, 117, 119, 129, 176, 179–181, 199, 212, 248
Jinping, Xi, 68, 185
Joas, Hans, 7, 242
John of Patmos, 97
Johnson, Daryl, 48, 49
Johnson, William, 79
Jonah, 7, 83
Jones, E. Stanley, 11, 130
Jove, 215, 216
Judaism, 18, 60, 85–86, 88, 93, 230
Julius Caesar, 221, 248
Just Mercy, 128, 249
Justin Martyr, 101, 212
Justinian, 103

Kabbalah, 90
Kadesh Peace Treaty, 198
Kalinga, 174, 175
Kama Sutra, 110, 160
Karadzic, Radovan, 129–30
Karma, 76–77, 79, 82, 110, 159, 183
Katha Upanishad, 76
Kauravas, 183
Kautilya, 175
Keats, John, 169
Kerala, 117, 147, 176–82, 198, 230, 238
Khan, Hazrat Inayat, 202
Khayyam, Omar, 170
kindness, 205–209, 226, 242–44, 248
King Cyrus, 8, 86, 88
King David, 99

King Jehoiakim, 85
King Josiah, 85
King Louis IX, 113
King Philip of Macedonia, 73
King, Martin Luther Jr., 10–11, 29, 48, 52, 97, 132, 148, 151, 210, 229, 249
KKK, 47, 48, 124–26, 151–52, 246
Klan, 48, 124–26, 250
Knānāya Christians, 176
Kochi, 176–79, 181, 239
Kodungallur, 176–79, 181
Kongzi, 65
Krishna, 183
Ku Klux Klan, 124
Kung, Hans, 102, 196, 197

Lao Tzu, 7, 68–69, 93, 143, 210, 220, 245
Las Casas, 119, 232, 248
Laudato Si', 36, 248
Lawson, James, 187
Lee, Harper, 88
left-wing, 15, 17, 26–27, 35, 40, 49, 50, 135, 138, 142, 151
Legacy Museum, 128
Leibniz, 89
Les Misérables, 175, 212–13, 222, 245
Let Us Dream, 227, 248
"Letter from the Birmingham Jail", 10
Levin, Joe, 126
Lewis, C.S., 23, 129, 236
Lewis, Congressman John, 151, 188
liberals, 40, 52, 124, 155, 161
Liberty University, 62, 133, 232
Life After Hate, 47, 48
Life After Life, 91, 92, 246
lion, 128, 208
loneliness, 50–51, 171
Long, Jeffrey, 92
Longfellow, Henry Wadsworth, 221
Lord Krishna, 183
Lord Rama, 218
Lord's prayer, 157
Losing Our Religion, 232, 246
love our enemies, 233
Loyola Institute of Peace and International Affairs, 239

Luther, Martin, 120
Lutheran, 120
Lyceum, 73–74

MacMillan, Margaret, 184
Mahabharata, 183, 208, 218, 245
Main, Fr. John, 227
Malabari, 180
Mandarin Chinese, 185
Marcus Aurelius, 224
Mark Antony, 221
Mars, 215–16
Marty, Martin, 40
Marxism, 64, 68
Maslow, Abraham, 32, 56–57
Master Kong, 65
masturbation, 110
May, Gerald G., 44
May, Rollo, 32
Mayo Clinic, 235
McAleer, Tony, 46, 48
McKinney, Janie, 152. See also Forsyth, Janie.
McMicken, Walter, 128
Medieval inquisition, 116
meditation, 30, 33, 43, 47, 52, 58, 61, 68–69, 80, 82, 154, 158, 171, 183, 193, 204, 227, 238
Meeink, Frank, 49
Menachery, George, 182
Mencius, 68
Menezes, 178
Merton, Thomas, 55–57, 70, 93–4, 109, 155, 164, 168, 238, 246
Messiah, 85
Messianic, 85
Milby, Jesse, 239
Milgram, Stanley, 40
Mill, John Stuart, 156
Minh, Ho Chi, 125
Mir, Miam, 63
Mongols, 114
monkeys, 189, 218
Moody, Raymond, 91, 213
Moore, Russell, 232
Moore, Walter, 78
moral conscience, 53
Mormon, 156

Mosaic Law, 85
Moses, 4, 96, 113, 216, 221
Mota, Nehemiah, 180
Mother Teresa, 94, 191, 246
Mr. Roger's show on PBS, 222
Mu Lian, 217
Muhammad, 9, 93, 165, 208, 221, 241
Murthy, Dr. Vivek, 50, 51, 246
Muslim, 41, 61–63, 90, 94, 112, 117, 180–81, 218, 221
Muziris, 176
mystical (mysticism), 17, 31–32, 55–57, 61–64, 90, 94, 102, 129, 182

Napoleon, 118, 198
narcissistic personality, 12, 237
National Memorial to Peace and Justice, 128
Nazi, 47, 49, 191
Nazranis, 176, 178, 179
NDE, 91, 92, 213, 214
Near Death Experience, 91, 170
Near-Death Experience Foundation, 92
Neptune, 216
neurotic guilt, 219
New Covenant, 85
New Testament, 8, 17, 88, 95, 106, 233
Nicholas of Cologne, 113
Nicomachean Ethics, 222, 241
Niebuhr, Reinhold, 19, 247
Nietzsche, Freidrich, 26, 34, 247
Nineveh, 83
Nobel Prize, 18, 59, 78, 169
non-violent direct action, 29, 97
nones, 55, 247

Oates, Wayne, 239
Odyssey, 215, 216, 244
Old Testament, 84, 86, 88, 110, 137, 184
opioids, 51
Oresteia, 75
Origen, 102, 103, 159, 251
Original Blessing, 18, 243
original sin, 18, 109, 179, 192
Orissa, 174

Orthodox(y), 35, 106–107, 129, 175, 179, 231
oxytocin, 51

Palestine, 112, 115, 129, 139
Palestinian Israeli conflict, 231
Palestinians, 13
Pandava, 183
Panikkar, Raimundo (Raimon), 197, 238, 244
panther, 208
Parable of the Sower, 201
Parable of the Talents, 217
Parable, 99, 170, 217–218
Paradesi, 180
paranoid personality, 235
Paris Peace treaties, 198
Parliament of the World's Religions, 190, 196, 238, 239
Parnia, Sam, 91
Pasternak, Boris, 166
patience, 2, 141, 143, 200–202, 204–206, 214, 221, 239
Patriarch Kirill, 175, 231
Paul, 2, 6, 8, 44, 53, 58, 92, 96–97, 108, 116, 129, 143–144, 225, 233, 243, 250
Pax Romana, 196
Peace of Westphalia, 121, 251
peak experiences, 57
Peck, M. Scott, 145
peepal tree, 80
Peloponnesian War, 184
People's crusade, 113
Perennial Wisdom for the Spiritually Independent, 89, 248
perfectionism, 43
perfectionistic or compulsive personality, 236
persistence, 200
personality disorders, 15, 19, 28–29, 44, 151, 167, 208, 235–237
Peter, 8, 58, 95–96, 98, 191, 233, 244
Pew Research, 36
Pharisees, 29, 30
Picciolini, Christian, 47

INDEX

PIG, 6, 14, 21, 23–24, 53, 94, 99, 131, 138, 160, 233. *See also* "problem of irrational gratification"
Pinker, Steven, 31
Planck, Max, 18, 177, 178
Plato, 7, 31, 70–71, 72–73, 77, 101, 103, 130, 248
Pliny the Elder, 176
Poetics, 72, 74, 241
poodle, 78
Poor Clares, 115
Pope Francis, 27, 36, 110, 116, 123, 129, 136–137, 175, 227, 232, 239, 248
Pope Gregory VII, 112
Pope Innocent III, 113
Pope Urban II, 112
Pope, 27, 36, 110, 112–18, 120, 123, 129, 136–37, 175, 179, 227, 232, 239, 247–48
pornography addiction, 161
Portuguese Inquisition, 118
prayer, 58, 63, 80, 147, 154, 180, 184, 205, 227
President Biden, 35
President George Washington, 38
President Reagan, 133
Presidential Medal of Freedom, 58
Prince of Peace, 173
Prince Siddhartha Gautama, 80
problem of irrational gratification, 6, 21, 24, 131. *See also* PIG
Prodigal Son, 100
Protestant Reformation, 120
Protestantism, 116–17
Psalms of David, 168
Putin, Vladimir, 175, 231

QAnon, 127, 251
Quakers, 122
Quantum Questions, 18, 31

Rabbi Gamaliel, 57
Rabbi Hillel (the Elder), 9, 57
Rabbi Rami Shapiro, 89
Rabia of Basra, 218
racism, 9, 11, 126, 135, 180
RADAR, 14, 25, 28

Rajaram, M., 182, 248
Rao, Seshagiri, 239
rape, 35, 105, 110, 121
rationalization, 27
Ravana, 218
real guilt, 219
Red Letter Christians, 190
Reed, Ralph, 133
reincarnation, 71, 73, 76–78, 102, 172, 183
religious extremists, 49
religious right, 135, 192
religiously unaffiliated, 55, 199
Republic, 72, 118, 248
Republican, 16, 38, 61, 124, 133–34, 192
Rethinking Life, 190–91, 242
Ricks, Thomas E., 131, 187
Riggleman, Denver, 34
right-wing, 15, 17, 26, 27, 35, 40, 49, 50, 133, 142, 151
Rishi, 75, 208
Rohr, Richard, 89, 239
Roman Empire, 103, 106, 121, 191
Roman Inquisition, 116
Rome, 46, 105, 115, 248
Rubenstein, Richard, 104
Rubin, Theodore Isaac, 150
Rudd, Kevin, 185
Rumi, 220
Runciman, Sir Steven, 114
Russia, 199

Sabarimala, 181
Sabbath, 100, 181
Sadat, Anwar, 62, 199
Sakunthala, 202
Salem, Abraham Barak, 180
Salerno University, 114
Samford University, 36, 244
Samsara, 82
Sanskrit, 76, 81, 174, 202
Sasse, 51, 52, 248
Sasse, Ben, 50
Satchidananda, 172
scapular, 29
schizoid personality, 237
schizotypal personality, 237

Schopenhauer, Arthur, 78, 95, 248, 250
Schrödinger, Erwin, 59, 78, 177, 233, 246, 250–51
Science Daily, 91, 247
Scott, Michael, 114
scribes, 29
seared conscience, 53
Second Axial Period, 238
Second Vatican Council, 123, 179, 238
secularism, 64
self-condemnation, 5
self-confidence, 203
self-control, 2, 76, 141, 214, 223–27, 239
self-hate, 11, 30, 49, 148–50, 207, 248
self-reflection, 26
self-respect, 66, 225
self-righteous prig, 23–24, 236
Sepulveda, Juan Gines de, 119
Serenity prayer, 19, 194, 204, 219
Sermon on the Mount, 11, 97–98, 106, 135, 151
sexism, 9
Shakespeare, William, 24–25, 88, 130, 159, 201, 221, 248
shame, 3–5, 10, 24–9, 39, 41, 43, 47, 68, 98, 146, 149, 188, 193, 204, 216, 230–31, 237
Shankara, 54, 59, 76, 177, 249
Shankaracharya, 59, 94, 177, 244, 250
Shapiro, Ben, 40
Shaw, George Bernard, 5
Sheen, Vincent, 130
Shikoh, Dara, 63
Shintoism, 60
Shirer, William, 130
Sicarii, 46
Sikhism, 60, 78
single-issue voting, 232
Sita, 218
skinheads, 46, 47, 48
Skinner, B.F., 32
Smedes, Lewis B., 195
Smith, Adam, 52
Smith, Huston, 66, 159, 221
Smithsonian, 9, 249

Socrates, 7, 30, 70–73, 77, 88, 130, 135, 152, 156–57
socratic approach, 70, 72
Solomon, 99, 110
Sophocles, 7, 203–204, 249
Sorcery, 116, 131, 141, 190
Southern Baptist Convention, 126, 138
Southern Baptist, 126–127, 136, 156
Southern Poverty Law Center, 126
Spanish Dutch treaty, 121
Spanish Inquisition, 117
Spinoza, 31
spiritual defect, 19
spiritual exercises, 205, 227
Spong, Bishop John Shelby, 18, 159, 239
Sponsel, Leslie, 189
Sri Mata Amritanandamayi, 178. *See also* Amma
Stanley, Andy, 16, 136
St. Augustine of Hippo, 107
St. Clare of Assisi, 115
St. Francis, 115, 116
St. Paul, 2, 6, 8, 37, 57, 59, 93, 95–96, 104, 109, 115, 129, 143, 158, 214, 220, 224, 239
St. Stephen, 57
St. Thomas Aquinas, 129
St. Thomas the Apostle, 117
St. Thomas, 117, 129, 176, 178–79, 182, 212
Star-Spangled Jesus, 134
Stephan, Maria J., 186
Stephen of Cloyes, 113
Stephenson, David Curtis, 124
Stevenson, Bryan, 128
Stevenson, Ian, 78
Stewart, Lyman, 123
Stewart, Milton, 123
still small voice, 4
Stockholm International Peace Research Institute, 196
stupor mundi, 114
substance abuse, 51, 149, 216
Sufi, 61, 63, 181, 196, 202, 203, 245
Sufism, 61, 90, 93
suicide, 46, 51, 125, 148, 204, 216

INDEX

Sun Tzu, 186
superego, 9–18, 21–26, 28–30, 35–36, 38–45, 47–53, 59, 61–62, 74, 82, 89, 94–95, 97–101, 108, 112, 120, 129, 131, 136, 144–52, 154–55, 157–60, 162–63, 166, 169, 171, 175, 182, 185, 189, 191–95, 204, 209, 212, 217–19, 228, 231–33
    Inquisition and harsh superego, 118
    fundamentalism and the KKK, 124
    Racism, Sexism, Fundamentalism, Militarism, Egoism, pride, 132
    Right wing and left-wing superego clashes, 138
    Superego can misguide, 200
Swaggart, Jimmy, 27
Swami Vivekananda, 197
swords into plowshares, 190
Syrian Church, 176, 178
systematic theology, 238

Tagore, Rabindranath, 169
Taj Mahal, 63
Tao Te Ching, 68–70, 93, 203, 210, 245
Taoism, 60–61, 67–70, 93, 203, 231
Taylor, Barbara Brown, 18, 94
Temple at Delphi, 73
Ten Commandments, 7
terrorism, 46, 49–50, 242
The Art of War, 186
The Axial Age and Its Consequences, 7
The Book of Analects, 68
The Brothers Karamazov, 117, 243
The Economist, 68, 162, 168, 249
The False White Christian Gospel, 192
The Fundamentalist Phenomenon, 62
The Fundamentals, 123
The Journal of Democracy, 186
The Kingdom, the Power, and the Glory, 133
The Light Beyond, 214, 246
The Middle Way, 5, 81
The Moral Majority, 62
The Origin and Goal of History, 64, 245
The Phenomenon of Man, 138
The Two Faces of Religion, 39, 239

The Way and its Power, 68
The Way, 24, 29, 33, 44, 54, 69, 76, 93, 124, 131, 149, 152–53, 155, 185–86, 192–94, 203, 207, 210
The World's Most Enlightening Region, 198
The World's Religions, 66, 159, 249
Theodosius, 106, 191
Thirukkural, 89, 110, 182, 202, 226, 248
Thucydides trap, 184
Thucydides, 184, 225, 249
Thunberg, Greta, 37, 251
Till, Emmett, 126
Tillich, Paul, 44, 92, 129
To Kill a Mockingbird, 17, 246
Tolstoy, Leo, 88–89, 106–107, 130, 182, 229, 250
    and the Kingdom of God within, 11
transitional sage, 7
Trappist, 56
Treaty of San Francisco, 198
Treaty of Versailles, 198
tree, 27, 61, 79, 108, 142, 207, 211, 242
Treece, Henry, 113, 114
Trump, Donald, 127, 139, 199
Turks, 112, 113
Twain, Mark, 12, 183, 230

U.N. Refugee Agency, 198
Ukraine, 139, 175, 199, 231
unhealthy pride, 203
United Nations Children's Fund, 198
United Nations, 198
Unity Church, 10
Universal Declaration of Human Rights, 198
University of Naples, 114
University of Virginia, 77, 150
Upanishads, 7, 63, 75–76, 78–79, 243, 251
Updike, Harvey, 38

vaccination, 1, 3, 133, 145, 178
Valjean, Jean, 212–13, 222
Vasco de Gama, 118
Vatican II, 109, 123

Vatsyayana, 160
Vavar, 181
Vedanta, 75, 78, 177, 249
Vedas, 59, 75–76
Venus, 215
Virgin Mary, 129
Voltaire, 132, 229, 250
Vulcan, 215, 216

Waging a Good War, 131, 187, 248
Waldo, Peter, 115, 116, 243
Wallis, Jim, 192, 245, 250
Walsh, Roger, 214
weak conscience, 53
wheel, 175
white supremacist, 47–48, 50, 126, 150
Whitehead, Alfred North, 72
Why Civil Resistance Works, 186
Wiesel, Elie, 239
Wilber, Ken, 18, 31
Wilkinson, David, 161
Williams, Roger, 34–35
Winans, 133
works of the flesh, 142
World Bank, 162

World Food Program, 198
World Happiness index, 195
World Health Organization, 198
World's Fair, 197
wounded conscience, 53

Xenophon, 70, 88

Yahweh, 84–85, 107
Yahya, Harun, 90
Yalom, Irvin, 218
yin/yang symbol, 69
yoga, 61, 80, 227, 238, 242
Yordan Zhekov, 44

Zacchaeus, 207
Zahnd, Brian, 134
Zealots, 46
Zechariah, 86
Zen Buddhism, 93
Zhekov, Yordan, 15
Ziglar, Zig, 215
Zoroaster, 7, 87–88, 210
Zoroastrianism, 60, 88

www.ingramcontent.com/pod-product-compliance
Lightning Source LLC
Chambersburg PA
CBHW050842230426
43667CB00012B/2114